DISCARD

Prison City

"Prisons and their surrounding communities tend to become close-knit and insular. They are sprinkled all across the landscape and are a little-understood aspect of American society. Ruth Massingill and Ardyth Broadrick Sohn ask, 'What's going on here?' *Prison City* opens windows of perception and truth with clarity and wit. Well worth reading."
—Sheldon Ekland-Olson, Rapoport Centennial Professor of Liberal Arts, University of Texas, Austin; Co-author of The Rope, the Chair, and the Needle: Capital Punishment in Texas, 1923–1990

"This clinical study of America's number one prison town of Huntsville, Texas, offers the sociological equivalent of X-ray charts of a patient who is very sick but in deep denial. It is our Dachau."
—Scott Christianson, Author of With Liberty for Some and Notorious Prisons

"A wire service reporter, who covered countless executions in the heyday of 'Old Sparky,' swore that the warden's last words to the condemned man were, 'Have a seat, please.' You will not leave the edge of your seat, wherever you are sitting, as you read this remarkable work of scholarship turned drama. The authors of *Prison City* have artfully combined the stories of a town where life is shaped—and life ends."
—Mickey Herskowitz, Co-Author of Dan Rather's Best Seller, The Camera Never Blinks

Prison City

PETER LANG
New York • Washington, D.C./Baltimore • Bern
Frankfurt am Main • Berlin • Brussels • Vienna • Oxford

Prison City

Life with the Death Penalty in Huntsville, Texas

Ruth Massingill
& Ardyth Broadrick Sohn

PETER LANG
New York • Washington, D.C./Baltimore • Bern
Frankfurt am Main • Berlin • Brussels • Vienna • Oxford

Library of Congress Cataloging-in-Publication Data

Prison city: life with the death penalty in Huntsville, Texas /
Ruth Massingill, Ardyth Broadrick Sohn.
p. cm.
Includes bibliographical references and index.
1. Texas. State Penitentiary at Huntsville. 2. Prisons—Social aspects—
Texas—Huntsville. 3. Prisons—Public relations—Texas—Huntsville.
4. Prisoners—Texas—Huntsville. 5. Correctional personnel—Texas—
Huntsville. 6. Capital punishment—Texas—Huntsville. 7. Death row—
Texas—Huntsville. 8. Huntsville (Tex.)—Social conditions.
I. Massingill, Ruth. II. Sohn, Ardyth Broadrick.
HV9481.H82T49   365'.9764169—dc22   2006038102
ISBN 978-0-8204-8891-2 (hardcover)
ISBN 978-0-8204-8890-5 (paperback)

Bibliographic information published by **Die Deutsche Bibliothek**.
Die Deutsche Bibliothek lists this publication in the "Deutsche
Nationalbibliografie"; detailed bibliographic data is available
on the Internet at http://dnb.ddb.de/.

The paper in this book meets the guidelines for permanence and durability
of the Committee on Production Guidelines for Book Longevity
of the Council of Library Resources.

© 2007 Peter Lang Publishing, Inc., New York
29 Broadway, 18th floor, New York, NY 10006
www.peterlang.com

All rights reserved.
Reprint or reproduction, even partially, in all forms such as microfilm,
xerography, microfiche, microcard, and offset strictly prohibited.

Printed in the United States of America

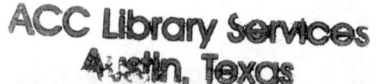

For Frank Q. Dobbs
1936–2006

On the set of Gambler V *in 1994, Bracketville, Texas.*

Frank understood perfectly that luck is the "head-on, three-way collision between opportunity, preparation and persistence," and his life was a testament to that philosophy. From Huntsville native son to Motion Picture Hall of Famer, Frank traveled far and accomplished much, but he always treasured his East Texas roots and his role as mentor to students at his alma mater, Sam Houston State University.

About the Cover

A place both stupefyingly ordinary and terrifyingly extraordinary, Huntsville's uniqueness is represented in this downtown photo. For more than half a century, a ramshackle burger joint called Mr. Hamburger served "killer burgers," made with two thick handmade beef patties and dressed with American cheese, lettuce, tomato, onions, pickles, mustard, mayo, and jalapeños.

Across the street from the happy clown sign, deadly serious business is conducted in the red brick buildings of the Texas Department of Criminal Justice compound. Housing for prison officers abuts the Walls Unit (building with clock), where weekly executions of real killers are carried out. Huntsville's status as the execution capital of Texas since 1924 has won the town the descriptive if not desirable CB sobriquet "Prison City," which inspired the title for this book.

Contents

List of Illustrations xi

Acknowledgments xiii

Introduction 1

Section I: From the Outside Looking In: Cultural Perspectives
  on Living in a Society Dominated by Capital Punishment 13
  Chapter 1: From Pleasantville to Prison City 15
  Chapter 2: Public Perceptions, Private Realities 41

Section II: Caught in the Middle: The Role of PR in Shaping
  Social Perspectives of the Criminal Justice System 63
  Chapter 3: The Criminal Justice PIO as Liaison between
    Myth and Reality 65
  Chapter 4: Death Row: Target of the Public's Macabre
    Fascination 103

Section III: Voices and Images from Prison City, Texas 139

Section IV: Voices from Within: Balancing Guaranteed Rights
  and Protection of the Innocent 169
  Chapter 5: Communication Inside the Walls 171
  Chapter 6: Communication Beyond the Walls 197

Summary 223

Section V: Conclusion: Empathy, Innocence, and Social
  Priorities 229

References 253

Contributors 257

Index 259

Illustrations

Big Sam Statue on Interstate Highway 45	1
Amnesty International demonstration during execution	13
Texas Department of Criminal Justice Administrative Headquarters	13
Sam Houston's rocking chair, *Sam Houston Memorial Museum photo*	23
Media trucks at execution, *TDCJ Media Services photo*	63
Patsy Woodall and Don Reid at *Huntsville Item, TDCJ Media Services photo*	63
New Zion Missionary Baptist Church	140
Joe Byrd (Peckerwood) Cemetery, *TDCJ Media Services photo*	140
Texas Prison Museum and Huntsvile Hornets stadium	141
Huntsville Kiwanis at the Walls in 1953, *TDCJ Media Services photo*	142
Convict construction, *TDCJ Media Services photo*	142
Former home of the Walls warden	143
Austin Hall on Sam Houston State University campus	143
The Walls unit in 1895, *City of Huntsville-Walker County Treasures photo*	144
Sam Houston State University bell tower, *SHSU photo*	144
Armed guard in the Walls watchtower in 2004	147
Picket officer in the Walls watchtower in 1960s, *TDCJ Media Services photo*	147
Goree girls chasing greased pigs at Prison Rodeo, *TDCJ Media Services photo*	148
Bullrider at Prison Rodeo, *TDCJ Media Services photo*	148
Sam Houston State University student housing on Sam Houston Avenue	149
The Walls in 1947, *City of Huntsville-Walker County Treasures photo*	149
Voodoo Tattoo sign on Sam Houston Avenue	151
Hallway shakedown for contraband, *TDCJ Media Services photo*	153
Media on lawn at execution, *TDCJ Media Services photo*	153
Wynn unit sign, *The Windham School District photo*	159
Prison graduation, *photo by Bambi Kiser, The Windham School District*	161
Old Sparky on display in the Texas Prison Museum	162
Control panel for Old Sparky	162
Holding cell for condemned prisoners, walkway to the death chamber, gurney for lethal injection, *Texas Department of Criminal Justice photos*	163
Double fence at Ellis unit, *TDCJ Media Services photo*	167
Hoe squad with "aggies," *TDCJ Media Services photo*	169
Texas Syndicate tattoo, *TDCJ Media Services photo*	169
Pistol range for prison guards, *TDCJ Media Services photo*	223
Goree girls band broadcasting on WBAP, *TDCJ Media Services photo*	229
Leadbelly mural in downtown Huntsville	229
Sam Houston grave, *Huntsville-Walker County Chamber of Commerce photo*	249

Photos not otherwise designated are the property of the authors. All photos were taken in the Huntsville area.

Acknowledgments

Prison City exists as tangible words and images because innumerable people contributed encouragement, information, and that most precious commodity—time—over the four-year span of this project. Although it is not possible to list everyone to whom gratitude is owed, the authors extend special thanks to the following:

Robin Andersen, who first saw the potential of this concept and whose enthusiasm has been unflagging,

Melody Davison, the "Renaissance woman" who was unfailingly upbeat while lending professional and practical assistance at every stage of the process,

Debbi Hatton and Tina Baiter, who contributed research, interviews, and personal profiles,

Sandy Rogers at the Huntsville Prison Museum and the folks at the Sam Houston Memorial Museum, who patiently searched out historic images and documents,

James Adams, J.D., who served as consulting legal editor, and Terry Horvath, J.D., who provided painstaking legal research,

The multitude of insiders and outsiders in Huntsville and beyond who shared their viewpoints through interviews and photos,

Sam Houston State University journalism students for surveying Huntsville community leaders,

Those volunteer readers and self-appointed cheerleaders who gave unstintingly of their time and positive energy,

KPFT-Houston, Pacifica Radio Foundation, for permission to quote from *The Ray Hill Prison Show* song,

Gryphon Enterprises of Austin, Texas, for innovative graphic design and production, and

The experts at Peter Lang who believed in this project and guided it through the rough seas of publication and promotion.

INTRODUCTION

A Tribute to Courage, dubbed "Big Sam," is the world's tallest statue of an American hero. The thirty-ton memorial was erected by artist David Adickes in 1994.[1]

The small-town, historic flair of Huntsville brings new meaning to "Texas Charm." There's truly something for everyone in Huntsville!
—City of Huntsville website

Huntsville, a tiny dot on the map, marks the location of an East Texas town of 35,000 residents. Motorists traveling seventy miles an hour on Interstate 45 could easily miss the exit sign about an hour north of Houston, but mention Huntsville to anyone in the state and there will almost assuredly be instant recognition. Go farther afield—New York, Canada, England, or France—and many have heard of Huntsville. Along with western motifs of tumbleweeds, longhorns, and cowboys, another icon of what has become the centerpiece of the U.S. criminal justice system looms large in the state of Texas—capital punishment. Huntsville has been called the execution capital of the world; 351 have been put to death there in the last twenty years.[2] More prominent than the sixty-seven-foot statute of Sam Houston standing guard at the edge of town, more enduring than the 130-year-old state university known for its criminal justice program, the execution tradition is inextricably tied to public perceptions about Huntsville.

On a global scale, the United States incarcerates more people than any other country in the world, housing more than 2 million prisoners—one fifth of the world's inmates[3]—at an annual cost in excess of $57 billion.[4] This prison population crosses every cultural border known to humankind. Many people, regardless of social strata, are touched by the criminal justice system, either directly or indirectly. Crime and punishment have become highly charged emotional issues successfully used for political gain by world leaders and by small-town politicians alike. For these reasons, Huntsville can be said to have broad social significance as a community that lives daily amid issues of international concern.

This book carefully explores the classic ethnographer's question of *What is going on here?*[5] *Prison City* looks beneath the placid surface of this small Texas town to understand the importance of Huntsville and the place it occupies in contemporary America. Although many of the situations and voices will resonate with natives of the state, this book is not just for Texans, but offers an opportunity to better understand how the Texas justice system is explained and interpreted, and how it has become a global metaphor for incarceration and capital punishment.

The prison population exists in a world apart from most peoples' experiences, but the insular society of the incarcerated represents an increasingly dominant force in the political, cultural, and economic landscape of American society. This stems in part from the sophisticated web of persuasive communication techniques used by public information officers who work in the criminal justice system. Community leaders in towns where prisons are the principal industry explain themselves through the media. Journalists cover the philosophy and practices of those working in criminal justice and tell the human-interest stories surrounding high-profile crimes. Victims and their families, as well as perpetrators and their friends and relatives, become the subject of news stories with relentless regularity. For all these reasons, penal institutions have become powerful influences on various groups outside the prison gates; they now occupy a major portion of U.S. media discourse.

Walking the line between perception and truth is a delicate balancing act for all the communities affected by incarceration and capital punishment, a dichotomy that is explored from various perspectives throughout this book. Also, the complex and ambiguous relationship between "insiders" and "outsiders"—both in a physical sense as well as in emotional and political senses—is a defining theme. The barriers that divide the inmates from the general population are more than physical; they are social, cultural, and psychological.

This book examines an essential topic from a variety of perspectives in the hope of bridging some of the discursive and perceptual gaps that obscure our understanding of criminal justice issues. In these pages, Huntsville elites articulate some of the disturbing truths about their town. Public relations efforts that shape perceptions of the criminal justice system and ways correctional officers view their work provide a different viewpoint. The physical insiders demonstrate the communication techniques used by incarcerated populations, and the resulting stories of crime, criminals, and victims show the power of the media. From this cacophony of voices we can hope to find a common ground able to facilitate humane policies that satisfy our demands for justice while also fulfilling the need for public safety.

Texas: A Culture like No Other

The myths surrounding the second-largest state in the union are as legendary and far reaching as its landscape. From its ironic humor and legends to its social enigmas, the stories found in these pages illustrate that the statement "Texas: It's a whole other country" is not just the state's advertising slogan but a way of life. While outsiders may eschew the concept as arrogant or ethnocentric, natives comprehend the complexity of thriving in a society built on pride and hard work. Texas culture is pervasive in the mindset of the lifelong residents who fiercely protect the family lineages of their communities, denoting the insiders and outsiders among their populations. In a state that prohibits hiring public school teachers who have not passed a course in Texas history, a person is first a member of his family, second a Texan, and third an American.

Regardless of pedigree, Texans understand that humor relies heavily on sly inside jokes, with submerged cultural references to shared meanings. Outsiders who hear only the text of the message miss multiple layers of nuance. Texans often tell humorous stories with an underlying moral in a gentle, self-deprecating manner and take some pride in the fact that only members of the culture will completely understand. In fact, many Texans, if pressed, would admit that their drawl becomes more pronounced and their speech slower when they are addressing an outsider who may need extra time to fully process the fine distinctions of the narrative.

This gulf between insiders and outsiders is a popular construct for many enduring parables, such as the tale about the newcomer who asked the local preacher what the locals were like. The preacher always came back with the question "What were the people like where you came from?" No matter how the newcomer described his former neighbors, the preacher would respond, "Well, you'll find the people here are about the same."

Nevertheless, Texans know they are not the same as those from outside the state, and they are secure enough in that knowledge to feel comfortable poking fun at themselves as well as their politicians and state institutions; no one is exempt. For example, residents' references to former governor George W. Bush as "shrub" are part and parcel of the Texas brand of humor and not a campaign of mean spirit. Many natives would say Texans are egalitarian both in their praise and in their cynicism. Power and position alone do not merit respect; it must be earned by being an insider who innately understands the context of the conversation.

By its sheer size, Texas is an amalgamation of many cultures. West Texas closely aligns itself with stories of the cowboy and cattle drives, while South Texas embraces its Hispanic roots, and East Texas prides itself on genteel southern hospitality. Ensconced in the piney woods of East Texas, Huntsville, with its azalea trails, white-columned homes, and historic statue, could be any town along the Mason Dixon line with one exception: it houses the headquarters for one of the nation's largest penal systems.[6]

While politicians in the state capital argue about budgets, and district attorneys build their careers on conviction rates, the inmate population in Texas grows by leaps and bounds, mirroring the national trend for the past thirty years.[7] No matter how many prisons Texas builds, it seems there are inmates to fill them. Feeding and housing more than 150,000 convicted felons[8] provides bread and butter for thousands of TDCJ employees and lucrative contracts for hundreds of subcontracted businesses. Prisons are a growth industry in Texas.

The story of Texas prisons is as complex as the Dallas freeway system and as ritualized as the Texas two-step. In many ways the prison system is symbolic of the state: a study in contrast, paradox, and irony. Beneath its multidimensional layers, however, it all boils down to insider versus outsider, politics versus ego, perceptions versus realities, and, deep beneath the surface, a unifying thread of fear.

Study Focus and Methodology

Purpose of the Study

The authors were drawn to this topic for several reasons, including their own fascination with the public's conflict over capital punishment. In addition, the authors lived in the field site, which hosts legal executions nearly every week at a rate surpassing the rest of the world,[9] so it was second nature to be curious about how this phenomenon affects the local culture. However, there is very little serious research about prisons' effects on communities and the ways residents discuss and process the reality of their unusual situation. The authors were in a unique position to complete a long-term, rigorous study of the community from the inside out since they had access to interviewees, documents, and details relating to the theoretical, policy, and practical aspects of capital punishment.

The study began by exploring one general research question: *What's going on here?* Although the question is simple, the potential answers are multidimensional and touch on values, beliefs, and attitudes connected to three distinct Huntsville communities: (1) leaders and elites, (2) Texas Department of Criminal Justice (TDCJ) public information officers, and (3) inmates. Other groups in the community also contribute to the culture, but these three emerged as significant because of their influences on internal and external communication about capital punishment, both inside and outside the borders of Huntsville. For instance, leaders and elites set communication agendas that relate to political, social, and economic decision making in Huntsville. The prison public information officers determine communication agendas for community, state, national, and international audiences. In turn, inmates design communication agendas that challenge the goals of the other two groups.

Research Procedure

Like most ethnographic studies, this research required extensive planning, rigorous multiple data collection procedures, and months of analysis and synthesis of data. During nearly five years of research, more than 100 individuals were consulted, some 70 people were interviewed, and in excess of 150 images were considered for the book.

The first research phase involved study of documents, including historical and current artifacts relating to the town's formation and its selection as prison city for Texas. Physical spaces in the community were mapped, including the local university sitting high on a hill on the south end of town, the crumbling former rodeo stadium where inmates once rode bulls for the entertainment of tourists, a cemetery for those who leave prison only when they die, an early slave market corner, the cemetery where Sam Houston rests, and the woodlands where the first visitors to the area came to enjoy rest and natural spring waters.

Important community events were attended, including somber weekly execution vigils on a corner facing the Walls and a modest celebration for prisoners graduating from college. Notations about everyday behaviors of the three groups also were part of this early investigation. Through this process the authors came to understand geographical boundaries that separated parks, residences, and workplaces from the Walls, which is just a short walk from the historic town square and band shell.

Next, a survey of positional elites was conducted to compare and contrast observational data with survey responses and to identify key informants about the town's culture. Through a multistage selection process, forty civic, political, religious, and social elites were chosen for interviews because of their elected titles or prominence in community activities. A small subset of residents identified as particularly visible or knowledgeable leaders was interviewed in person to provide a list of communication topics for agenda setters in town. The survey questions were administered in the same order with the same wording by trained interviewers, and the answers were content-analyzed with standard tests conducted to ensure coding reliability. Themes were extracted and common characteristics identified. Results indicated that many elites simply ignore the town's main industry—the penal institution. Instead, they see Huntsville as a small town just like many in eastern Texas where the courthouse square records not only history but evokes common themes shared with other rural communities across the state.

The final stage of the research involved in-depth personal recorded interviews with selected community members in their natural settings (that is, their living rooms, offices, the prison environment, and so on). The general open-ended questions for the semistructured interviews were developed through analysis of the data collected in the first two phases of research. However, the questions were regarded only as *probes* for the respondents, who were urged to tell their stories in their own words. By the time the interviews were conducted, the purpose of the study was well known, and trust between the authors and the respondents had been established. The recordings were transcribed and analyzed for common frames, with miniature case profiles emerging from the data.

Reflections

What became clear from analysis was that individuals who had been selected previously because they appeared to fit into one of the three categories of citizens actually span several social and conversational borders. Therefore, readers will encounter individuals speaking in more than one section. This is a rhetorical device as well as a strategy to provide readers with a richer picture of featured community speakers.

Community opinions are as divergent as the state's geography is varied. What community members have in common is conviction; each is certain of the rightness of his or her viewpoint. Variously, the people who appear in these pages cite the cold, hard logic of statistics and bottom-line economics; they tell heartrending stories of regret and atonement. They justify political expediency and the realities of public office, and they explain the generations of tradition that underlie all Texas institutions, especially the prison system. The term *Prison City* is a facile stereotype, but these voices indicate that the truth is much more complex and nebulous.

Paraphrasing is used only when context is being created by the authors or when framing is needed for enhanced understanding of the emerging themes. The authors prefer to let the community members speak in their own voices with local language and colloquialisms enriching the descriptions and explanations of community concerns.

The authors have taken an objective rather than an advocacy stance to the research findings. Readers are asked to review data through a cultural lens filtered by community multivocality rather than by rigid research hypotheses or politicized agendas.

Section I: From the Outside Looking In

In this section the reader meets one of the most vocal complainers and activists against capital punishment in the entire state. His comments are balanced by the optimism of a city manager who sees the prison as a good neighbor and a clean industry. Both men are relative outsiders compared to the female former mayor, who has an impressive appreciation for the history and value of her community and puts its major industry into a social and economic context. Readers also hear the voice of the district attorney describing a local teenager who threw a young mother and her living child into a grave. He explains how this case among others turned him from pacifist to prosecutor. Grandmothers, professors, local church ladies, and prison teachers add their voices to the community conversation about capital punishment and how the world views their town. Profiles of "typical" town leaders and observations about how race impacts communication patterns in the town are included.

This section also focuses on the history and background of how Huntsville became home to the Texas penitentiary system in the late 1840s and how townspeople today cope with living in a company town whose borders are dominated by seven prisons, including the oldest of them, the red-bricked Walls unit where executions take place. The descriptions, interviews, and historical notes provide both a geographical and sociological picture of the boundaries surrounding capital punishment in this small East Texas community where the most famous hero is frontiersman Sam Houston. This six-foot-six-inch giant of a man, who died in Huntsville, still casts his shadow over the piney woods around the town and the university named for him. After helping win Texas's independence from Mexico, Houston settled in Huntsville to practice law and politics, retiring from public life when he failed to secure Texas support for the Union in the Civil War. Houston retreated to his pastoral home, where he and his Native American friends appreciated the area's natural beauty with numerous springs and abundant game in the dense forests.

Today, the town still maintains a rural beauty amid severe economic and social problems innate for a community dominated by prisons. Huntsville is compared to other company towns like Middletown, with more than its share of domestic violence, economically disadvantaged school children, and symptoms of hypervigilance contributing to high rates of alcoholism and drug use. The town leaders responsible for reaching out and comforting families affected by capital punishment describe what they think are important values and beliefs in the community. A university scholar's research about local newspaper crime stories is featured, along with comparisons to other cultures' word choices apropos of capital punishment.

Readers also will encounter clashing voices from insiders and outsiders who know where the community boundaries are and have developed strategies for negotiating the unseen signposts in their town. The speakers are reflective about the roles they play and demonstrate intuitive understanding of how they are viewed outside their borders. They appreciate their privilege as well as their burden and remain largely patient as they repeatedly answer the question *What's going on here?*

Section II: Caught in the Middle

This section explores the role of public relations in framing and influencing public perceptions of the Texas criminal justice system. It is based on a series of interviews with public information specialists within the Texas Department of Criminal Justice and conversations with representatives of their many publics. The goal is to take an inside look at how the prison's public information officers (PIOs) frame media messages to reflect the agency's mission and to retain public support for Texas's criminal justice system. The crisis nature of prison PR and the security-conscious work environment create one of the most unusual jobs in the field for these liaisons between the prison and the public. In this politically charged environment, official communication by the institution must be carefully woven to reflect the chosen image.

Reporters who cover the prison beat offer both their professional and their personal opinions about criminal justice issues. Their voices range from those of veteran Texas reporters who have covered hundreds of executions to the broader perspective of national reporters and the dismay of international reporters. In addition to the PIOs and the criminal justice reporters, interviews were conducted with a cross section of others touched by TDCJ's public persona. Conversations with an award-winning L.A. filmmaker with deep roots in Huntsville, and with "town and gown" representatives—blue-collar workers and local university professors—address the myths and realities surrounding this institution that dominates the social landscape of Huntsville and shapes the image most people have of Prison City. Tensions between the mass media and the public information office are analyzed, as is the emerging role of women as prison spokespeople. The contrast between public perceptions of the criminal justice system and present-day realities is a thread that winds throughout.

Since death row is the predominate image most nonresidents have of Huntsville, the second chapter of this section is devoted to the public relations issues surrounding the death penalty and executions in Texas. Questions concerning media coverage of capital punishment are explored from contrasting viewpoints. Reporters speak about professional rewards and personal costs of covering the prison beat. By contrast, the PIOs give a candid behind-the-scenes look at their often difficult jobs and share anecdotes, from mournful to comical, of experiences with prisoner-clients. Whether founded on myth or fact, Texans' attitudes toward crime and punishment as well as their fascination with capital punishment are prevalent perceptions the PIOs must address.

Section III: Voices and Images from Prison City

To give visual texture to this ethnographic narrative, a selection of images—current and historical—gives a mind's-eye view of the town, the prison, and some of the people whose voices are heard in the book. These images are complemented by a handful of ethnographic miniature case studies that transport the reader deeper and deeper inside Prison City. The journey begins with a glimpse of the life view of local families in which several generations work for the prison in this twenty-first-century company town. Next, readers vicariously visit the local tattoo parlor frequented by prison guards and attend a prisoner college graduation. Finally, from deep inside the prison, a death row inmate describes his existence behind bars through an autoethnographic narrative.

Section IV: Voices from Within

From activist David Ruiz to journalist Jorge Renaud, convicted felons have used communication channels to index their experiences in the criminal justice system. Prisoners have become communication experts, using technologically advanced and astute persuasive theory to get their messages past the border defined not only by prison walls but also those created by the stigma of the "inmate" label. The myth that "what goes on inside the prison stays inside the prison" is debunked as the voices of prison employees, family members, and Huntsville businesspeople explain the complex relationship of interdependence forged by necessity. Sometimes the information is educational, eye-opening, and heart wrenching. One commonality quickly becomes readily apparent: the prison system requires innovation.

Prisoners detail creative ways to circumvent prison policies, wives describe unusual wedding ceremonies, and a couple tell how they met and fell in love while visiting incarcerated family members. These true stories are indeed stranger than fiction. This section also provides a discussion of communication pathways that have proven successful in disseminating the voices of those who call TDCJ either a place of torture or a place of residence.

While the Constitution provides the legal framework for defining U.S. citizens' legal rights, the court system has preferred to embrace a hands-off approach regarding incarcerated populations. Prison officials are vested with power to interpret how the courts' rulings pertain to their units. This approach is the primary reason each prison unit is as unique and distinctive as a major metropolis. From prison argot to body art and "kites," this section examines the distinctive forms of communication inmates use in confinement.

The second chapter of this section explores the great lengths to which family members and loved ones of inmates will go to get their messages inside the walls, illustrating the adage "If there is a will there is a way." This section demonstrates that prison sentences are served by the convicted as well as those who love them outside the walls. Communication is facilitated by both traditional and new technologies, which are explained through dialogues with TDCJ mailroom employees, who describe the tedious process of reading inmates' correspondence; a former inmate who has created a nationally recognized radio show for prisoners and their families; and Internet conversations with women who have fallen in love with men who will spend the rest of their lives behind walls. These dialogues all serve to answer the question *What really goes on here?*

Section V: Conclusion

The final section, written by a nationally known peace and justice studies scholar, gives a broader national perspective on divisive prison issues and examines how popular media shape public perceptions of capital punishment. In the ever-evolving world of public policy in criminal justice, these reflections set the stage for future studies of the topics presented in this book and compare public attitudes about crime and punishment to criminal justice realities.

Prison City was written to shed light on a number of controversial, though little-understood, issues hidden behind prison walls. Here are refections on questions of crime and punishment, vengeance and forgiveness. Do the criminal justice practices of the culture of Huntsville—and, by extension, America—reflect a society bent on unproductive vengeance, or does the "eye for an eye" stricture foster a safer society for those outside the prison walls? It is hoped that readers will find their own answers to these questions as they listen to the multitude of voices in this book.

Notes

[1] Sam Houston Statue website, August 15, 2006. Available at: http:www.samhoustonstatue.org/.

[2] "Year by Year Death Row Statistics," Texas Execution Information Center Statistics. Available at: http://www.txexecutions.org/stats/asp.

[3] "How the Rockefeller Drug Laws Harm Society," January 2004 position paper. Available at: http://www.interfaithimpactny.org/positionpapers/womenprison.htm.

[4] Marc Mauer, "Comparative International Rates of Incarceration: An Examination of Causes and Trends," June 20, 2003. Presented to the U.S. Commission on Civil Rights.

[5] L. R. Gay, Geoffrey Mills, and Peter Airasian, *Educational Research* (Columbus, Ohio: Pearson Prentice Hall, 2006).

[6] Paige Harrison and Jennifer Karberg, "Prison and Jail Inmates at Midyear 2003," *Bureau of Justice Statistics Bulletin*, May 2004.

[7] Mauer.

[8] Richard Willing, "USA's Prison Population a Record, but Growth Slowing," *USA Today*, November 7, 2004. Available at: http://www.usatoday.com/news/nation/2004-11-07-women-prison_x.htm.

[9] ACLU, "Executions and Exonerations by State since 1976," February 6, 2004. Available at: http://www.aclu.org/capital/general/10425pub20040206.html.

Section I
From the Outside Looking In:
Cultural Perspectives on Living in a Society Dominated by Capital Punishment

While the prison system provides "bread and butter" for about one fifth of the residents, community leaders must cope with controversy and public criticism.

Chapter One
From Pleasantville to Prison City

Well, over the fifty-five years I've lived here, I have found the motto describing Huntsville that I coined some years ago still fits. It's "Huntsville, where an evil elite rules by deceit."
—George Russell, entrepreneur and self-described local Don Quixote

Huntsville's Many Contrasts

Huntsville is a small town like many others in America—except this small town hosts frequent executions. Just a few short blocks from the town square that includes a county courthouse, band shell, and historic log cabin sits the historic red brick building known as the Walls, where convicted Texas inmates spend their final hours before death sentences are carried out. Visitors are often stunned by the harsh mission of the town compared to its surrounding rural beauty, which includes vast pastures, beautiful woods, and wildflowers.

On a hill overlooking the Walls is Sam Houston State University (often called Sam), named for one of the town's most famous citizens. History is important to Huntsville natives, with Houston immortalized in a huge statue at the town's entrance and his gravesite a favorite visitor destination. While some faculty and students seem oblivious to the town's main industry (capital punishment), many professors are active in preserving local history, and the university enjoys statewide recognition for its criminal justice program, which provides training and research information for law enforcement officials.

Huntsville may be extraordinary in its domination by penal institutions, yet it still shares many characteristics with other small towns. For instance, Huntsville insiders include members of founding families who still reside in the town. And, just like in small towns everywhere, members of the inner elite circle do not necessarily agree with each other about significant issues. Disagreement is a well-established Huntsville tradition. Residents still like to recall how their beloved Sam Houston became estranged from town leaders in 1862 when he objected to Texas fighting on the side of the Confederacy. After being stripped of his political power in Austin, he returned to Huntsville, where he found he was not only shunned but had difficulty securing housing from residents who weren't sure they wanted him living there again. Today, debate remains a big part of the leadership agenda in the community, and although there might be universal agreement about the outcome of the Civil War, there definitely is disagreement about capital punishment.

The Town Critic

While most civic, social, and economic leaders in Huntsville focus on its pastoral beauty and friendly people, George Russell is considered by his foes at city hall to be the town's biggest public relations nightmare. A self-described "social outcast for decades,"[1] he is an outspoken critic of Huntsville leaders, capital punishment, and local environmental destruction. He appears regularly at city council meetings to voice his complaints and authors hundreds of websites where he vents his frustrations. On one site, called PoliticalWhores.org, he took on former Texas governor George W. Bush, with whom he says he shared a makeshift jail cell in Huntsville.

According to Russell, the town sponsored a charity event called a "jailathon," which he points out with some sarcasm could only have been dreamed up by Huntsville leaders. Governor Bush agreed to be locked into a "cell" at the mall with other town leaders, to be "bailed out" by donations. Russell says he paid a "rather large sum to be incarcerated alone with the man who would later follow in his father's footsteps [as president of the United States]."[2] Russell says he showed Bush pictures of clear-cutting in national forests in an effort to influence him to talk to his father about environmental preservation.

It didn't work.

Russell reports that "Dubya" (which is how many East Texans refer to the forty-third U.S. president) became angry, denied that the photos were of national forests, and accused him of lying. "Furthermore, he said he had no intention of passing the photos on to his father, and I might as well leave because I was wasting his time and mine,"[3] Russell says.

Such rebuffs don't discourage Russell, who is often the subject of controversy concerning Huntsville, which he calls the "City of Death." Besides capital punishment and the environment, Russell is interested in religion and the Universal Ethician Church, which he founded on his land near Lake Livingston, east of Huntsville. Services are held there, and he maintains a green cemetery where bodies can be buried in cardboard or other biodegradable containers. While Russell might be described as eccentric or unorthodox, he is nobody's political fool. For instance, he succeeded in having his church ground "hallowed" by burying at least one person there, thereby stopping a nine-mile power line planned for the area. This ended up in a battle before the Texas Public Utility Commission, and the power co-op's Austin attorney accuses Russell of giving him a major "headache" by stalling an important public project.[4]

Campus Town

Most town elites point to the local university with pride, but Russell has only contempt for what he views as a lack of leadership from Sam Houston State University. A political science professor, a drama professor, and a criminal justice professor have "guts and integrity," but "most of the rest have their heads in the sand," according to Russell. "This town is really run by a tiny clique of bullies, uneducated, ignorant bullies. If these folks up here [at the university] would stand together, they could defeat the monster. Huntsville could become a leader in prison reform. But it ain't gonna happen. 'Cause of these spineless…"—his sentence trails off as he gives an exasperated shrug.[5]

While Russell may not have respect for much of the university faculty, the student body boasts at least one well-known celebrity among its alums. Dan Rather, longtime anchor and managing editor for the *CBS Evening News* before his 2005 retirement, is a graduate. CBS established a Dan Rather Scholarship Fund for a student majoring in either print or broadcast journalism, with Rather requesting preference be given to a student who works on a paid or volunteer basis for the campus newspaper, the *Houstonian*.[6] The communications building, where journalism is taught, is named for Rather, who has appeared in university promotional materials. Many of today's students have backgrounds similar to his.

Rather was born in 1931 in Wharton, Texas, and is a 1953 journalism graduate.[7] The former TV newsman says he always wanted to be a newspaperman and worked on his high school newspaper, yet he enrolled at Sam to play football. Most kids he knew growing up in Houston Heights didn't finish high school, and for them college was an impossible dream.

Rather says that if it had not been for his love of playing football he might have joined other young boys in the oil fields, where he was a roughneck by the age of seventeen.[8] However, playing college football at Sam Houston State was not in his future, and after spring practice he was cut from the team. When he told his journalism professor and mentor Hugh Cunningham the news, the professor was delighted and encouraged Rather to major in journalism, and so he did—sometimes working three jobs to pay for tuition.

Rather confesses that he was a "clumsy bad writer," but he is grateful for the education he received at the university that still caters to first-generation students like Rather. "This was an average cow college, a backwater. I'm not denigrating it in any way, because I owe it a great deal," he says.[9]

Although the students study in the midst of the state's prison system and know that executions are held just down the hill from their classrooms, there is little daily preoccupation with with the town's dominant industry.

Another well-known Texas journalist, syndicated columnist Molly Ivins, held a teaching fellowship at Sam Houston State University several years ago. Ivins said she had insight about the perseverance Rather (as well as other graduates) always demonstrated. "None of the students read a daily newspaper. The best ones maybe read a newsweekly. None could write well. None were prepared to go out and meet the world. But I thought they would turn out to be good reporters because they knew they'd have to work their asses off to get anywhere."[10]

Today, the university is more than a cow college, but the student body is not very far removed from the scrappy profile Rather and Ivins describe. Many are first-generation and self-supporting students who come to Huntsville because enrollment at the main state university in Austin is very competitive, living expenses in Huntsville are economical, and commuting to jobs in Houston is possible. Some of the students even work in the prison system, which is grateful for the steady labor supply. Although the students study in the midst of the state's prison system and know that executions are held just down the hill from their classrooms, there is little daily preoccupation with the town's dominant industry.

In fact, there isn't much conversation about the fact that the campus library and state death house are located just a few blocks from each other in the center of town. If outsiders bring up the topic, locals acknowledge that it may seem bizarre to newcomers, but to Huntsville residents and students that is just the way it is. Journalism students occasionally put out special capital punishment editions and instructors invite prison public information officials as guest speakers, but there are no specific journalism curricula for writing about or reporting on capital punishment.

Taking the Talk to Europe

If Russell is accused of causing trouble in Huntsville, he claims it is nothing compared to what Huntsville is accused of in Europe. He likes to spend time in Gioviano, Tuscany, where he finds his spiritual oasis. "The only place I seem to get along with folks is in Italy. I think people seem to be a little more civilized [there]," he says. He tells of being asked in Italy where he is from and answering, "La Citta di Morte." He says people immediately knew that Huntsville, Texas, was his home. "So we have created a reputation as the death capital of the free world that has extremely negative implications on our image. And that's the polar opposite of the image we should be portraying."[11]

Russell is not the only resident to complain of an international negative image for Huntsville. Writing in their 2003 book, Virginia and David Owens say, "In other parts of the country, and especially in Europe, claiming this town as your home is almost like saying you grew up in Three Mile Island or Chernobyl."[12]

Although he wasn't born in Huntsville, Russell's fervor and enthusiasm for local history matches any native's. He laments that Sam Houston and other early settlers didn't win the vote to have the capital instead of the penitentiary located in Huntsville. For Russell this decision was "perhaps the biggest disaster to befall Huntsville."[13] He speculates that the magnitude of the inheritance probably wasn't recognized in the 1850s because there were fewer criminals. He mentions the Civil War and the relocation of the town's first college (Austin College) to Sherman, Texas, as major contributors to what he says has been the town's loss of heritage and gentility.

Critical as he is, Russell has invested both time and money in the town. His family's income came from some unusual sources. In addition to teaching at Sam Houston State University, Russell says his father "also created a side business in his garage called Educational Filmstrip Network, producing and distributing educational films to schools across the country. In the late 1980s, the company went video, changed its name to Educational Video Network, and business exploded."[14] Russell points proudly to a 2004 DVD that lists him as an associate producer. The documentary, called *Liberty Bound*, premiered in Italy and includes footage about Huntsville. Film narrator Christine Rose identifies local sites in her hometown, mentioning that the 1980 movie *Urban Cowboy* was filmed at the former prison rodeo site in downtown Huntsville.[15]

> *"In other parts of the country, and especially in Europe, claiming this town as your home is almost like saying you grew up in Three Mile Island or Chernobyl."*

Today George Russell is a business owner with so much property in the historic hilltop area of Huntsville a sign declares the neighborhood Russellville. While he is not opposed to making money, Russell is adamantly against anyone making money from executions. He hopes he is a role model to "show people you can survive even though you're bucking the system. And [I am] hoping other people will say, heh, they haven't chased Russell outta town. They may have chased everyone else outta town, but if you stand your ground you might do a little good."[16]

The Other Side of Huntsville

Kevin Evans, city manager of Huntsville, loves the garden views just outside his tall office windows. The deep jungle green of large plants mixes with dogwood buds on a spring morning. He notes that the grass and grounds are sometimes tended by prison inmates. Inmate crews do high-impact city "maintenance jobs from time to time. They'll clear this creek [behind the city building], and they bring work parties any time we ask them. It's just their part of their contribution to the community," he observes. "Every industry has problems and solutions at some point. TDCJ has chosen to work very closely with this community to keep the problems to a minimum and the solutions to an absolute maximum," he says.[17]

One prison official remarks, "I know the prison generally comes up when they are looking at doing projects, because we do have basically free labor, and we do a partnership with the city."[18]

Evans sees the prison as a good neighbor. "It is a very clean industry; it is a solid industry; it's a basic industry." He admits it's unfortunate it deals in an area a lot of people are uncomfortable with, but he highlights the upside. "We've got the headquarters; we've got some of the best units in the state; we've got some of the best employees at TDCJ in the country. They work hard and they are very much a part of this community. We're here to serve them."[19]

Although Evans has lived in Huntsville only a short time, he is already a booster for the community he sees as both unique and historical. "For either a Texan or a student of Texas history, this is one of the places things got started. A quick pass through the cemetery will tell you that." Naturally, Sam Houston is at the top of the list of famous Huntsville residents, Evans points out, but "he's not the whole list."[20]

> *"You've got an itty-bitty town with few residents who have to gear up for this enormous influx of people day to day. In some ways it's the best of all worlds and other times it's tough."*

Evans readily admits that for years Huntsville was seen only as the prison town where executions were carried out and this has been an enormous public image problem to overcome. To him, "That's not all this town has to offer." He views the prison system as one of the largest and most important industries in the community that provides a reliable economic base. He believes that the prison and the university together "give us not only a stable but a very unique base."[21]

Managing Huntsville

Evans says it is a tough job to handle the needs of the 35,000 residents of Huntsville, pointing to the challenges of an infrastructure to serve 8,362 prisoners as well as some 15,000 students. The burden is borne by the small number of permanent residents who ante up property taxes, while the state-owned lands of the prisons and university are not taxed. The city has to supply water, streets, and police and fire protection for a city in which about 40 percent of the property is not on the tax rolls.

The largest single taxpayer in Huntsville is Wal-Mart, with an assessment in 2004 of almost $16 million—nearly 2 percent of the total tax valuation for the city.[22] Texas Department of Criminal Justice staff estimates their monthly payroll at $18.4 million,[23] with about 2,600 weekly visitors to the prison who add to the coffers while stopping in the county seat.

Evans explains that the daily traffic generated by the prison-university combination is "phenomenal." He guesses that thousands of nonresidents—sometimes as many as 75,000 a day—visit Huntsville for business. "We have to be prepared to take care of water, wastewater, and street use for a lot more than just 35,000 folks," he says, adding, "so you've got an itty-bitty town with few residents who have to gear up for this enormous influx of people day to day. In some ways it's the best of all worlds and other times it's tough."[24]

Employment Figures for Huntsville*

Employer	Number of Employees
Texas Department of Criminal Justice	6,744
Sam Houston State University	2,458
Huntsville Independent School District	974
Huntsville Memorial Hospital	540
Wal-Mart	517

*Figures provided by Huntsville city manager, March 21, 2005.

City officials like Evans worry about pay cuts at the prison, since even a small economic fluctuation can impact the city enormously. An interagency council of leaders of city and county governments meets monthly to keep everyone informed of any changes in community income.[25] The founder of this monthly meeting is Jane Monday.

Public Relations as a Community Concern

Mayor from 1985 to 1991, Jane Monday established the breakfast get-togethers as a communication tool. She has written several history books about Texas, including one about Joshua Houston, a slave belonging to the Houston family who became a free man and later served on the city council and as a county commissioner. His son established one of the first

Prison City Close-Up

Sam Houston Memorial Museum photo

"Ask Martin...to call at the Penitentiary and order the large chair (Rocking)...and let it be sent to the Boy at the tan yard, and have a seat put in it...let the back be high, and lean back so as to make it pleasant... I do not expect to complain of any want of elegancies, or comfort, if I live to reach home and find you and the family well!"
—Sam Houston letter March 20, 1858

Almost 150 years after Sam Houston ordered this custom-made rocking chair from the Huntsville prison workshop, inmates still manufacture a Sam Houston office furniture series, including the $455 judge's swivel chair with a screen-printed gold state seal, which can be seen in Texas courtrooms across the state.

Since Sam Houston's day, the prison factories have grown into thriving enterprises that produce a wide range of products for internal use and for external sale to tax-supported agencies, counties, cities, schools, and hospitals. Texas Correctional Industries (TCI) includes divisions for graphics, furniture, metal, and textiles. In 2005, TCI's forty-one facilities generated $78 million in revenue.[26]

TDCJ's statutory objectives for its manufacturing operation are twofold: (1) provide inmate laborers with valuable skills, and (2) reduce the agency's costs by producing products and services for use within the prison as well as for outside sales.[27] As a result, the Texas prison system is largely self-sufficient. "We make the cells the inmates live in; we grow cotton and weave it into fabric for towels, blankets, and clothing," explains Jayne Thurman of TCI's marketing division. " We even make the toothpaste they use. As far as inmates go, we manufacture everything."[28]

From the license plates that most people associate with prison manufacturing to the razor wire that tops prison fences, from janitorial supplies to leather saddles and officer uniforms, the range of products is extensive. Prisoners are not paid for their work, but according to TCI's annual review, training programs "reduce idleness and provide opportunities for offenders to learn marketable job skills and work ethics."[29] ✪

schools for African Americans in the state of Texas. Monday calls Joshua a "hero" because he "speaks for many blacks whose stories are lost." His records were kept as part of Houston's archives because "they knew they were important from the very beginning."[30] While Sam Houston owned slaves, he was not a supporter of the Confederacy and in fact was relieved of his post as governor of Texas for refusing to take the oath to the Confederacy in 1861. When he returned to Huntsville from Austin the following year, he had difficulty finding anyone who would rent or sell him a house.[31] Eventually, he leased a home known as the Steamboat House because of its unusual architecture. He died there a year later, and his funeral was held in the upstairs parlor.[32]

Monday, a founder of the Texas Prison Museum in Huntsville, has also served as chair of the Texas State University System Board of Regents, which oversees Sam Houston State University. She is a strong advocate for the town and for the prison system, noting that because of the prison industry city payrolls are stable. However, like Evans, she also mentions the disadvantage of having so much town property under state ownership because the state doesn't pay property taxes. She sees this lack of a good tax base as particularly hard on the school system, which also derives most of its income from property taxes. It is difficult for entry-level teachers and young guards and their families to live well. Although some prison staff have access to institutional housing at reasonable rates, many at the lower end of the economic scale or in entry-level positions have to live in mobile homes.

Serious Issues Engage Leaders

Town leaders like Monday recognize that the town has difficult challenges. One is a lack of support for youth in the community with few recreational facilities.[33] Professor Mary Evelyn Collins, who teaches speech and rhetoric at Sam Houston State University and is active in civic and charitable organizations, thinks it is difficult to "get your children through puberty in this town without something happening to them. They have so little. To be really active in public school these days requires you to have a significant amount of money."[34] She mentions a five-year-old study that revealed that "students seven through twelve don't feel connected with their school at all. It is a major flaw. It doesn't matter if they are white, black, or Hispanic, they don't feel a strong connection to school [and there are no adults] they trust. To me it is a very scary thing so many students can't identify a teacher, a minister, a Sunday school teacher, or anybody they can go to with an important issue in their life."[35] (See the close-up of a high-school murderer at the end of this chapter.)

Local Educational Concerns

Judy Ellis, a local retiree and grandmother, is president of the board of the Elkins Lake residential development a few miles south of town, and she too is concerned about children in the community. Both her husband, now retired from the military, and her daughter are former Huntsville teachers. Her daughter, who also lives in Elkins Lake, home schools her children rather than sending them to the public schools in Huntsville. Ellis says both her husband and daughter were troubled by large classes and a negative atmosphere for healthy social interaction in the local schools.[36]

> *In Huntsville "one out of every 127.2 children and youth are neglected or abused compared to one out of every 198.8 at the state level."*

Ellis and her board oversee a wooded preserve where some twelve hundred residents live in comfortable homes far away from the Walls and some of the social and economic problems of Huntsville. The golf course is popular, and a large club facility includes recreational amenities for children and an upscale dining area for families. Both past as well as current presidents of the university live in the preserve along with many other community leaders.

The contrast for some families living in Huntsville can be dramatic, according to Professor Collins. There are no boys' or girls' clubs in Huntsville. Collins mentions one public school teacher "who had a heart for working with middle schoolers"; the teacher started a couple of programs, but it was overwhelming to find adult volunteers, because of the kind of community Huntsville is. Collins explains that potential volunteers like retirees were busy playing golf, and others who might have been interested in volunteering were employed full-time at university or prison jobs. She also mentions that some possible volunteers were "so overstressed working in the prison they just couldn't volunteer."[37]

Ellis, Collins, and other town leaders are familiar with the term *hypervigilance*—the emotional changes wrought by jobs such as those of correctional officers. At shift's end correctional officers go directly from the prison to their homes and families. The heightened emotional state necessary to be watchful of prisoners can quickly turn to depression and increase the potential for violence at home.[38] Some town leaders believe that alcohol and drug abuse as well as domestic violence may be related to hypervigiance in Huntsville. The Texas Department of Criminal Justice's policy puts the jobs of those accused of domestic violence in jeopardy. A community report speculates that many problems are not even reported because of "financial dependence on the abuser" and families' fears that identifying offenders will threaten the family income. The report's figures show that in Huntsville "one out of every 127.2 children and youth are neglected or abused compared to one out of every 198.8 at the state level."[39]

Furthermore, Huntsville's average income is lower than the state's median, largely because the Texas Department of Criminal Justice pays its employees less than the state average.[40] The report also indicates that more than 50 percent of the school district's students are "classified as economically disadvantaged"—higher than the state level—while the average per-pupil expenditure is lower than the state average. More than 18 percent of the students do not graduate from high school.[41]

Parks and Prisons Draw Visitors

City Manager Evans is aware of these problems, but he points out that the last ten years have been good for the city. Evans says that the convention bureau and chamber of commerce have done a good job of publicizing the town's attributes—also part of the story of Huntsville. According to Evans, "The community as a whole has worked very hard. Sam Houston State has worked very hard. They have just done great things!"[42]
And indeed he is right. There are plenty of attractions for visitors in Huntsville: art tours, a graveyard tour featuring Sam Houston's final resting place, a downtown walking tour, and even a historic driving tour with stops at the Sam Houston Memorial Museum complex, Houston's Woodland Home, his log cabin law office, and period gardens. In addition, every April a popular folk and cowboy music festival draws visitors. Across from the Sam Houston Memorial Park is the Homestead restaurant, which not only serves excellent meals but appeals to tourists because it is housed in a hand-hewn pine log structure built in 1834 by German immigrant Lemuel Collard, who fought in the Texas revolution against Mexico.[43]

Touring the Town

Other interesting sites include King's Candies, located on the spot where the first Masonic Lodge stood and where Sam Houston attended meetings. Chicken salad sandwiches are a specialty, but most people come for the huge sodas or sundaes and handmade candies. Next door to King's on the north side of the town square is the site of the original Gibbs Brothers' store. It is the oldest business in Texas in continuous operation by the same family at the same location.

It was opened as a mercantile store in 1841, and Sam Houston not only shopped there but liked to sit outside and whittle. On the west side of the square along Sam Houston Avenue is the Texan Cafe, specializing in substantial breakfasts and hefty lunches accompanied by favorite side dishes of mustard greens, freedom fries, and sweetened ice tea, East Texans' favorite beverage. The walls of the Texan Cafe are covered with enlarged photos from the 1800s showing that the square has not changed much in terms of looks or its appreciation for hearty food. However, no Texas town is complete without barbecue, and Huntsville has one of the best selections in the state.

Barbecue like No Other

New Zion Missionary Baptist Church Barbecue is one place that draws people from all socioeconomic groups, including Huntsville town leaders. In the early 1970s Annie Mae Ward began cooking her barbecue, now so legendary it was part of a 2005 *USA Today* story about the best places in the nation to find good cooking.[44] Her barbecue has been featured on CBS, in statewide newspapers, and in *Texas Monthly*. Iron smokers outside a small annex next door to the church puff oak wood smells into the surrounding air. Legend has it, when Ward first fired up the aromatic barbecue to feed lunch to her husband, who was painting the church, the smells pulled people off the highway, and she ended up selling his lunch to strangers.[45]

Church members Mae and Horace Archie took over in 2004 when Ward's health declined. They turn out about nine hundred pounds of pork ribs, brisket, sausage, and chicken a week.[46] Members of the church serve side dishes of potato salad, pinto beans, and white bread with pickles, with red onion slices optional. Iced tea is also part of the meal along with various pies. Profits from the barbecue have provided air-conditioning for the church hall and other items for the congregation.[47]

However, not only the smells and tastes of Huntsville draw praise; the sights also inspire positive comments. For instance, famous blues artist Leadbelly (Huddie William Ledbetter) is immortalized in a huge mural on the side of a building at 1221 Sam Houston Avenue. In 1916 he was in a Texas jail for assault, but he escaped and later killed a man in a fight. He was sentenced to thirty years of hard labor for his crimes, but after seven years the governor pardoned the musician when he begged for clemency with a song. By 1934 his tunes "Midnight Special" and "Rock Island Line" had made him famous.[48]

The downtown walking tour takes visitors past antiques stores and bronzed Texas-shaped signage to identify early homes, a restored spring used by both Indian tribes and early settlers, and a log cabin on the site of the first homestead in Huntsville. There is also an art tour, but probably one of the most popular tourist attractions is the prison driving tour that takes visitors past all seven prisons, including the Walls unit where executions take place just two blocks from the courthouse square. The crumbling remains of the famous rodeo stadium are still visible.

Prison Rodeo Was a Major Attraction

Former mayor Monday grew up seeing everyone associated with the prison system as friends of the family. She remembers looking forward to the first Sunday in October in particular because that is when the prison rodeos started. "Every October you just knew everybody in the world would be here in town. You didn't drive at certain times because you knew the streets were going to be blocked off. It was a major fundraiser for most of the nonprofits in town,"[49] she says.

The Walls prison rodeo was started in 1931 as "recreation for inmates and entertainment for staff and their families." By 1933 almost fifteen thousand visitors were turning up in Huntsville for the Sunday shows, still considered among the most successful public relations events ever for a prison. At first only experienced inmates were allowed to participate, but by the 1940s any male inmate with "guts and a clean record for a year" could join the tryouts.[50] Rodeo performers earned $2 in 1933 and $10 in 1986 just for participating—and even more for winning. It was not without risk, however. Two inmates died in the arena and others suffered broken bones and various injuries.

Prison officials erected wooden stands and charged admission. Proceeds subsidized school textbooks, dentures, and Christmas turkeys for needy residents. Huntsville restaurants and stores reaped healthy profits on rodeo Sundays, as did inmates who peddled arts and crafts on the midway. By 1950 the wooden stands were replaced by concrete and steel. When it was forced to close in 1986 after engineers condemned the stadium, the rodeo was grossing $450,000 a season from some fifty thousand fans.

Halftime shows with inmate music had been replaced by featured singers like Loretta Lynn, Tom Mix, and Willie Nelson. The event engaged much of the prison community, with farm inmates rounding up "wild steers from river bottom pastures. At the Goree unit women sewed the cowboys' zebra-striped uniforms. Printers and journalists from the Walls produced souvenir programs, and leatherworkers tooled saddles and chaps for riders whose families could not provide equipment."[51]

The Walls as a Historic Site

During the Civil War, the Walls unit imprisoned captured Union soldiers. According to the visitors' brochure, "Sam Houston, whose son was imprisoned at a union POW camp, would often stride through the big prison gate, booming encouragement to the captured soldiers."[52] Interesting trivia included in the brochure lists the youngest inmate as a nine-year-old boy sentenced in 1884 for robbery and an eleven-year-old girl sentenced the same year for administering poison. The most unusual offense listed is "worthlessness."[53]

Visitors to Huntsville taking the prison driving tour will undoubtedly make a stop at the Joe Byrd Cemetery, dubbed Peckerwood Hill. The twenty-two-acre prison cemetery is just east of the SHSU campus. According to the tour brochure, the "most infamous prisoner ever to be buried here was Satanta, a Kiowa Indian chief." Convicted of killing seven white settlers in 1871 during the Salt Creek Massacre, his death sentence was commuted to life. Unable to tolerate confinement, he died in 1878 by diving headfirst onto a brick wall from a second-story window in the Walls. He was buried in Peckerwood, but for eighty-five years his tribe tried to have his body returned to Oklahoma. Finally, in 1963 the tribe received legislative approval. After a traditional ceremony, inmates exhumed his bones and a tooth. These remains were reburied in Fort Sill, Oklahoma, where two thousand Kiowas paid their respects to him in a special ceremony.[54]

Prison Museum Successful

One of the most successful public relations attractions in town is the Texas Prison Museum off I-45, managed by former Walls warden Jim Willett, who spent thirty years with the Texas Department of Criminal Justice. Until recently the museum was located in a building downtown on the courthouse square. Willet said he and others felt that if they built a museum off the interstate on the west edge of town, people would be more willing to visit. He was right; even without advertising and even though museums in general were reporting fewer visitors, there were 23,000 visitors the first year and 24,000 the second year.

> *"Most come in thinking the electric chair is what they want to see." But the display on contraband—weapons inmates have made illegally—seems to capture visitors' interest the most.*

A guest book indicates that most visitors heard about the museum from friends. Willett reports that most "come in thinking the electric chair is what they want to see."[55] But the display on contraband—weapons inmates have made illegally—seems to capture visitors' interest the most. The museum houses belongings of famous Texas inmates. There is a gun used by outlaws Bonnie and Clyde, a guitar that belonged to Leadbelly, and items owned by musician David Crosby (of the Byrds and Crosby, Stills, and Nash), who was incarcerated in Huntsville in the 1980s for possession of cocaine and weapons violations.

While the museum draws Texas families and seniors, it also is a popular stop on the vacation itineraries of Europeans, who generally feel the need to tell Willett they "don't agree with this execution stuff in Texas."[56]

Early Roots: Pleasant Gray Settles In

Huntsville natives take pride in their pre-prison history. Many descendents of early residents are active in both civic and social activities. Traders visiting the Huntsville area in the 1800s found a clean spring for drinking water, friendly Bedias Indians, and abundant piney woods thickets for hunting. Pleasant Gray, one of the early explorers, founded the town of

Huntsville in 1835 on land he bought from the Mexican government.[57] He built an Indian trading post in a small grove of oak trees close to a prairie, where Gray's Indian customers could graze their ponies while bartering with him.[58]

The town square has not changed much since its founding. The Walker County Court House sits on land deeded to the city by Gray for one cent. Instead of horse tie-ups, the courthouse is now surrounded by free parking spaces that are rarely filled—unless a newsworthy execution has brought outsiders to town.

Crossing the Borders into Town

Huntsville's main entrance is via I-45, which connects Dallas and Houston. Motorists arriving from the south pass through beautiful forests of the Huntsville State Park before being greeted by Big Sam (Houston), "the world's tallest statue of an American hero,"[59] visible for nearly seven miles—day or night, thanks to spotlights that come on at dusk. The sixty-seven-foot-tall white concrete statue weighs over thirty tons and was dedicated in 1994. The statue, too, has not been without controversy. Local citizens found it hilarious when shortly after the statue was erected town leaders noticed a part of Sam's anatomy was not proportional and demanded it be corrected so it would not continue to embarrass Elkins Lake matrons who confronted its imperfections every time they entered or exited their neighborhood.

There is disagreement among amused citizens as to exactly what needed correction on the statue. Some claim that Big Sam was taken down and his trousers readjusted for a problem with overendowment, while others insist that the statue's trousers appeared concave and needed enhancement. Even after renovations, the trousers continued to cause comment because every time it rains unsightly stains appear on the front of them, according to local lore. Whatever the true account, the statue stands proudly on its ten-foot Texas sunset granite base for all motorists to see as they approach or leave Huntsville.[60]

In addition to the Houston statue, travelers headed for Huntsville will pass multiple prison facilities—including the Estelle unit on seven thousand acres, the Ellis unit on eleven thousand acres, where maximum-security and repeat offenders are held, the Byrd unit on fifty acres, and the Wynne unit on fourteen hundred acres, which also houses the Windham School System's administrative offices for inmate education.

Just Outside Huntsville

While public school teachers in Huntsville may deal with children of families suffering the effects of hypervigilance, teachers in the Windham School District (WSD) face a whole different set of challenges. The WSD, a "separate and distinct" entity from the Texas Department of Criminal Justice, was established in 1969 by the state legislature to provide academic, life skills, and career/technology education to inmates. It is one of the largest correctional education systems in the nation, with more than thirteen hundred employees in eighty-eight prison units. In 2003 and 2004 WSD served over 76,000 student inmates, with the typical student functioning below the seventh-grade level.

Research studies have shown that illiteracy is a strong indicator of recidivism. For every one thousand releases of nonreader young property offenders, the state estimates "$12 million in re-incarceration costs compared to $7.2 million for young property offenders who can read."[61] Clearly it is cost-effective to provide education for illiterate prisoners.

Felix Buxxkemper, principal at the Estelle unit ten miles north of Huntsville, says that priority for education is given to those inmates who cannot read and write at the sixth-grade level and are within five years of release. The thirty-year veteran administrator and leader of this unusual school district says the job tends to draw teachers who have five to ten years of experience in the public school system and love to teach but don't care for paperwork, or for overseeing lunchrooms and school bus lines.

Linda Masters is one of the teachers who found her calling in the prison classroom. She teaches literacy and has written a novel based on her experiences. Her day starts at 5 A.M. when she arrives to greet twenty-five students who will study with her from 5:15 to 8:15. No guards are in the classroom with her, but they are in the hallway if needed. Buxxkemper says that only inmates who have "behaved" and earned the privilege of attending school are allowed to take classes, so problems requiring supervision are rare. After a fifteen-minute break, Masters meets her next class of twenty-five students, who are with her until 11:30. She spends forty-five minutes organizing for the next day or doing lesson plans and then leaves shortly after noon, when another set of teachers arrives for the afternoon and evening sessions.

Wanda Mayes, one of the night-shift teachers, says her inmate students are not so different from those she teaches at the community college, although college students can come and go as they please and are not delivered to class by guards. Mayes says that two or more guards are always posted outside her classroom in case she needs them, but rarely has she needed to call on their help because if a student is extracted from her classroom he loses the privilege to attend classes.

"I like teaching the prisoners, which is why I keep doing it. They are older, streetwise, and more mature, so they are attentive and get their work done,"[62] she says, noting that their motivation is very different from that of traditional college students. She has students who rise at 2 A.M. for jobs in the mess hall yet arrive with assignments in hand at 6 P.M., eager to learn during her three-hour class. Mayes also says she has never caught an inmate cheating on an exam. Many inmate students want to read library resources like law books and dream of writing their own appeals. She says they also see classes as a way to move from jobs in the mess hall to become inmate librarians.

Another motivation is the chance to see people who are not near them in their cells or work areas and to catch up on news. Mayes said she once had a problem with the students talking among themselves, so she requested that they speak loudly enough for everyone to hear. They told her she didn't want to hear what they were saying, but when she insisted they told her details about why X killed Y inmate. She says she has learned not to ask them any information not related to classwork. She describes her teaching world as a city where everyone has his place and forms bonds. The only difference, she says, is that the bonds are continually shifting because people come and go daily, so there is little or no stability in their lives.

Literacy teacher Masters recounts an anecdote about a student who brought a letter from his daughter every Monday for Masters to read to him because he couldn't afford to pay another inmate to read it. One day he arrived crying, and proudly told her, "I read this all by myself." Another story Masters relates involves a student who was convinced that humans were plants not animals because he thought people were "human beans." Such misunderstandings are usually straightened out by parents before kindergarten, but Masters takes nothing for granted. One day she asked for a show of hands of those who had been shot. Everyone raised his hand. Some even volunteered to show their wounds.

Masters thinks teachers quickly learn to develop classroom examples to reflect the students' common experiences. She observes that there is also an obligation to provide illustrations and examples from "the free world," since students are hoping to reenter the outside world after they serve their sentences. Masters finds her job very rewarding. "Teaching people to read and to find a whole new world, I'm proud of that. And they are proud of themselves. It is not that they are stupid; they are uneducated." A number are also dyslexic. A University of Texas medical branch study indicated that the prevalence of dyslexia is higher in the incarcerated population than in the general public.[63]

> *"Ninety percent of these offenders get released and return to their communities. They are either going to be a positive contribution to the community or a negative one. If you just lock them up and don't provide any rehabilitation or training it's tough when they get out."*

Masters's biggest frustration is public misunderstanding about the job she and her peers are doing. "Some people think we come up and babysit. Every teacher is very serious about students and about the job they do," she emphasizes. Her dedication is echoed by Marjie Haynes, director of the Windham Division of Instruction. She thinks people don't appreciate the value of education for this particular population. If she could, she says she would tell the public, "Ninety percent of these offenders do get released from prison and return to their communities. They are either going to be a positive contribution to the community or a negative one. If you just lock them up and don't provide any rehabilitation or training it's tough when they get out." Haynes believes that investing in prison education ultimately saves both money and potential victims.[64]

Unlike other school systems, Haynes emphasizes, hers must teach basic academic skills as well as help students prepare to reenter and reestablish themselves in society and with their own families. This requires a focus on life skills and cognitive intervention to restructure criminal thinking. One of the classes involves parenting. "We've found so many [who] want to do well, want to be good parents, but don't know the proper methodology," Haynes says. "You just see a cycle. I remember going to a unit nearby and seeing a man and his father incarcerated together…a generational cycle." Haynes points out the need to interrupt that pattern. "The thought was, if they could learn how to parent differently, perhaps that would help break the cycle."[65]

Maintaining the Balance

Huntsville's history is among the richest in Texas—perhaps in the nation. Its citizens have included Native Americans, early settlers, war heroes, and former slaves who helped form a community known today as the state's prison town. Its residents take their role as keeper of a major institution seriously, which has brought both curses and accolades from outsiders. However, no matter how one regards this community, the reality is that residents are faced with major challenges related to the responsibilities they carry for the rest of the state. Some of these include becoming educational leaders in one of the most challenging school districts in the country, or leaders for social change and historical preservation, while others accept the challenge of the work required to keep the prison institution functioning.

Hypervigilance has resulted in social problems affecting families, and a lack of adequate tax support has cut needed resources. Town leaders have acknowledged these and other problems with a directness and openness rare in most political settings. Leaders argue over solutions to problems, but there is agreement about the town's colorful history, beautiful lakes and forests, and desirable mix of citizens—farmers, retirees, small business owners, and university professors—who are as important to the community fabric as the prison system.

While the integration among town, university, and prison has been difficult, leaders have been creative in finding ways to respond to opportunities and have maintained good humor in the face of almost constant teasing or even hostility from outsiders. Huntsville leaders work hard to straddle boundaries—geographical as well as sociological.

Not much is hidden in Huntsville—the prison, the execution chamber, and occasional twinges of racial tension are visible, as are the efforts to draw tourists to the historical, culinary, and natural assets of this rural town. In a company town constantly faced with outsiders who ask *What's going on here?* town leaders share details about living in the community. Their observations are sometimes surprising but always reflective and brutally direct.

> *I'm a very strong advocate for TDCJ. I grew up here. The prisoners, the administrators of the prison, the officers—they were all friends of our family. We never knew what it was like to not have the Walls. It was a normal situation.*
>
> —Jane Monday, former Huntsville mayor

Prison City Close-Up

"A Crime the Death Penalty Was Designed to Punish": Student Killed Mother and Child

One local high school student, notorious as an example of what can go wrong when adult mentors are scarce, is Raymond Cobb. In 1993 he murdered a young Huntsville mother and her child. On March 3, 2005, Cobb was one of seventy-two death row inmates in the nation whose sentence was commuted by the U.S. Supreme Court because they were under eighteen when they committed their crimes. Of the seventy-two prisoners with commuted sentences, twenty-nine are in Texas.[66]

Walker County district attorney David Weeks handled the prosecution and ultimately won the death sentence against Cobb for the case that he called "the most horrendous thing I have ever seen."[67] Weeks, a graduate of the University of Virginia with a philosophy degree, got his J.D. degree from the University of Houston. His philosophy background helps him as a lawyer and enables him to "rationalize most anything." But, three weeks after the Supreme Court ruled on Cobb and other young offenders sitting on death row, Weeks was not feeling very philosophical. "Raymond Cobb just got his case commuted to life because he was seventeen when he killed a twenty-three-year-old mother and buried her sixteen-month-old baby alive."[68]

Background on the Crime

Cobb lived with his mother north of town, and was active in the youth group at University Heights Baptist Church, where he sang in the choir. He had never been in trouble at school; in fact, some described him as "a quiet boy, a little on the outskirts of the teenage clique."[69] Two days after Christmas in 1993, Cobb was alone at home with just a week to go before starting his final semester of high school. "He would later claim he drank several beers that afternoon, smoked some marijuana and topped it off with tequila."[70]

He crossed the road and entered the home of Lindsey and Margaret Owings. Margaret, a decorated Navy veteran, was in her sewing room. She confronted Cobb when she discovered him dismantling her stereo. He stabbed her in the abdomen and the heart,[71] then dragged her body to a wooded area for burial. Returning to the house, he found sixteen-month-old Kori Rae asleep. He carried the child to Margaret's grave, threw her in the hole he had dug, and tossed her mother's body on top.

"The way he carried out the crime tells you more than what his physical age was. There are people younger than eighteen out there who are as scary as anybody you can come across," Weeks observes. "They're just wired differently. If there ever was a crime that the death penalty was designed to punish, that was it."[72]

After committing the murder, Cobb returned to high school, improved his grades, and graduated on schedule in the spring of 1994. He moved to Odessa, Texas, to be with his father, who had already served two sentences in prison.[73]

Cobb was one of seventy-two death row inmates in the nation whose sentence was commuted by the U.S. Supreme Court because they were under eighteen when they committed their crimes.

Cobb lived with his crime for two years before confessing to his father. He led investigators to the gravesite and produced Margaret Owings's gold wedding ring, taken from her finger.[74] In February 1997 a Huntsville jury convicted him, and he was sentenced to die. Since the 2005 ruling by the Supreme Court spared his life, he is living out his sentence at the Polunsky unit in Livingston, just east of Huntsville.

Cobb's picture and a letter dated April 29, 2005, appear on a death row site where he tells visitors he is twenty-eight years old and would like pen pals. He reports that since being in prison he has become self-educated and learned to enjoy reading books about history, philosophy, and psychology. He still likes to sing and listen to music. His letter has been translated into German for an international audience.[75] ✪

Notes

[1] George Russell (Huntsville business owner and local activist), interview by Ardyth Sohn, Huntsville, Texas, March 21, 2005.

[2] Ibid.

[3] Ibid.

[4] Craig Malisow, "Outside the Box," *Houston Press*, October 28, 2004. Available at: http://www.houstonpress.com/issues/2004-10-28/news/feature_print.html.

[5] Russell interview, 2005.

[6] "CBS Establishes CBS/Dan Rather Scholarship Fund at Sam Houston State University, Rather's Alma Mater," October 11, 2000. Available at: http://www.shsu.edu/~pin_www/T@S/2000/RatherEndow.html.

[7] Rather Communications Building. Available at: http://www.buildingshsu.com/rather_communication_building.html.

[8] Dan Rather, "Academy of Achievement: A Museum of Living History," May 5, 2001. Available at: http://www.achievement.org/autodoc/page/rat0int-4.

[9] Ibid.

[10] Gary Cartwright, "Dan Rather Retorting," *Texas Monthly*, March 2005.

[11] Russell interview, 2005.

[12] Virginia Stem Owens and David Clinton Owens, *Living Next Door to the Death House* (Grand Rapids, Michigan: William B. Eerdmans, 2003), 14.

[13] Russell interview, 2005.

[14] Malisow.

[15] Christine Rose, *Liberty Bound* (Blue Moose Films, 2004).

[16] Russell interview, 2005.

[17] Kevin Evans (city manager), interview by Ardyth Sohn, Huntsville, Texas, March 21, 2005.

[18] Michelle Lyons (TDCJ public information officer), interview by Ruth Massingill, Huntsville, Texas, March 29, 2005.

[19] Evans interview, 2005.

[20] Ibid.

[21] Ibid.

[22] Ibid.

[23] Huntsville Leadership Institute, March 21, 2005.

[24] Evans interview, 2005.

[25] Ibid.

[26] "Manufacturing and Logistics Division," *TDCJ 2005 Annual Review*. Available at: http://www.tdcj.state.tx.us/mediasvc/annualreview2005/supportsvcs/manlog.html, 2.

[27] Ibid.

[28] Jayne Thurman, telephone conversation with Ruth Massingill, November 3, 2006.

[29] "Manufacturing," 1.

[30] Jane Monday (city leader and former mayor), interview by Ruth Massingill, Huntsville, Texas, December 2, 2003.

[31] "Historic Step by Step Driving Tour," Huntsville Convention and Visitors Bureau, Huntsville/Walker County Chamber of Commerce, distributed March 2005.

[32] Sam Houston Memorial Museum, audio history, March 2005.

[33] Research study by Ardyth Sohn and students in Journalism 499, "Political Communication Topics," Sam Houston State University, fall 2001.

[34] Mary Evelyn Collins (Sam Houston State University professor and local activist), interview by Ardyth Sohn, Huntsville, Texas, March 23, 2005.

[35] Ibid.

[36] Judy Ellis (Elkins Lake neighborhood leader), interview by Ardyth Sohn, Huntsville, Texas, March 23, 2005.

37 Collins interview, 2005.
38 "Huntsville's Promise," Huntsville city council publication, October 23, 2001, 13.
39 Ibid., 12.
40 Ibid., 6–7.
41 Ibid., 19.
42 Evans interview, 2005.
43 Homestead House Menu, March 2005.
44 "New Zion Missionary Baptist Church Barbecue," *USA Today*, May 24, 2005.
45 Alison Cook, "The Church of the Immaculate Barbecue," *Houston Press*, July 28, 1994. Available at: http://www.houstonpress.com/issues/1994-07-28/cafe.html.
46 "New Zion."
47 Cook.
48 "Downtown Historic Walking Tour," a publication of the Huntsville Convention and Visitors Bureau Huntsville/Walker County Chamber of Commerce, distributed March 2005.
49 Monday interview, 2003.
50 "Texas Prison Rodeo," *The Online Handbook of Texas*. Available at: http://www.tsha.utexas.edu/handbook/online/articles/view/TT/xxt1.html.
51 Ibid.
52 "Prison Driving Tour," a publication of the Huntsville Convention and Visitors Bureau Huntsville/Walker County Chamber of Commerce, distributed March 2005.
53 Ibid.
54 Ibid.
55 Jim Willett (former warden), interview by Ruth Massingill and Ardyth Sohn, Huntsville, Texas, March 22, 2005.
56 Ibid.
57 "Downtown Historic Walking Tour."
58 Ibid.
59 "Stand with Sam," brochure, Sam Houston Statue Huntsville Visitor Center, distributed March 21, 2005. Available at: http://www.huntsvilletexas.com.
60 Accounts collected from several current and past city leaders, interviewed by Ardyth Sohn, March through August 2005.
61 Windham School District, "Annual Performance Report, 2003–2004," 1.
62 Wanda Mayes (Windham School District teacher), interview by Debbi Hatton, Athens, Texas, July 2, 2005, and Windham interviews by Ardyth Sohn, Huntsville, Texas, March 23, 2005.
63 Marjie Haynes (director, Division of Instruction, Windham School District), interview by Ardyth Sohn, Huntsville, Texas, March 23, 2005.
64 Ibid.
65 Ibid.
66 Scott Gold, "Death Row Cutoff Age Fuels Debate in Texas," *Los Angeles Times*, March 3, 2005. Available at: http://www.detnews.com/2005/politics/0503/03/A06-106348.htm.
67 Ibid.
68 David Weeks (Walker County district attorney), interview by Ardyth Sohn, Huntsville, Texas, March 21, 2005.
69 Owens and Owens, 51.
70 Ibid.
71 Ibid.
72 Weeks interview, 2005.
73 Gold.
74 Owens and Owens, 52–54.
75 Raymond Cobb #999221 (inmate at Polunsky unit), April 29, 2005. Available at: http://www.deathrow-usa.us/RaymondCobb.htm.

Chapter Two
Public Perceptions, Private Realities

The two largest employers in this town are TDCJ [Texas Department of Criminal Justice] and the university [Sam Houston State University]. So, we're a government town. People refer to us as a company town because of the prison system.
—David Weeks, Walker County district attorney

Not Your Typical Town

While it is true that there are several government employers in town, the one most associated with Huntsville is the Texas Department of Criminal Justice (TDCJ). This makes it a unique "company" town specializing in prisoners and capital punishment rather than manufacturing, mining, or other more benign products or services. This also sets up a very distinct boundary between insiders and outsiders—even within the town itself. Some residents consider themselves insiders because they and their relatives have always worked inside the prison, while other insiders provide leadership for community services supporting those who are incarcerated or are working for the prison system.

Almost a quarter of the citizens in Huntsville are employed by TDCJ, and those not directly involved are well aware of the dominance of the prison system in the community.[1] Reminders are everywhere. For decades, guards on horseback have supervised inmates wearing distinctive white uniforms while doing manual labor for projects beyond the prison boundaries.

The sound of a mournful siren blowing throughout the day communicates details about inmate whereabouts. One siren means it is time for a count of inmates; two blasts mean the count is accurate and all is clear. If there is no second set of sirens, something is wrong.[2] However, civilian residents barely acknowledge the sounds or the meanings of them. For insiders what is seen and heard in Huntsville is normal and expected and only those who cross the borders as outsiders make jokes about or comment on the strangeness of the circumstances.

The Huntsville Walls unit, located only two blocks from the square, dominates the town's geographical borders. Besides housing the infamous death chamber, the Walls also serves as the single discharge point for the entire prison system. When inmates are released from anywhere in Texas, they are brought by bus to Huntsville. Prisoners ready for release are kept at the Walls until processed out through the famous gates to freedom.[3] While most states and towns have put prisons in isolated areas, Huntsville's Walls unit is integrated into the center of the community. The Walls is not hidden physically, socially, or psychologically from local residents.

Recently released prisoners who walk the length of a city block to Huntsville's Greyhound Station to buy a ticket out of town are as much a part of the local landscape as Friday-night high school football games. While the central location of the prison seems strange to some, it serves as a vivid contrast to what sociologist Morris Janowitz calls shifting penal boundaries:

> In the simplest terms, the prison has moved from an institution at the periphery of society, remote, isolated, with distinct boundaries, under the control of personalistic and authoritarian leadership. It was an organization with a strong emphasis on informal and interpersonal mechanisms of control. Over time, it has shifted more to the center of the larger society; its boundaries have become more permeable and its older control mechanisms have given way to more rational, bureaucratic and legalistic arrangements.[4]

While other states may have been "shifting" prisons to a more figurative central location in society, Texas and Huntsville always have had prisons literally and figuratively inside their communities. Lorna Rhodes's ethnographic study notes that prison expansion in the last quarter of the twentieth century "produced an institutional complex of almost unimaginable size and complexity. Although prison growth has recently slowed, the prison complex remains a massive—if partially hidden—presence that matters to our public life in a myriad of both obvious and subtle ways. Large-scale incarceration has its most obvious effects on those directly involved as prisoners, workers and their families and communities."[5] Huntsville, Texas, is an interesting case study of a town that has adjusted to the very tensions mentioned by Rhodes. The geographic boundaries between prison and the traditional community are blurred in Huntsville, making it impossible to separate sociological borders.

"The prison as a social system does not exist in isolation any more than the criminal within the prison exists in isolation as an individual, and the institution and its settings are inextricably mixed despite the definite boundary of the wall," observes researcher Gresham Sykes.[6] Rhodes agrees, pointing out that penal institutions include not just prisoners, correctional workers, and the public, but also auxiliary industries and "workers arranged around prison systems, the legal and human rights organizations that help prisoners and the media."[7] Huntsville includes all those variables and is an interesting mosaic of how various publics come together to define the town and its major industry.

> *Recently released prisoners who walk the city block to Huntsville's Greyhound Station to buy a ticket out of town are as much a part of the local landscape as Friday-night high school football games.*

Walker County district attorney David Weeks regularly contemplates the larger sociological context of his role in the community as a town leader. Raised as a pacifist by Mennonite parents, he was drawn to law as a way to articulate his beliefs. "I didn't start off with prosecution in mind," Weeks explains. "I was planning on becoming Perry Mason. I wanted to protect poor, downtrodden innocents. But, as I gained more experience in the system, I learned the real truth, which is most defendants are guilty."[8]

Weeks agrees that Huntsville is unique. Although its major industry is prisons, it is also a university town, a rural farming and ranching community, and a place offering lakes, golf courses, and a variety of recreational facilities. This combination draws favorable reviews from outsiders, too. *The Rating Guide to Life in America's Small Cities* and *Demographics Daily* have both placed Huntsville among the nation's top dream towns with the highest quality of life. *Money* magazine named Huntsville one of its thirty-five ideal communities in which to live. Huntsville also is registered as a wild bird sanctuary,[9] and many residents spend pleasant hours producing outstanding vegetables and flowers that flourish in the mild climate.

While Weeks enjoys the history and rural beauty of his town, he also is very aware of community challenges and admits that drugs top the list of the community's major problems. "That's everywhere. The drug problem impacts everything and because of that we end up with a lot of property crimes," Weeks says. "Surprisingly, compared to some of our surrounding counties our crimes of violence are lower, and I'm not sure why."[10]

Local leaders are continuously dealing with outsiders who have little or no understanding of their town. Weeks believes that some of the major misperceptions people outside Texas have about executions in Huntsville involve confusion about the legal system's workings and the role his office plays. "We get calls—particularly from overseas—they all think my office personally prosecutes these death penalty cases." While such calls can be annoying and time consuming, he thinks the biggest misperception is that local residents are obsessed with the death penalty. "Folks around here probably discuss it more than most places. Whenever we have an execution it's reported in the paper, and we have people on both sides of the issue."[11]

Weeks mentions Dennis Longmire as one of the most recognized town leaders opposed to capital punishment. A criminal justice professor at Sam Houston State University, Longmire has stood on the northwest corner of the street behind the yellow ribbon blocking access to the Walls almost every time an execution has occurred for nearly twenty-one years. The respect and tolerance community members show one another is probably best illustrated in how local law and order proponents regard Longmire. Weeks is direct in his discussion of the professor, whom he sees as driven by integrity rather than publicity.

"We're on different sides, but we have a great deal of respect for each other," Weeks explains. "Dennis lives out his beliefs. When there's an execution, he's there with his votive candle. I don't care whether it's a big public brouhaha, or it's somebody nobody cares about, Dennis is there. We disagree, but we do so in a civilized, respectful manner."[12]

Another Longmire fan is retired TDCJ public information manager Larry Fitzgerald. "You know, it's really kind of funny, but I always respected Dennis. Rain or shine, he was out there protesting every time. Now, Dennis and I team up as expert witnesses. Dennis will testify to the execution's dangerousness, and I testify to the conditions in prison, the day in the life of a prisoner. But Dennis and I, we've kind of laughed. He was out there protesting while I was walking people to their executions, and now we're working together."[13] (See the close-up of Longmire at the end of this chapter.)

Community Responses to What Happens in Town

While other Huntsville leaders may not join Longmire on the protestors' corner, they are not oblivious to what happens at the Walls. There are church-sponsored prayer programs the day of an execution, and a facility called the Hospitality House provides shelter for families of inmates. Charles Freddy Walters, a former missionary, oversees the Hospitality House. Its support comes from local as well as statewide church groups that contribute food for guests who prepare meals in the kitchen or even take food with them when they depart. "We have a number of ladies [on fixed incomes] who come once a month, and they take a month's worth of groceries when they leave, " Walters says. "They tell us if it were not for those groceries, they could not visit their loved ones [in prison]."[14] The entire Walters family, including a teenage son who helps out when children visit, is involved in the outreach program. They occupy an eight-hundred-square-foot apartment in the house.

The Huntsville Hospitality House is always open to minister to the families of three distinct inmate populations: those being executed, those on death row, and those being released.

Walters said the Hospitality House joined the Chamber of Commerce in 2004 to better publicize the work it does and to solicit more help with projects. Occasionally, university sororities organize a food drive, and Crossroads Baptist Church in The Woodlands near Houston has provided supplies. Other churches come quarterly, once a month, or once a year with donations. Summer is usually the most difficult season, Walters explains, because people are busy and forget to help.

The Hospitality House was built in twenty-four hours in 1986 by a number of Texas Baptist groups. There are now twelve such facilities around the state. The Huntsville house is seven thousand square feet, with sixteen rooms and forty-eight sleeping spaces and costs $2,000 to $2,500 per week to operate. While local churches contribute money, Walters says, "A lot of individuals contribute also."[15]

Walters estimates that some five thousand people stay in the house each year. The only qualification for spending a night is that the guest must be a friend or family member of someone in a Huntsville or Livingston prison. Unlike other facilities that are only open on weekends when general population visitation is allowed, the Huntsville Hospitality House is always open to minister to the families of three distinct inmate populations: those being executed, those on death row, and those being released. Walters says the prison chaplain sends a letter to families of inmates scheduled for execution. The letter gives information about the day of the execution and also includes a note from Walters describing his facility and inviting families to stay there.

Families generally arrive at the house around 1:30 on the day of the execution. "We always have a pot of soup fixed for them on that day," Walters explains. "There is a family chaplain from TDCJ who is here with them, counseling and providing support."[16]

At around 3 P.M. the chaplain, who has been with the condemned inmate, comes to the house and explains to family member witnesses what will take place. While the chaplain is with the family, a spiritual advisor is with the prisoner. Then the chaplain and spiritual advisor switch places. The spiritual advisor arrives at the house at about 5 P.M. to collect witnesses and help them check in at the prison. After the execution, the family returns to the house, and the chaplain brings the prisoner's personal effects to the family. Next, they move to the funeral home if they want to view the body. Generally, that's the last contact Walters has with the family.

"We feel our best ministry is done on the day of the execution because the family can walk in that door at 2 P.M., and at 7 P.M. when they leave we're crying and hugging and have formed a bond," Walters says. "We get calls from them every once in a while letting us know how they're doing."[17]

Walters says inmates about to be released often contact him and ask if they can live at Hospitality House until they get settled. While they are allowed to shower there, released inmates are never sheltered at the Hospitality House. "The city government did not want it to be a halfway house," Walters says.[18]

The Hospitality House focuses on children, too, and one of its programs provides Christmas gifts collected by local churches and civic organizations for children of prison inmates. "We give them to the families when they're here, so they can say it's from their daddy or from Santa Claus," Walters explains.[19]

Crossroads Baptist Church also provides the house with 150 bags of Christmas presents for women family members of inmates. "They're working trying to keep a household, to keep the children in clothes, to send money to their husbands in prison, and a lot of times they don't have resources for themselves," Walter says. "So [the church] puts together a nice bag with a Bible, house shoes, bath products, stationery—things they wouldn't go out and buy for themselves."[20]

Additionally, at the first of the school year, Walters says, "local churches donate school supplies for the children."[21] An average of about twenty-five children stay at Hospitality House each month, with more youngsters visiting during summer breaks.

Community Reaches Victims, Too

The needs of families of the victims of crimes are also a concern in Huntsville, and town leaders dedicated to that effort include Jim Brazzil, who gained international experience when his church sent him to Ukraine in 1992 to minister to inmates. He has been a TDCJ prison chaplain and now is program administrator for Victim and Community Support and Education. Brazzil's responsibilities include contacting victims when offenders have an execution date.

As director of Victims' Services in Huntsville, Brazzil explains that his agency notifies victims sixty to ninety days before the execution. "We need to know who in [the] family wants to witness the execution. There are five family slots. If there's more than one victim, then there are six slots to be split between two or more families."[22] He says that victims' family members who wish to see the execution are invited to his office and shown a video to prepare them, "and of course we're on the phone with them constantly."[23]

On the evening of the execution, Brazzil prepares family members and sees that they are escorted into the death chamber. After the execution, Brazzil conducts "a debriefing to make sure they're okay mostly, and to prepare them for the future." TDCJ then offers an opportunity to hold a press conference before "sending them on their way. If we need to make accommodations for them overnight, we do that as well. And then we follow up with them, and we stay in contact. We offer our services, whatever they [need]."[24]

While the Miranda Act provided rights for offenders, Brazzil says Victims' Services has only been around for about twenty years and is still evolving. "We get involved with the victims after the offender has been incarcerated," Brazzil observes. "Everything we have in our organization is victim driven."[25] He does not think the public has any misconceptions about Victims' Services. "I just don't think they have any conceptions at all. Most people don't know we're here. The state constitution has amendments for victims' rights, and most people do not know that."[26]

Brazzil is proud of the work his four-person unit (the smallest in the state) does in Huntsville. "I think we're on the cutting edge of true healing or restoration for victims, and that's what we're trying to accomplish. Oftentimes their freedoms, their joys, everything has been robbed, and they have lost a sense of power in their lives. We try to give it back to them."[27]

Brazzil and his staff try to educate the community and specifically local agencies about programs that might be helpful, such as the victim offender mediation dialogue (VOMD), which can be accessed through the TDCJ website, and victim notification services (VNS), which maintains a twenty-four-hour hotline seven days a week for victims anxious to know when an offender is eligible for parole or if an inmate has escaped or died. Another program he mentions is called victim impact panels, which also has a page at the TDCJ website. This program collects victim stories. "If we feel it's a good story, we will take those victims into prisons, parole offices, police departments, or schools, and we let them tell their stories."[28] In addition to these official programs aimed at stimulating public discussions about capital punishment, the media are a strong and influential factor in directing community conversations.

Community Media, Leaders, and Agendas

In Huntsville one newspaper has recorded town happenings for more than 150 years. The *Huntsville Item*, started in 1850, is the second-oldest continuously published newspaper in Texas.[29] While the local newspaper dutifully covers preexecution stories and assigns reporters to witness and report on all executions, it neither advocates nor protests capital punishment. English professor Helena Halmari's research focusing on linguistic characteristics of news stories in the *Item* provides some interesting observations.[30]

In an interview with a reporter from the Sam Houston State University student newspaper, the Finnish native observes that "Language reflects our thought patterns….Therefore, the way in which stories are written directly reveals the beliefs of those who wrote it." She points out that the newspaper's ideology is reflected in its reporters' "word choices, syntactic patterns, repeated juxtapositions of meanings and the highly predictable episode structure in execution narratives."[31]

For example, she notes that the newspaper refers to a convicted murderer as a "killer," while those carrying out the execution are referred to as officials or an execution team, thus reminding readers that nobody executes anyone in Huntsville but rather executions merely take place there. Another example she gives is the inclusion in some news stories of information about inmate tattoos. "Tattoos in American society are sometimes associated with criminal background and undesirable socio-economic status,"[32] she says. The inclusion of such details gives readers a framework with which to categorize inmates.

In an article about her research, Halmari writes, "While clearly and consciously, the *Huntsville Item* is fulfilling its function as a neutral reporter of local events, it simultaneously, through an intricate play with the language employed, justifies the executions that its home community is choosing to, or has chosen to, carry out."[33]

Halmari identifies four themes with "implicit underlying messages: Lethal injection is a humane execution method; executed people are bad and deserve to die; no one person is responsible for carrying out a sentence; and even if the executed person was bad, he may have changed and capital punishment sends him to his Savior."[34] While acknowledging that crime is a popular news topic and that events like executions related to crime are newsworthy, Halmari's four themes are consistently repeated in news stories and represent a decidedly positive public relations "spin" on the topic.[35]

In a related research study, Halmari and Jan-Ola Ostman explore the *Huntsville Item* coverage of the 1998 execution of Karla Faye Tucker, the first woman in over a century to be executed in Texas. Tucker's execution challenged newspaper managers because she was a young, attractive, born-again Christian—and a pickax murderer. While the majority of the Texas population supports the death penalty, religion and good manners matter a lot too.[36] The *Huntsville Item* was faced with the delicate task of reporting the execution of a Christian woman whom the court said deserved to die to a readership that includes citizens vocally opposed to executions as well as regular churchgoers (many of whom have livelihoods connected to correctional facilities).[37]

According to Halmari and Ostman, the *Item*'s capital punishment coverage generally includes: facts about the execution, reasons for the execution, a description of the crime, the inmate's last words, and quotes from the victim's family. The two researchers think that "the purpose of the reports is to allow the citizens of Huntsville to 'feel good' despite what happens in their town and to consider an execution 'nothing out of the ordinary.'"[38]

The authors note that in the Tucker case, however, the *Item* was more multidimensional than usual and reported on the two sides of Karla—the good person and the bad person. Halmari and Ostman say that the pro–death penalty views presented in the paper were framed as representing the views of the *Huntsville Item* and the local residents, while the anti–death penalty views were framed as "guest" or "foreign" views.[39]

> ***The newspaper refers to a convicted murderer as a "killer," while those carrying out the execution are referred to as officials or an execution team, thus reminding readers that nobody executes anyone in Huntsville but executions merely take place there.***

For over three decades, mass communication researchers have speculated that "issues ordinarily are created, not in the mass media, but either in professional groups or political institutions. Through one or more of these channels, issues become familiar in the community."[40] Whether the *Huntsville Item* was "framing" its coverage of the Tucker execution or simply maneuvering its way through news content with international as well as national political agendas is not clear in the study. The authors do point out that the newspaper made an attempt to "give a more versatile picture of the person to be executed—Tucker is portrayed both as a pickax killer and as a converted Christian."[41] A local newspaper can set or reflect agendas, and there is evidence in other studies[42] that internal self-censorship by reporters, editors, and publishers to conform with community leaders' viewpoints can and does occur. Media seek commentary from local leaders who are in a position to influence and shape perceptions of the public.

At least one local leader doubts that the media and town leaders ever cooperate on setting agendas. "There's a bias against the media [here]," says Fitzgerald. "I don't know if that's just Huntsville [or] if that's East Texas. It's almost like, 'Well, my daddy didn't like the media, so I don't like the media.'" This doesn't mean Fitzgerald himself didn't try to impact both media and public agendas about capital punishment when he was TDCJ public information manager. "I think I tried to make Huntsville something other than the execution capital of the country. I tried to include as many stories as I possibly could that [Huntsville] was a victims' rights capital rather than an execution capital."[43]

Whether other elites have similar agendas is not clear; however, Robert S. and Helen M. Lynd, in the landmark Middletown studies, found that the media present information "in any way that will not offend their chief supporters." The study found that Middletown's dominant interests affected "not only advertising and editorial comment, but the actual news."[44] Other researchers also have reflected on the phenomena during several decades of observing the environment in which media operate. "The news media do not operate with total autonomy but are themselves an integral part of the political system. The existence of communication channels exerts an influence on what elites feel they must disseminate, on how they act, and how they communicate with members of various other elites and sub-elites."[45]

Clearly, Huntsville leaders are not immune to interactive influences between themselves and the local newspaper, which carries partial responsibility for defining and rationalizing the community's main industry.

Community Agendas

The sources and motivations for community topics of interest have been explored for more than thirty years via agenda-setting theory, which asserts that the media can suggest topics about which the public thinks or concerns itself.[46] Researchers such as Maxwell McCombs, a professor and Jesse H. Jones Centennial Chair in Communications at the University of Texas at Austin, extended that theory to explore how the process works for different content and in different settings, including small towns.[47] While agenda-setting hypotheses were not formally tested in Huntsville, issues of importance to town leaders were monitored and studied for connections to newspaper topics. In an early consultation with McCombs[48] about this project, he suggested simply asking leaders, "If you had a friend who knew nothing about Huntsville, how would you describe Huntsville to them?" This proved an interesting and revealing approach to discovering community agendas.

In describing their town, over half of the respondents did not mention the prison system at all, instead focusing on the Big Piney woods, friendly people, advantages provided by the local university, the town's rich history, and its ideal location as a small town close to a major city. The eighteen respondents who did mention the prominence of the Texas Department of Criminal Justice in Huntsville were diverse in their descriptions, with two calling it the "city of death" and the "capital of capital punishment," while several others mentioned the importance of prison jobs and the advantage of having a state agency's headquarters in their town.

Who Is a Town Leader?

Forty Huntsville elites were selected for this survey. Interviewees all held elected or appointed leadership positions or were frequently mentioned by other leaders because of their active roles in the community. Following are highlight demographics of those surveyed:

- 60 percent were between the ages of forty-six and sixty-five;
- 76 percent were male;
- 87 percent were white;
- 40 percent earned over $100,000 annually;
- 58 percent held graduate degrees;
- 24 percent had bachelor's degrees;
- 26 percent were Republicans;
- 21 percent were Democrats; and
- Almost 100 percent said they were "religious," with Baptists, Catholics, Methodists, Church of Christ, Episcopalians, and Unitarians represented.[49]

In summary, the survey results indicated that Huntsville's typical town leader is a white male, about fifty-six years old, with some graduate education, earning about $78,000 annually. He is a Republican who has lived in Huntsville for at least thirteen years. He belongs to a Baptist or other Christian church and is employed by the state government.

Leadership Perspective

One person who is not a typical town leader is Gary Crawford, a black man in his early forties, born and raised in Huntsville. He is a former city council member who made an unsuccessful bid for mayor, but he is thinking of again running for city council. Crawford, a big supporter of his hometown, calls Huntsville a "good place to live. It's an historic place that's got a lot of families that have been around here a long time. There are worse places you can be," he says. He admits the town is a "good old boys' kinda place; it's an East Texas thing. The strange thing I found out is the good old boys' network is divided up into different little groups that don't like each other. The good old boys don't all get along."[50] Still, he insists Huntsville is a nice place and says that the same sort of exclusivity exists in any historic town in East Texas.

While Crawford recognizes the cliques, he says he doesn't really fit into one himself. As a city council member he represented Ward Three, where most black citizens in Huntsville live. Crawford always thinks of himself as caring about the town as a whole, with no special interest groups more important than others. However, Crawford is not a stranger to racism and he recalls when the schools in Huntsville were segregated and racial divisions were common. "I remember when I was a kid there were certain places—Dairy Queen, Dandy Dog, Tastee Freeze—where you had to go around to the side window [instead of the main entrance]. I never understood that, but it was just part of growing up; it was just the way it was here, and that's been done away with."[51]

Occasionally there are still racial incidents, and Crawford commented on a March 2005 episode when city councilwoman Judy Kayse made a reference to lynching in front of local black men. Her words drew heated responses from the NAACP and calls from some for her resignation. Crawford said, "I don't have any hatred toward Judy. There are a lot of Judys. There are a lot of people worse than Judy who act like they are your friends, and they are not. I would rather sit down with the Grand Dragon of the KKK in uniform and know who he is than sit down with someone who says he is a friend [but isn't]."[52]

Crawford makes connections between racist behaviors in general society to behaviors he has observed in the prison system. He thinks the prison system demonstrates the same sort of prejudices as the outside world. He says behaviors inside prison do not differ much from behaviors outside the Walls. "If I am guarding yellow people and I start treating them bad, [then] I say, 'These yellow people are nasty, these yellow people are crooked; a no-good yellow person is worthless.' If I go to Wal-Mart in Huntsville and I have to deal with yellow people, how do I differentiate that yellow person from the yellow person [in prison]? I treat 'em the same way."[53]

Crawford also worries that Texas is not focused on why people end up in the TDCJ system. He says it starts with the school district, because state funding for education is inadequate. "Tell me this; [why] spend more to have an inmate at TDCJ than you would spend to give him a quality education? What's worth more? Let's stop 'em at the front end."[54] In particular he is upset that pay for teachers is low in Huntsville and believes his town "should have the same quality of teachers they got in River Oaks or in Dallas." He mentions the number of Huntsville students who have problems at home because a parent works for TDCJ. "As you go into that house [where a problem child lives] you'll find a parent that's been involved with TDCJ some kinda way. It's a perpetual problem."[55] He sees it as sort of a toll paid by families who have wage earners employed by the prison. However, he is not surprised by the extraction of such a toll. "I guess it's like anywhere else. Some people live around chemical plants, and they don't view it as being dangerous because they live around it all the time. It's just a fact of life."

Crawford is very aware of the contradictions the prison economy presents for his city. "Looking at it from an economic standpoint, prisons are good and bad." In Crawford's view, as one of the largest employers in the community the prison system sets the pay scale; other area employers do not have to up the ante. The "average Joe" simply has to accept the area wage scale,[56] and Crawford says the scale is set too low.

In his opinion, the city should negotiate more advantages from the Texas Department of Criminal Justice. He would like to see the prison system give the city some of its land for development. "Lease it to the city for a dollar or let us sell it. Don't get me wrong, TDCJ inmates do some labor here in town, but [that's] a miniscule amount when you look at how much money we are losing because we can't tax [TDCJ] property."[57]

Crawford wonders why there are not more programs to deal with community problems and, like Weeks, he puts illegal drug use at the top of his list of challenges for Huntsville leaders. "Huntsville has a drug problem. I'll tell you about it. You know how many rehab facilities are in this town? Close your eyes; how many do you see? None. There's not any."[58]

While Crawford and other leaders identify many effects of having a prison system dominate the town, on a practical level finding enough local workers to staff the facilities is a major challenge.

Guards Are a Tough Recruiting Target

TDCJ's decision in 2003 to eliminate most overtime pay to correctional officers and instead issue "comp" time for the first 240 hours of overtime earned each year resulted in significant savings for the agency. While overtime pay cost $36.1 million in 2002, it only cost $2 million in 2003. However, because of staff shortages, when officers earn compensatory time it is difficult to schedule because they cannot take time off unless there are enough employees to cover their shifts.

Whether it is the new overtime rule, the stress of the job, or the salary cap, 5,511 correctional officers (21 percent) quit in 2004. "Turnover is a consistent problem in prisons," says Richard E. Griffin, an attorney with

Jackson Walker in Houston and former chairman of the Arkansas prison system in the 1970s and '80s. "You get tired of having urine thrown at you and being cussed, and everything that goes on in a prison unit, and not being able to do something about it."[59]

> *"Turnover is a consistent problem in prisons. You get tired of having urine thrown at you and being cussed... and not being able to do something about it."*

One of the best recruiting venues for the prison system is the university, with a ready supply of first-generation college students who rarely have families wealthy enough to pay all tuition and costs at Sam Houston State University. Students take whatever jobs are available to pay the bills, and the prison system actively recruits from the university. "There's been a long-standing relationship between the department and young people attending school at Sam Houston State University," says TDCJ public information officer Byron Hays.[60]

According to Ken Johnson, section director for employment, TDCJ tries to match student schedules to work shifts so students can both work and attend classes. Initial screening of potential applicants is done online through the TDCJ website. After a successful interview, new employees attend a five-and-a-half-week academy course before undergoing one hundred hours of on-the-job training. Full-time correctional officers start at $1,816 per month. Benefits, vacation time, and sick leave are part of the job package, as is Homes for Heroes, a home loan program. While most prison guards are male, 38 percent are now female, according to Johnson.[61]

Huntsville native David Pollis, an eleven-year veteran of TDCJ, paid for his education at Sam Houston State University by working as a night transfer officer. "You've got to be knowledgeable about what you're supposed to do. The inmates are going to test you on everything—you're going to be put into situations you can't imagine," Pollis says.[62]

One guard who has been tested is Jake Linney, a white twenty-four-year-old SHSU student who admits there have been times when he has brought episodes and attitudes from his prison job home with him. He describes an instance when he joined a team of officers who used gas plus leg and arm restraints to control a prisoner.

"At the time, the adrenalin is going ninety miles an hour, but you get home [and realize] that offender could have had a knife; he could've stabbed me. I could be dead right now. They don't have store-bought weapons; they make it all. They have spear guns. They have knives; they call them shanks. They have all kinds of weapons that are probably just as powerful as guns," he says.[63]

Linney works in a unit where prisoners are taken off their psychological medications when they first arrive to see if they really need them. "It's a money kinda thing for TDCJ. If they [prisoners] are really psychotic, they can switch on you like that, and all we have is a little can of gas. If they really are psychotic, a can of gas isn't going to stop 'em."[64]

Since he grew up in an almost treeless area of South Texas, Linney says he loves Huntsville because of the piney woods. While his job is stressful, he is sometimes amazed at the talents of inmates and describes one man who was such a good artist he could duplicate every detail in a photograph.[65] Linney said he told the man he should get out of prison and start drawing for a living. The man wryly replied, "I've got a ninety-year sentence."

Linney earns $800 a month for eighty hours' work while he studies for a math secondary education degree at Sam Houston State University. He jokes, "If I can deal with these offenders, I can deal with high school kids; they can't be much worse."[66] While he needs the salary to pay his expenses, he doesn't think it is nearly enough.

"Our governor, Ricky Perry, said monkeys could do our job. I would like to put him in a gray uniform and stick him in there. If you are a cop you get paid real well. We're doing the same jobs as cops."[67]

Beneath the Surface: Contrast and Challenge

Huntsville is a clash of both environmental and community fabrics. The lush meadows and forests draw national notice for their beauty, while brutal heat and sudden storms can flood an area within minutes, changing the landscape from welcoming to dangerous. Likewise, university and community amenities have drawn retirees looking for golf, water sports, and historical connections to Texas, while the prison looks for people to work as guards. Outsiders may be horrified by the realities of the prison system, but insiders demonstrate leadership in responding to the social responsibilities their town encounters on a daily basis. While boundaries are clear in Huntsville, there is movement between and among various communities forced to communicate and respond to one another in civil ways.

The local newspaper has developed innovative responses to cover capital punishment news in one of the most unique settings imaginable. A number of institutions and individuals share roles in setting agendas for community constituents. While no one disputes the enormous impact the prison system has on Huntsville, individuals and organizations demonstrate calm resolution to meeting challenges with the scarce resources available. Huntsville is an ordinary community responding to extraordinary tensions that test even the most able and responsive leaders.

Those leaders include the professionals trained to deliver messages to publics outside Huntsville, the public information representatives for the Texas prison system who are headquartered in Huntsville. In addition to being long-standing members of the community, one of their major challenges is dealing with myths and legends perpetuated by outsiders (including the media) concerning prisons, Huntsville, and Texas in general. As insiders who deal on a daily basis with outsiders from all over the world, these public information officers may have one of the most interesting and unusual public information jobs in the world.

I'm not there for the condemned so much as I'm there for me and for us as a society. I think someone needs to witness injustices when they're happening, and I think every time it [an execution] happens, it is an injustice.
—Dennis Longmire, SHSU professor and capital punishment protestor

Prison City Close-Up

A Constant Witness:
Twenty Years of Protesting Executions

Dennis L. Longmire dresses casually on execution evenings, in Birkenstocks with a large hat framing his bearded face. The SHSU criminal justice professor speaks in a quiet voice perfect for lecturing and punctuates his discourse with examples, facts, and philosophy. Even when he speaks passionately about his beliefs, there is a calmness surrounding him. He admits he schedules his life around executions and attends almost every one. "Even when I'm out of town, I do take a moment at six o'clock [when executions occur] on the day of the execution to reflect."[68]

On execution nights, Longmire starts his vigil on the protestors' corner around 5 P.M. By 6:15 or 6:30, when the execution is over, Longmire goes to his grandson's soccer game, another meeting, or to class if he's teaching that night. The frequency of executions, Longmire admits, causes stress in his personal life. "It's always difficult to think we're going to be putting someone to death who is really a reformed human spirit. Other times, the person we're executing has made no effort at redemption; they may even claim guilt, but almost with pride. Sometimes they say, 'Damn it I did it, and I would do it again if I had the opportunity,'" he remarks.[69]

In the last two decades, Longmire estimates he has been present on the protestors' corner for probably 90 percent of the executions. Since 1976, when the U.S. Supreme Court reinstated executions, Texas has executed more people than any other state. During Governor George W. Bush's tenure, more people were executed—about one every two weeks—than under any other governor in the United States. Up to 80 percent of Texans strongly favored capital punishment during Bush's time as governor,[70] and in a 2004 Gallup poll 50 percent of Americans said they favored the death penalty over life imprisonment for murder.[71] However, Longmire believes that more than two decades' worth of research shows that Texans' support of capital punishment as a deterrent to crime is unjustified.

Longmire, who finished his Ph.D. in 1979, says, "By 1979 research had demonstrated the death penalty was no more effective as a deterrent than a long prison sentence—it's not an effective public policy instrument."[72]

While passionate about his beliefs, Longmire does not support confrontational politics. "I don't challenge the prison system for being murderers, and sometimes advocacy groups will be there on the corner with bullhorns chanting...challenging the correctional officers. To me, that's counterproductive."[73]

While he opposes capital punishment, Longmire is sympathetic to townspeople who work at TDCJ, observing, "I've seen correctional officers get on their knees, cross themselves, and say a prayer. Then they get back up and do their duty. So I know some of them don't agree with what's going on, but they're just trying to make a living and feed their families."[74]

> **"I've seen correctional officers get on their knees, cross themselves, and say a prayer. Then they get back up and do their duty."**

While Longmire has his admirers, he also knows there are people, including other professors in criminal justice, who do not support him. "My colleagues are the people who most object to what I do on the corner. I believe my bias against the death penalty influences everything I do, but I'm aware of it, and I'm cautious about it."[75]

Longmire particularly monitored his behavior when he was associate dean for academic programs in the Criminal Justice College, and during those times he was silent during his vigils on the protestors' corner. "My good sense told me the wrong article in the wrong newspaper could cost this university millions of dollars just because somebody from an administrative position down here spoke against a highly popular issue. So during the early years, I was quiet."[76] Now he is willing to speak out.

"If you talk to the officials in the prison system, they'll tell you, 'The man with the candle out there with the hat on, he's here all the time.' They're consciously aware what they're doing is being objected to, not just by someone with a bullhorn, but by a professor they respect. I always articulate my objections as broadly as possible and make it clear it's not the prison that's the problem; it's the legislature, and it's the people who put those folks in office—that's the problem."[77] ✪

Notes

[1] Virginia Stem Owens and David Clinton Owens, *Living Next Door to the Death House* (Grand Rapids, Michigan: William B. Eerdmans, 2003), book jacket.
[2] Michelle Lyons (public information officer), interview by Tina Baiter, Huntsville, Texas, May 19, 2005.
[3] Owens and Owens, 97.
[4] Morris Janowitz, "Foreword," in James B. Jacobs, *Stateville: The Penitentiary in Mass Society* (Chicago: University of Chicago Press, 1977), x.
[5] Lorna A. Rhodes, *Total Confinement: Madness and Reason in the Maximum Security Prison* (Berkeley: University of California Press, 2004), xiii.
[6] Gresham Sykes, *The Society of Captives* (Princeton, New Jersey: Princeton University Press, 1958; repr., New York: Atteneur, 1966), 8.
[7] Rhodes, 8.
[8] David Weeks (Walker County district attorney), interview by Ardyth Sohn, Huntsville, Texas, March 21, 2005.
[9] Owens and Owens, viii.
[10] Weeks interview, 2005.
[11] Ibid.
[12] Ibid.
[13] Larry Fitzgerald (TDCJ public information manager), interview by Ruth Massingill, Austin, Texas, March 17, 2005.
[14] Charles Freddy Walters (overseer of Hospitality House), interview by Tina Baiter, Huntsville, Texas, March 21, 2005.
[15] Ibid.
[16] Ibid.
[17] Ibid.
[18] Ibid.
[19] Ibid.
[20] Ibid.
[21] Ibid.
[22] Jim Brazzil (program administrator for Victim and Community Support and Education), interview by Tina Baiter, Huntsville, Texas, July 18, 2005.
[23] Ibid.
[24] Ibid.
[25] Ibid.
[26] Ibid.
[27] Ibid.
[28] Ibid.
[29] *Huntsville Item*. Available at: http://www.itemonline.com/about us/.
[30] Audrey Wick, "A Discourse on Death," *The Houstonian*, February 20, 2001, 1, 6.
[31] Ibid.
[32] Ibid.
[33] Helena Halmari, "Discourse of Death: The Function of the Local Newspaper Coverage of Huntsville, Texas, Executions in Language and Ideology: Selected Papers from the 6th International Pragmatics Conference," vol. 1, edited by Jef Verschueren, International Pragmatics Association, Antwerp, Belgium, 1999, 203.
[34] Ibid.
[35] Ibid.
[36] James W. Marquart, Sheldon Ekland-Olson, and Jonathan R. Sorensen, *The Rope, the Chair, and the Needle: Capital Punishment in Texas, 1923–1990* (Austin: University of Texas Press, 1994), 190–91.
[37] Helen Halmari and Jan-Ola Ostman, "The Soft-Spoken, Angelic Pickax Killer: The Notion

of Discourse Pattern in Controversial News Reporting," *Journal of Pragmatics*, 2001, 805-23.
   [38] Ibid.
   [39] Ibid.
   [40] Ibid.
   [41] Ibid.
   [42] See, for instance, Maxwell McCombs, *Setting the Agenda: The News Media and Public Opinion* (Cambridge, Massachusetts: Polity Press, 2004).
   [43] Fitzgerald interview, 2005.
   [44] Robert S. Lynd and Helen M. Lynd, *Middletown* (New York: Harcourt, Brace, 1929), 475.
   [45] Sidney Kraus et al., "Critical Events Analysis," in *Political Communications: Issues and Strategies for Research*, ed. Steven H. Chaffee (Beverly Hills, California: Sage, 1975), 202.
   [46] Bernard C. Cohen, *The Press and Foreign Policy* (Princeton, New Jersey: Princeton University Press, 1967), 13.
   [47] See also David Protess and Maxwell McCombs (Eds.), *Agenda Setting: Readings on Media, Public Opinion, and Policy Making* (Hillsdale, New Jersey: Lawrence Earlbaum, 1991).
   [48] Maxwell McCombs, private discussion with Ardyth Sohn, spring 2001.
   [49] Study was completed by Ardyth Sohn and journalism students at Sam Houston State University in fall 2001.
   [50] Gary Crawford (former Huntsville city council member), interview by Melody Davison, Huntsville, Texas, June 21, 2005.
   [51] Ibid.
   [52] Ibid.
   [53] Ibid.
   [54] Ibid.
   [55] Ibid.
   [56] Ibid.
   [57] Ibid.
   [58] Ibid.
   [59] Terry Langford, "State Prison Guards Tough to Keep," Houston Chronicle, March 26, 2005. Available at: http://www.solutionsfortexas.info/id309.html.
   [60] Kelly Jakubowski, "Student Prison Guards: TDCJ Holds Job Fair for Students," The Houstonian Online, May 3, 2005. Available at: http://www.houstonianonline.com/media/paper229/news/2005/05/03/Huntsville/Student.Press.
   [61] Ibid.
   [62] Ibid.
   [63] Jake Linney (Texas Department of Criminal Justice employee), interview by Melody Davison, Huntsville, Texas, July 8, 2005.
   [64] Ibid.
   [65] Ibid.
   [66] Ibid.
   [67] Ibid
   [68] Dennis Longmire (criminal justice professor and anti–capital punishment activist), interview by Melody Davison, Huntsville, Texas, June 21, 2005.
   [69] Ibid.
   [70] Erika Casriel,"Bush and the Texas Death Machine,"*Rolling Stone*,August 3, 2000, 29–34.
   [71] David W. Moore, "Public Divided between Death Penalty and Life Imprisonment without Parole," *Gallup Poll News Service*, June 2, 2004.
   [72] Longmire interview, 2005.
   [73] Ibid.
   [74] Ibid.
   [75] Ibid.
   [76] Ibid.
   [77] Ibid.

SECTION II
CAUGHT IN THE MIDDLE:
The Role of PR in Shaping Social Perspectives of the Criminal Justice System

Most executions barely ripple the placid surface of everyday life, but high-profile cases attract the "media circus." Prison coverage has always been a routine part of the news landscape for Huntsville Item *reporters such as Patsy Woodall and Don Reid, who covered 189 executions during his career.*

Chapter Three
The Criminal Justice PIO as Liaison between Myth and Reality

Typically, people talk about someone breaking out of prison. If they break out of prison, they ain't gonna hang around here long...they're gonna leave as fast as they can because everybody here is associated with the system somehow. I guess you could call that a myth. The reality is, it's actually a lot safer here.
—Kevin Evans, Huntsville city manager

This is prison city; lock your doors at night and don't walk anywhere by yourself—it's not safe, especially if you're a female.
—Summer camp instructor to high school students

"My Kid Can Beat Up Your Kid"

Texas tough is more than a catchy slogan for selling Ford trucks to Texans; it is a pervasive attitude that spans generations, from toddler to octogenarian, and is woven into the multiple cultures across the state. Politicians frequently include tough-on-crime planks in their campaign platforms, and that message plays well, particularly in the rural districts. In most parts of the state the very surroundings are unfriendly; there are critters such as snakes, roaches, mosquitoes, and fire ants to combat. Perhaps that's why the majority of Texans feel safer if they possess firearms: According to a 2004 Scripps Howard poll, 52 percent of the state's residents own guns, up from 48 percent in 2000. Texans also like to carry guns in their purses, pockets, or vehicles; 61 percent support the state's concealed handgun law.[1]

This tough stance extends to the medium of personal billboards—bumper stickers—where Huntsville vehicles have been known to sport the line "My kid can beat up your kid" and, of course, the perennial favorite, "When guns are outlawed, only outlaws will have guns."

Some shade-tree political analysts—the old-timers who gather for coffee on small-town courthouse squares—speculate that Texas evolved in the last thirty years from a "yellow dog" Democrat state (where voters would vote for a yellow dog if it were running on the Dem ticket) to a Republican-dominated state in part because Republican politicians used the fear appeal of gun control laws to win votes from the blue-collar constituency.

Livelihood for many in that constituency is already precarious—Texas is a right-to-work state, so the unions that do exist have difficulty recruiting and building power bases. Since many jobs have no sick leave or insurance benefits, state agencies such as the Texas Department of Criminal Justice are desirable employers. The job market is uncertain in many communities, where economies fluctuate from boom to bust with the rising or falling fortunes of oil, land, and, more recently, technology. Residents do not find their own lives to be easy; they take an almost perverse pride in a bulldoglike tenacity to overcome financial as well as personal obstacles.

"It's not our role to mold public perception. PR people try to influence and persuade through the media."

Many families have lived in Texas—often in the same community—for generations. Some have never traveled out of the state. In rural areas especially, many live on inherited land and may be "land poor," which means having property but insufficient cash flow to pay taxes. Their own struggles foster intolerance for anyone who lies, steals, or won't work. It is the nature of the state culture to value independence and a strong work ethic; Texans in general are not sympathetic toward felons and are strongly opposed to "coddling" prisoners. In Grimes County, thirty miles west of Huntsville, a painted roadside sign demonstrates this attitude with the warning "You'll do time for crime in Grimes County." According to a Texas crime poll conducted in 2004 through the Criminal Justice Center at Sam Houston State University, more than 75 percent of the state's citizens support the death penalty; in Huntsville the number is much higher, perhaps as high as 95 percent.[2]

Within this politically charged environment, official communication by TDCJ must be woven to reflect the chosen image and retain public support while combating public misperceptions regarding the criminal justice system.

Public Relations vs. Public Information

In a state that is proud of its tough stance on crime and criminals and has the incarceration and execution figures to prove it; the state prison population has grown from 32,000 to more than 150,000 in the last twenty years.³ TDCJ's public information officers' (PIOs') jobs might seem to be an uphill battle against generations of ingrained ideas about the role of criminal justice and the function prisons should play in society. In many cases public perceptions do not match present-day realities, but the PIOs say that correcting those misconceptions is a struggle.

One of the first erroneous notions is that TDCJ hires public relations people. In post-Enron Texas more than ever, PR implies "spin doctors" and information manipulation—in other words, lying—in many Texans' eyes. Since that is not the kind of public servant activity the populace wants to finance with tax dollars, officially there are no PR practitioners in the Texas criminal justice system.

"We don't see ourselves as public relations people," says Mike Viesca, director of the TDCJ Information Office from 2003 until 2006. "We see ourselves as public information. We're not here to promote any kind of thought as it relates to criminal justice. We work with the news media to get them information to write their stories."⁴

Viesca's predecessor, Larry Todd, made the same distinction between PR and PI: "It's not our role to mold public perception. PR people try to influence and persuade through the media. Public information people provide accurate and timely information."⁵ According to Todd, there is a need for more in-depth information. He expressed the concern that reporters often focus on more sensational criminal justice topics and ignore complex—but vital—issues like the state budget.

Nevertheless, the media are the public the PIOs serve and they are neither "our enemy nor are they our close allies," TDCJ employees are reminded in a forty-seven-page handbook for working with the news media.⁶ PR basics are spelled out in the introduction: "When we react with candor, we establish credibility. When we fail to communicate, we leave a void which frequently becomes a negative story and thus a poor perception of our agency."⁷

Reporters such as Mike Graczyk of the Associated Press, who has worked with the agency for years, develop a high level of comfort in the media-PIO relationship. Some say those alliances are too cozy, bordering on "you scratch my back and I'll scratch yours." Nevertheless, the process of prison reporting tends to fall into a predictable routine. "I've had a pretty good relationship with [the PIOs]," Graczyk says. "They know I'm not going to screw them and I hope for the same thing." He believes the prisoners are willing participants in this reciprocity too. "They use us, we use them. We all use each other to get the story."[8]

A Unique Public Information Job

This important information function is the responsibility of a handful of PIOs who are charged with promoting the institution's four-pronged mission: (1) to provide public safety, (2) to promote positive change in offender behavior, (3) to reintegrate offenders into society, and (4) to assist victims of crime.[9] This is a sweeping directive for a sprawling and complex state agency with more than eighty facilities staffed by 39,000 employees across 268,000 square miles, almost five times the area of New York State.

The staff responsible for proactive as well as reactive public information activities for the prison system and the prison's school system consists of three and a half positions—all except the director are based in Huntsville. Essentially, their jobs are focused on external media relations, although they also coordinate some internal communications, as Viesca explains: "We certainly keep everybody internally in the loop if there are certain issues in the news media that are popping up. I try to give division directors a heads up [about] stories that affect their particular area."[10]

Job requirements for the director's position include eight years of full-time, wage-earning experience in business administration, criminal justice, journalism, law enforcement, public administration, or public information.[11] There is a high preference for government agency experience, which apparently weighed heavily in the selection of Viesca, who was previously deputy press secretary for the Texas attorney general and also worked in the Department of Transportation as well as in television as a news producer.

Experienced PR people, who can read between the lines of the official job description, would realize that the director's job is a highly political position that requires a delicate balancing act between internal pressures and media requests. In Austin Viesca has been described as a "consummate politician," which is neither a compliment nor a condemnation in the state's capital but does allow him to negotiate the political waters with relative ease. Even so, in the spring of 2006, Viesca was unexpectedly "reassigned" to an internal communication role in the agency.

The staff in Huntsville is more involved in hands-on public information activities: setting up media interviews with prisoners, providing press kits, responding to media requests from far and near, and, of course, the more controversial role of being media escorts for executions, sometimes as often as every week. A background in media and a degree in a communications field are requisite. A mix of media backgrounds in the department is desirable. "When I came on, they were looking for someone with newspaper experience to write the press releases," says public information director Michelle Lyons, who had previously covered the prison beat for the *Huntsville Item*. "The main requirement was experience."[12]

Lyons remembers she took a four-day course offered by one of the national correctional institutes specifically for prison PIOs. "They gave us a lot of different crisis situations, then they would have us stand up and give a news conference. The other PIOs would just hammer at you. They were a lot more vicious than most reporters because they knew which questions would push your buttons."[13]

The demands on the public information office ebb and flow, depending on the prison-related issues in the news and on the execution schedule, but at least one staff member is always on call.

Likewise, Bambi Kiser, the communications coordinator for the Windham School District, brought practical experience to her job. Previously, she taught high school journalism; now she tries to persuade the media to tell positive stories about education and rehabilitation in the prison, which often cuts against the grain of public perception. "It's hard for people to understand the value of what we do," Kiser says. "People are quick to think, 'They committed a crime, they are locked up, and we shouldn't spend any more time and money on them.'"[14]

In reality, the State of Texas was a pioneer in prison education. Huntsville native Frank Dobbs recounts how his photographer father was hired in the 1940s to document conditions in the Texas prison system, which had been the focus of a "series of scandals over living conditions and housing and unexplained deaths." As part of the process of cleaning up the system, Texas became the first prison system to offer a complete education. "If your sentence was long enough, you could go from illiteracy to a college degree," Dobbs says. "That was first done in Texas, [but] it gets very little acknowledgment or credit because it doesn't suit the public persona of the ugly Texan."[15]

The job demands on the public information office ebb and flow, depending on the prison-related issues in the news and on the execution schedule, but at least one staff member is always on call. "Deadlines don't take a vacation, so that's why we are always available to answer questions even after hours—twenty-four hours a day," Viesca says.[16] During regular working hours, the staff processes hundreds of media requests for interviews, often sparked by news events. "A lot of times their cases draw the interest," Viesca says. "Maybe it's the anniversary of a certain event. Often, perhaps, they have a court ruling that changes their case."[17] Texas has a more open policy than some states when it comes to interviews with inmates, according to Viesca. Several states, including California, do not allow one-on-one interviews with offenders. Invariably, a rush of reporters request interviews with Texas death row inmates just before their executions. "It happens in waves; we'll have a month where there is no execution and then a month where there are five, and we get a lot busier," Lyons says.[18]

The staff in Huntsville is better able to stay aloof from the political undercurrents of prison controversies, but like all state employees their jobs are at the mercy of legislative budget cuts, which are affected by the state's political leadership and public opinion. The tough-on-crime attitude has made the political fortunes of many Texas politicians, including George "Dubya" Bush, but some politicos feel uncomfortable with that stance and with the image it conveys, both within the state and beyond its borders. "A lot of us became embarrassed about the state's reputation for being bloodthirsty," says Texas senator Rodney Ellis, who successfully sponsored a bill in 2001 to require DNA testing. "But being tough doesn't mean you have to be bloodthirsty."[19]

More recently, Ellis lauded the governor's appointment of a special criminal justice advisory council to study potential flaws in the state's justice system—from arrest to final appeal—and to recommend changes. The panel was charged with reviewing issues that have received unfavorable media coverage and sapped public confidence in the state's prison system, including the death penalty, mishandling of evidence by city crime labs, fairness and accessibility of the appellate system, and use of new technologies.[20] Some cynics declared the creation of the nine-member commission to be PR motivated since the governor was facing a difficult reelection campaign. Governor's spokesperson Kathy Walt says the panel was directed to take a broad look at the state's criminal justice system rather than examine individual cases. "This council is going to look at the criminal justice system as a whole and how to make improvements."[21]

Viesca professes to be unfazed by the creation of the commission: "I think a lot of the concerns that have been raised are in the areas leading up to incarceration and not as a result of it: the appellate process, the trial itself. To me, that's where the focus is."[22] The behind-the-scenes politics are always a cause for speculation—after all, this is a state where the dead rose from their graves to vote for former president Lyndon Johnson. When President George W. Bush requested a review in 2004 of death row convictions of Mexican nationals, skeptics said Mexican oil, not justice, was the incentive.

If the PIOs' jobs are complicated by ever-changing political pressures, one thing remains constant: the onslaught of tired jokes they hear from both friends and strangers. Lyons was working in the PI office when she married, which led to teasing about where she found her groom. Although her husband is not associated with the prison system, she takes the quips in stride: "Yes, he is an inmate, and I know where he is at all times," she says with a good-natured smile. But, in reality, "those jokes get kind of old," she admits.[23]

In self-defense, residents get in the habit of making their own jests. Dr. Dennis Longmire, who has been standing on the "protest corner" across from the Walls for practically every execution since he came to Huntsville to teach criminal justice at Sam Houston State over twenty years ago, says wryly that he only intended to "do five years in Huntsville," but he met a woman whom he eventually married and she explained that Texas women did not leave the state, so his five years turned into a "life sentence."[24] Most residents are accustomed to hearing, "Oh, they let you out for the weekend?" when they first tell people they are from Huntsville.

Although everyone realizes the jokes are not malicious, they are a constant reminder that the overriding public perception of Huntsville—despite the best efforts of the university and city PR people—is that of prison town. Frank Krystyniak, Sam Houston State University's PR director, says he occasionally fields calls from concerned parents about the proximity of the prison to the university campus. He uses the "prison towns are safe places" response. "The closest problem was several years ago when an inmate escaped from a unit around Trinity (fifteen miles east of Huntsville, population 2,721) and drove through our campus," Krystyniak says. "His truck played out and he forced a female student to drive him to Pasadena in her car. But, inmates don't hang around—they try to get out of here."[25]

Not only do most inhabitants regard the town as safe, the very building where the public information department is housed is considered a "secure" building—the doors are always locked. Employees enter with a passcard, but visitors must call for clearance to enter. The two-story red brick administrative building fronts on 11th Street, the "main drag" that connects the downtown square to Interstate 45, the link between Houston and Dallas. Passersby see a red, white, and blue sign that boasts: "TDCJ is a great place to work."

Lyons says being next door to the Walls created problems that led to a decision several years ago to limit access. "Because the Walls unit is where the inmates are released every day, we had a problem with a lot of family members coming into the building and trashing the restrooms or break rooms [while] waiting for their relatives," Lyons says. The locked doors also protect the PIOs from unexpected media drop-ins. "We have a lot of foreign journalists who show up unannounced and most of them just want to come in and argue, so it really has worked to our advantage that the building is locked down," Lyons explains. "The reporters don't question it; they just look at it as another security measure related to a prison system."[26]

Uncooperative and Unlovable Clients

While the PIOs are sometimes besieged by antagonistic reporters, their "clients"—the prisoners—can be hostile and uncooperative as well. The PI officers process hundreds of media requests, and the majority of the prisoners agree to be interviewed. Sometimes, however, when the reporter, accompanied by a PIO, arrives, the inmate has a change of heart. Occasionally, an inmate will focus on the PIO as an object of hate. That was the case with John King, the "Jasper dragster" who was convicted for his role in assaulting a black man and dragging him to death on a chain tied to the bumper of a Ford pickup.[27]

Larry Fitzgerald, who was the PIO at the time, remembers that King first declined to be interviewed and then changed his mind and consented to an interview with AP reporter Mike Graczyk. "Graczyk came to talk to him," Fitzgerald recalls. "As was my practice, I was always in the room. I didn't care what the inmate said, [and] out there at Polunsky, you can't hear what's going on anyway because it's done on the phone. When we got through, Graczyk said, 'Boy, he hates you.' He had called me a liar, just all sorts of things. You know, I don't really care what Mr. King thinks of me. But, if I had to go back and witness [an execution], that's the one I would choose. I'd just like to see him get his."[28]

The PIOs don't censor their prisoner-clients' conversations with the media, but they monitor for illegal activities, such as selling interviews, which inmates often try to do, particularly to the foreign media.

Reporters, particularly female reporters, must deal with occasional heckling and crudeness in the course of their day. Walt, blond and elegant, who was dubbed "Megababe" by an inmate, a nickname that stuck during her years covering death row for the *Houston Chronicle*, remembers, "There were times when I would walk down the unit and people would yell things— they're a little more graphic than construction site workers."

Walt says she sometimes wondered if the situation might get out of control, but it never did. "TDCJ was careful and would never have allowed me or any other reporter to be taken into an area where that was likely to happen."[29] Kelly Prew, reporter for the *Huntsville Item*, says that most prisoners who agree to interviews are respectful. "They're very reserved and polite and they say 'yes, ma'am'."[30] One advantage female reporters have, according to Prew, is that male prisoners are more likely to grant interviews to women. With women prisoners, on the other hand, the reverse is true.

The PIOs don't censor their prisoner-clients' conversations with the media, but they do monitor them for illegal activities, such as selling interviews to reporters, which inmates often try to do, particularly to the foreign media. "If we find out about it, we terminate it because it is absolutely not allowed," Lyons says. This is where the PIO job laps over into investigative work. "It's difficult for us to prove. We had a situation where we thought it was occurring and we were trying to prove it by looking at [deposits in] his commissary trust fund." Payments are sometimes made to inmates' family members, which is difficult to find and prove, Lyons explains.[31]

By Texas law, inmates are not allowed to profit from their notoriety, but many try to do so, especially death row prisoners. Personal items offered for sale range from fingernail clippings, offered by "railroad killer" Angel Maturino Resendiz, to items of clothing. Murder memorabilia listings sometimes turn up on eBay, the international auction site sometimes called the world's largest garage sale. Lyons remembers a death row inmate who tried to auction off a witness spot for his execution. The PI officers had the listing pulled from eBay. The witness slots are the property of the condemned, but they have no monetary value. "You can put whomever you like to witness your execution, but you're not allowed to take money for it," Lyons says.[32]

In the end, it's a power game; for the most part, the prisoners' lives are regulated around the clock. What they can control is whether or not they grant interviews and what they say in those interviews.

Exercising this sliver of power does not make them loveable characters to frustrated reporters, and it puts the PIOs in an uncomfortable spot—caught in the middle.

Stress and Adrenaline

Although the PIO job is in an often unfriendly environment with criminals for clients and prurient public interest driving much of the media coverage, the public information officers find their jobs to be exciting in a way unique among public relations positions. Fitzgerald, who was known for providing pithy sound bites during his eight-year tenure in Huntsville as public information manager, said it best: "I have often described this job as like playing Russian roulette. When that phone rings, you don't know; it could be a hostage situation, it could be an escape, it could be a riot, it could be a homicide...there's just no telling. It's the most exciting job I have ever had because usually every day there's some kind of adrenalin rush."[33]

As for the psychological toll the PIO job exacts, Fitzgerald never anticipated working in a prison system, but when that's where his career path led he adopted the same philosophy that served him well as a broadcast reporter covering such disasters as plane crashes, car wrecks, and fires. "Just don't take it home with you," Fitzgerald says. "What do you do when you go home? How do you handle it? Very easily. Watch television and go to bed."[34]

On the subject of job stress, Lyons's only comment was that she gets frustrated when she doesn't have time to disseminate as many positive stories as she would like. "It stresses me out that I would like to give people a better understanding of some of the good things we do."[35] Taking a longer view, Charles Brown, who joined the public information office in 1967 and recently retired, attended every execution for decades. Looking back, he is philosophical: "Well, it's part of your job; you have to divorce yourself from the things you dislike. But, if I was going to be the spokesman for the agency, then I would rather be there to see what happened so I could report it [to the media]."³⁶

Reporters, too, feel the pressure of covering prison news day in and day out. "It was a very emotionally draining beat to cover," Walt recalled. "It's not just covering the inmates, it's covering the victims—that was the most gut-wrenching—having those people cry their hearts out."³⁷ Vagaries of Texas law create injustices *Item* reporter Prew finds difficult to accept. "The 'tough on crime' mentality is just laughable. In Texas one of the criteria is it has to be a child under five years of age to constitute a capital crime. We're tough on crime in Texas, let me tell you. If you're five and you die, we've got you covered, but if you're six…"³⁸

Bad News vs. Good News

High-profile breakouts, riots, or hostage situations can electrify public opinion and generate massive media coverage, creating long, stressful workdays for the PI staff. At that point, the job becomes primarily reactive to the bad news of the crisis. "Unfortunately, in this type of arena, a lot is going to be reactive," Viesca says. "We have certainly tried to introduce some proactive measures so we can see a balance of news coverage out there, where we are not just associated with the negative."³⁹

The agency's policy is not to stonewall even if the news is unpleasant. "Bad news is like garbage; the smell does not improve with age," warns *TDCJ's Media Relations Manual*, which warns that attempts to hide negative stories result in broader and more damaging media coverage when the information does come to light.⁴⁰ This is classic textbook public relations, accepted in theory by administrators and politicians alike but sometimes forgotten in an actual crisis. The PIOs say they try to follow this edict, although Viesca is clearly wary of writers "with agendas." Like any PR professional, the PIOs do not necessarily tell reporters all they know. Lyons points out that she is still in the news business, just as she was when she was a newspaper reporter.

"One of the biggest differences is the amount of information I find out is a lot greater. I learn a lot of stuff that I wouldn't as a reporter and then we have to decide what we're able to release and what we aren't."⁴¹ But the PIOs know truth will out: "If something bad happens, we're not going to lie about it—there is no point," Lyons says. "You might as well just take the blows and move on. The bottom line is in this type of public relations, there are going to be a lot more bad things in the news about us than there are good."⁴²

―――――― *Prison City Close-Up* ――――――

Good News Bears Reporting:
A Day in the Life of Bambi Kiser

Bambi Kiser, communications coordinator for the Windham School District (WSD) since July 1994, often works in tandem with the PI office to set up media interviews and tours. Although her office is cozy and personalized, Kiser is careful not to display family pictures in her workspace. This is a precaution, because offenders are in and out of her office daily performing janitorial duties and Kiser does not want to chance putting her family in danger. "I might put up pictures of my sister's kids," Kiser jokes, "but not my own."[43]

Kiser fills both external and internal PR roles for Windham. In addition to distributing press releases and being media liaison for the ninety prison campuses across the state, she produces Windham staff publications, updates the website calendar and bulletin board, and provides supervision and editing for the offender newspaper, the *Echo*.

Unlike the negative news Lyons's office often delivers about TDCJ, most of the information Kiser provides focuses on how education in the Texas prison system helps reduce recidivism rates. Kiser's hardest job is selling the WSD to the public, because there are numerous misperceptions about the prison education system. "We would never lie about what we do," Kiser says. "We would never hide what we do. But we can lose everything over a misconception."[44]

Kiser spells out some of those misconceptions: Offenders receive free college educations; tax money is wasted on providing education to prisoners; and workshops where offenders learn job skills are air-conditioned. Perhaps the most difficult myth to dispel, Kiser says, is the conviction held by many Texas taxpayers that offenders cannot become productive citizens of society.

The motto of the WSD is "Fighting Crime through Education," and numerous success stories have come out of the WSD's academic, vocational, and cognitive programs. These stories give Kiser opportunities to promote the positive effect of Texas's criminal justice system. One of the highlights of her job is attending graduation ceremonies, where prisoners' accomplishments range from earning certificates in vocational training to earning a bachelor's or a master's degree. (See "Graduation behind Bars" in section 3.)

Overall, Kiser sees her role as a traffic director who helps reporters get the most accurate information possible about Windham. ✪

On the proactive, "good news" side, the job is driven by efforts to tell the story about education and rehabilitation successes. These efforts often involve coordination with the Windham School District, the Texas Education Agency program housed within TDCJ that focuses on academic, vocational, and behavioral change for more than 83,000 prisoners across the state. Although the program is separate from the public information office, Bambi Kiser, the Windham communications coordinator, works closely with the PI staff to arrange media coverage since reporters must enter prison facilities to talk with inmates or staff about educational programs. The two offices also work together to promote various proactive initiatives such as Go Kids, a mentoring program for children of incarcerated parents, and the "media honor roll," which recognizes print and broadcast reporters who cover prison education issues. Kiser says she sees the media seeking balance. "After a lot of bad news [about prisons], the media want something different. They say, 'Tell me something good.'"[45]

Lyons says she, too, tries to direct media toward the agency's activities in the areas of probation, parole, and education, "because there are a lot of stories out there we need to tell."[46] She says it is often difficult to generate interest in positive stories such as the Wynne unit program in which inmates repair and update donated computers for use in low-income school districts. "Well, that's great, but it's hard to get reporters to write about that though the same people are here five seconds later if we have a hostage or if we have an escape. Sometimes it's frustrating."[47] Lyons says she just keeps sending out proactive stories and usually finds the greatest success with smaller Texas newspapers where a well-written release with a local connection often makes it into print.

What Is News?

TDCJ's *Media Relations Manual* advocates anticipating "incidents—events in which the news media has interest and initiates an inquiry."[48] The website is very specific about the PIO's responsibilities: "The PIO may report to the news media any incidents of serious violence including assaults which result in fatalities or major injuries, riots, and disturbances that involve major disruptions of prison operations."[49] The PIO must carefully follow state open records laws while respecting the inmates' legal rights to privacy. Offenders cannot be identified as recipients of substance abuse treatment; only their general state of health or the nature of an injury can be discussed.[50]

Especially at units far from Huntsville, the warden may be designated to respond to reporters' questions, in coordination with the PIO.

The TDCJ *Media Relations Manual* cautions, "Reporters have an uncanny way of learning about incidents at our institutions through numerous sources. We are often placed in the position of responding to their inquiries rather than notifying them."[51] The PIOs like to get out in front of the media barrage whenever possible, contacting some of the longtime prison beat reporters when an issue of interest arises. "One of the tricks of doing media is establishing a good rapport with one or two reporters you really trust," says Fitzgerald, who built good working relationships with a number of Texas journalists while in Huntsville. "My philosophy was I'd rather be the one to tip [the reporter] off, rather than him be the one to start questioning me."[52] Over the years, the PI officers worked to build and maintain media credibility. Brown remembers that he never went "off the record" for background. "If a media person came to me, 'Hey, Charlie, what about so and so?' and I could answer, I would. I didn't play games. Because of that, we developed a great rapport. They knew I was telling the truth."[53]

Because of security issues, natural disasters loom larger in the prison community than in the surrounding area. Fires, floods, hurricanes, and tornadoes can disrupt the day-to-day routines and create the possibility for incidents. "Anytime there is a hurricane, we get a lot of calls about evacuating the prison in Galveston," Lyons says.[54] Frank Dobbs, whose mother was warden of the women's prison in Huntsville in the 1950s and '60s, remembers a citywide power blackout that caused consternation in the unit one night.

The teenage Frank Dobbs was drafted to carry a Coleman lantern and accompany a guard who checked every cell to be sure no one had escaped under cover of darkness. "It was the middle of the night and every prisoner was required to come to the front of the cell. Many of them were not wearing much. I was thinking what a great story I would have to tell in school the next day."[55] Media interest is fickle, however; when Dobbs saw the morning news, the big story was that university students had taken advantage of the blackout confusion to "tear the town up"—a night-long panty raid grabbed all the headlines. "And I was holding a lantern and following a guard through the prison all night and missed it all," Dobbs says with regret.[56]

―――――――― *Prison City Close-Up* ――――――――

Growing Up in Prison:
When the West Was Still Wild

In the early 1950s, my school bus stopped just inside the entrance to Goree to pick up two little boys. Goree was the state's sole prison for women. Its warden was Velda Dobbs, [and] the two little boys were hers. I would look with furtive awe every morning, wondering what it was like to live inside a prison compound and have convicted criminals cooking your meals and cleaning your room.
—Virginia Stem Owens (from Living Next Door to the Death House)

Sixty years later, one of those "little boys" remembers: "When I am asked about my childhood, I always say I grew up in the slammer and it usually stops the conversation cold. I moved to Huntsville as an eight-year-old and was involved in one way or another with the prison system through college.

"Both my parents were prison officers. My mother was a warden of the women's penitentiary for twenty-six years, so I grew up surrounded by arch-villain females. I also worked behind the scenes at the Texas Prison Rodeo when I was in high school. That's how I developed my interest in cameras and photography.

"The rodeo always happened every Sunday in October. But for the other eleven months all the bucking bulls and horses were kept on the thousand-acre prison farm at Goree. An elderly black cowboy named Willy was in charge. He did all the things a cowboy does anywhere in the western states, except at night they locked him up, and in the morning they unlocked him. Willy was a state-approved trustee who kept an eye on us, which usually meant putting us on a horse and taking us with him while he worked.

"So, we had horses and we had a thousand acres. I discovered all my friends were eager to be cowboys in a movie. They didn't think you had to act to be a cowboy; you just had to wear a big hat and not fall off the horse. So I sold parts to my friends: five dollars for a walk-on, ten dollars to get killed. Everyone who paid ten dollars had a good death scene. There was a lot of mayhem in that movie, but it worked. We certainly covered our costs.

"I later realized that to Texans, the West will always live and western movies will always be the pinnacle of the art. To the rest of the world, they've become old fashioned and are no longer appealing. But in Texas, they will last forever."[57] ✪

—Frank Q. Dobbs, award-winning filmmaker

Executions, once a sure media draw, have become more commonplace and therefore less newsworthy. Some critics even view this as an underlying purpose of the carefully regimented, sanitized, and structured death process. Prew, who covers executions for the *Huntsville Item*, agrees that the number of executions detracts from the news value of each one. "I'm at an execution I'd say on the average of once a week, sometimes twice a week." Occasionally, two executions are carried out in the same day. It becomes a challenge for the reporters to write distinctive stories. "The cases do run together because the descriptions of the cases are very similar," Prew says. "Sometimes we have weeks where there are four executions and it's hard for me as a reporter to keep them separate. So to the public, the ones who actually pay attention, I think it's mundane unless it affects their community. And that's sad because each case is a human life."[58]

Although the execution routine is unchanging, the reporters' styles are not the same. Some, like AP Texas correspondent Graczyk, take a factual approach, while others, such as Prew, look for a human interest "hook" and use description to paint a word picture. "I often think if I can put a bit more emotion into it people might be a little more willing to pay attention."[59] Graczyk, by contrast, works hard to keep his stories straight down the middle and doesn't appreciate the "spin" a lot of reporters inject into their stories.[60]

People are often curious about the reporters' personal stance on the death penalty. A few, like Prew, openly voice opposition; some reporters deny having an opinion on the issue, and others, such as Graczyk, are careful never to voice an opinion. Although Graczyk's preference on this issue is the topic of much speculation and conjecture among both reporters and PIOs, in the two decades he has been covering executions, he has never let his personal convictions intrude in his professional life. In interview after interview, Graczyk declines to answer this question. "I gain nothing by taking a side," Graczyk says. "If the inmate thinks I'm for the death penalty, then he's not going to want to talk to me; similarly, if the D.A.s think I'm totally against the system, then they won't talk with me either."[61]

Some automatically assume the PIOs are either in favor of executions or just don't care one way or the other. A middle-aged, sweet-faced woman standing on the "protest corner" in Huntsville during an execution was soft spoken and empathetic about the plight of death row inmates but became vitriolic when Lyons led the media witnesses from the administration building to the execution chamber in the Walls unit. "How can she do that job?" the woman asks, her voice filled with scorn. Such fissures in this small community are glimpsed occasionally but usually are masked as those with diametrically opposing views chat over church pews and grocery baskets about mundane topics like the weather, babies, and holiday plans. Still, the prison culture abiding in the community raises unanswered questions.

> *"Sometimes we have weeks where there are four executions and it's hard for me as a reporter to keep them separate."*

Eric Thompson has been covering executions for KPFT, the Houston affiliate of Pacifica Radio, since 2003 and he sees the contrast between the PIOs' public face and the actual situation as bizarre. "In the back of my mind, I can't help but be interested in how people are so methodical [when] someone is going to be dying and their paperwork makes them complicit in this death. But they always seem to block it out and are almost oddly smiling, cheerful, like 'It's just another day here and thanks to all the visitors for coming out to the Walls.'"[62] An East Texas native who instinctively understands the social conventions of the South, Thompson still is curious about what emotions underlie the businesslike way the PIOs conduct media relations on execution days. "They're just jovial about it. Are they actually happy the execution is that day or are they acting happy because there are so many media around and to act concerned would show some kind of concern for the process and they don't want to wrestle with that?"[63]

Reporters talk of media "insiders," those who routinely cover the executions, as opposed to "outsiders," onetime witnesses. Graczyk is the ultimate insider, having covered more than two hundred executions and counting. The *Huntsville Item* reporter is always in the inner circle, too. Julia Stuart, reporter for the *London Daily Mail*, came to Texas in the summer of 1998 to cover the execution of Robert Anthony Carter, who was seventeen when he shot and killed a gas station cashier. In a story about her reactions to Huntsville and the execution, Stuart describes the Texas reporters and PIOs cozily eating birthday cake minutes before the execution, relaxed and laughing.[64] Graczyk makes the distinction that they were eating leftover cake, not having a birthday party and says the foreign media see the American system as "brutal and barbaric" and view those reporters who routinely cover executions as "part of the process, as opposed to observers."[65]

Paradoxically, the brutality of executions is the focus of a growing body of criminology research that suggests that execution publicity may actually increase violent crime. Dr. Dennis Longmire, a criminal justice professor at SHSU, explains that this "brutalization research looks not only at the process of execution, but also at how widely it is publicized. It traces violent crime rates after the execution for a series of weeks and correlates with the volume of media coverage." The result, Longmire said, is a short-term but significant increase in violent crime.[66]

Is Media Coverage of TDCJ Issues Fair and Balanced?

Both reporters and PIOs agree that the answer to that question varies. Kathy Walt, a *Houston Chronicle* reporter before taking a job as spokesperson for Texas governor Rick Perry, looks at this issue from two viewpoints. "It's certainly easier to pay attention to inaccuracies in the media. If we see a story that misrepresents the governor's position, it stands out. As a reporter, if one of my colleagues misquoted or misrepresented someone's position, it wasn't my fight. When I was with the *Chronicle*, I would read other stories about prison issues and I would think there is a tendency to go for the worst scenario and that is just news. It is never news that the plane landed; it is just news that the plane crashed."[67]

Lyons says that Texas media generally provide fair reports because they understand Texas laws and the "mentality of the people." In Lyons's opinion, "They understand Texans are not bloodthirsty, let's-hang-them-up-in-the-town-square kind of people."[68] Out-of-state and foreign journalists are a different story, however. "I don't care that they slam us; that's their right, but it's just not fair—the things they say are just not true," Lyons says.[69]

Sometimes reporters are condescending toward the thirtysomething Lyons. She recalls a CNN correspondent who referred to her as a "cub reporter" despite her years of newspaper experience, and a *Rolling Stone* reporter who commented that Lyons had "seen more deaths than could be healthy for her tender young age."[70]

When the topic of fair and unbiased prison reporting arises, AP correspondent Graczyk's name is invariably invoked, both by the PIOs and by other Texas reporters. Graczyk has a reputation for being generous to colleagues and is admired by both current and former PIOs. "For younger reporters who have never been through this before, it is sometimes traumatic," Graczyk says. "For many of them, it is their first time to watch someone die, so I try to help them through it."[71]

Although this attitude has earned the AP reporter a special place in the fraternity of reporters, the Associated Press's coverage is not universally admired. Jim Marcus, administrator of the Texas Defender Service (TDS), a nonprofit organization that represents death row prisoners, finds AP coverage lacking in depth and understanding. He says that most of the reporters who cover death row issues regularly do a good job but are hampered by the necessity of making their stories understandable. "You can't use words like *habeas corpus*," says Marcus, who adds that media coverage of his organization is much more supportive than in the 1990s, when the attorneys would find death threats on the answering machine.[72]

Pacifica reporter Thompson thinks many reporters' stories, although not inaccurate, do not tell the whole story in context. It is a question of time and effort, in his opinion. "I have a problem with the media people lining up to be thrown a bone; they're just waiting for somebody to hand them the story. The only press kit you're picking up is from the prison press office, and they are spoon-feeding you. You're in their yard; you're minding their rules; their officers have their guns making sure you don't stand on their sidewalk. A large percentage of the media is very happy to take the press release, dress it up, and reread it—it's lazy but it's very easy."[73]

Lyons says that editorials in particular often contain erroneous information. "You know it's being written by a person who's never witnessed an execution."[74] That is probably true; Houston-based *New York Times* correspondent Ralph Blumenthal explains that what reporters write and what appears on the editorial page may be diametrically opposed in viewpoints. "There's a difference between the editorial interest of a newspaper, which is determined by its owner, and the coverage, which is often determined by editors and reporters," Blumenthal points out. "Usually, reporters and editors are free to pursue their journalistic instincts, and the ownership confines itself to the larger editorial pages and business decisions."[75]

Media Relations

Personal communication, as well as traditional media publicity and Internet resources, are the primary methods for communicating with the media on a day-to-day basis. In times of breaking news, press conferences are also used. Internet technology means huge savings in copying and mailing costs and makes the small staff more efficient according to TDCJ webmaster

Andrew Davis.[76] The news release, sent by fax or email, is still a staple, especially when it can be localized. Most press releases are sent via email, which increases the chance of getting stories published: "A lot of these small papers will literally cut and paste from the email," Lyons says.[77]

Lyons spends a lot of her time fielding calls and emails from reporters, ranging from those across town at the *Huntsville Item* office to those at news bureaus and publications halfway around the world. Generally, she prefers to deal with U.S. reporters by phone and to communicate with foreign media by email.

Requests for prisoner interviews must be submitted in written form and can take as long as two weeks to process. Blumenthal remembers a situation where he needed an interview for a story he wanted to do in the next few days, but the official procedure made it impossible. "I found that a little onerous… it seems to me there is a way of expediting it and making it more open," Blumenthal says. "But I think they're not particularly interested in making journalists' lives easier. They're running a big prison system and maybe opening up the system to outsiders makes their lives more difficult."[78]

Brown recalls that media access to prisoners prior to the mid-1980s was much more complex. Prison administrators were reluctant to allow media inside the units and, predictably, media stories were critical and often, Brown says, inaccurate. "For a long time, it appeared as though the media were out to get the system, and I think that was because they were shut out; if you got fifty percent accuracy, that was good." With a change of administration in 1984, the prison system was opened to media and the results were favorable for TDCJ. "A lot of the reporting got better because the reporters could come in and see for themselves. Then the stories got more benign." With the resumption of executions in Texas, the PIOs organized "media days" to make access to inmates more manageable.[79]

But some kinds of access are still off limits. Television stations frequently request permission to do direct satellite broadcasts from the units, but those are not allowed; recording—radio, TV, or telephonic media—must be done in advance. Live television or radio as well as direct satellite broadcasts are not permitted from any Texas prison. In fact, both still and video photographers are monitored carefully to protect checkpoints and other security measures. Even if a photographer is visiting a unit in some other part of the state and a PIO is not there, a TDCJ officer is assigned to watch the photographer at all times. "It's especially difficult with TV reporters who try to pretend they're not shooting, but you can look at the camera and see the little reel moving,"

Lyons says. "We have to watch that a lot."[80] Identifiable images of offenders can only be used with the written consent of the inmate. The office does not provide video news releases; Viesca is of the opinion "they don't work; no one uses them."[81]

Viesca is enthusiastic about the benefits of communicating with media via the office's website. In the mid-1990s, the Texas legislature mandated that all state agencies must have a presence on the Internet, so TDCJ created and launched its site in 1997. Web designer Davis says that consistency for the five-thousand-plus page site was central to his design. "Because it's so prosaic, I felt it needed uniformity for people trying to navigate through it so there is a commonality between the different divisions and they know where to find things." The site is well used, both by media as well as by the general public. Davis says that in the beginning he handled all emails for the agency, but as people became aware of the wealth of information available he began to receive hundreds of emails daily. "It's really grown into a major conduit between the agency and the public."[82]

Some kinds of access are still off limits; live television or radio as well as direct satellite broadcasts are not permitted from any Texas prison.

Media outlets are able to download press information from the site, access news release archives, review inmate interview policies, and scan published news clips. The death row page is especially useful to reporters. Since execution stays are frequent, the online execution schedule tells media and protestors alike when to head to Huntsville. The Internet makes it possible for the PIO staff to handle media even during high-profile executions or breaking news. "Using the Internet is an easier way for us to get our message out to a large audience, and I'm really talking about a worldwide audience," Viesca says. "We get calls, inquiries from Switzerland, from Germany, everywhere; they're curious about the criminal justice system."[83] Having answers to frequently asked questions and background information on the website saves the PIOs a lot of time so "when they do call us, their questions are narrower. With the limited resources we have, using the web is really a good way to go," Viesca says.[84]

National reporters find the web information useful as well. Blumenthal comments on the abundant online information. "I find it helpful you can look up the cases of all four-hundred-something people on death row. You can get a synopsis of what they were convicted of; you can get a biography, execution date, et cetera. So there's a lot of information; you don't even have to call the office."[85]

Some media, particularly national or international reporters, accuse the TDCJ public information office of "framing" messages to protect the "Texas Death Machine."[86] Viesca responds, "Well, we remind those reporters this agency carries out the sentence given to the individual and that's the role we play. We do it very professionally. Of course, we don't let our personal feelings get in the way. There were victims involved in these crimes. Because of that, this individual has ended up where he or she is. Just put some perspective on the process. That helps."[87]

Blumenthal sees his role as explaining the Texas system to *New York Times* readers, a worldwide and generally well-educated audience. "It's a state obviously in the forefront of the death penalty and it has probably one of the tougher takes on punishment in the country. So, I see my job as trying to explain that and understand that for the readers."[88] This media watchdog role is vital in the effort to keep abuses from occurring. Blumenthal points out that everything to do with prisons is outside the experience of most middle-class people and it is up to reporters to shine the light of media exposure on the system. "Unless reporters are getting access to the prisons and are writing about it, people have no idea what is going on. When there are secretive places unavailable to the press, that's when brutality occurs and prisons become the private domains of wardens and guards—it's very unhealthy."[89]

Prison Myths Abound

> *Due to the aura and mystique of the Lone Star State, reporters from other states and countries like to see and explore the workings of Texas and its prison system. The Public Information Office...serves to dispel many myths.*
> —TDCJ website[90]

Because the world inside a prison is outside the experience of most Texans, perceptions of life behind the walls are often colored by images presented in the popular media, hearsay, or pure misinformation. Of course, the State of Texas has long been the focus for larger-than-life personalities, tall tales, and Wild West images for some Americans, and certainly for people in other countries. When it comes to the Texas prison system, even the state's residents—the primary audience for the PIOs—labor under a variety of misconceptions, ranging from how prisoners work and live behind bars to how state funds are used. Working to replace those myths with facts is a constant and sometimes futile effort.

Myth #1: Prisons Are Country Clubs

Perhaps the most widespread misconception is the "country club myth," the idea that prisoners work little if at all and live in air-conditioned comfort with cable TV and Internet access. The actual circumstances are a country mile from that image; the story the PIOs try to communicate is that offenders are required to work and have few amenities. But many Texans have not gotten that message.

For example, a mid-July visit to blue-collar Huntsville watering holes such as Shenanigans yields dismissive comments about the town's prison population: "Yeah, those criminals have it easy, a roof over their heads and three square meals a day, watching soap operas in the afternoon, and playing basketball for recreation while the rest of us are sweating to earn an honest dollar—and my taxes paying for it all."[91] These workers are having an after-work beer—or two—to dull the memory of spending the day in the broiling sun or in the hot box of a prison unit, and they are resentful of those they view as "getting off easy." Gary Crawford, former city council member and employee of the local cable company, voices a common opinion: "You can go lay up all day if you don't want to work. If you had to fix roads by hand—hard labor—you'd eliminate some of the repeat offenders who would rather take the easy way out by having somebody take care of them the rest of their days."[92]

Perhaps some of the confusion arises because of the differences between the federal and Texas prison systems. "The federal prison system by and large is air-conditioned," explains former PIO Fitzgerald, who is now an expert witness on Texas prisons during criminal trials. "Federal prisons are a much easier place to do time. No, our prisons are not air-conditioned—we are not in the business to provide that kind of comfort, and the taxpayers wouldn't stand for it."[93] Because of the summer heat, a majority of Texans "in the free" spend May through September moving between air-conditioned houses, vehicles, and workplaces as much as possible as the temperatures soar into the triple digits. The TDCJ employees suffer as much as the prisoners. A former guard remembers working on the unit in the summer. "It's hot! And they got those big lights in there that stay on all the time too and that's a lot of heat." Temperatures in cells can go as high as 120 degrees in the height of summer. Exceptions to the no-air-conditioning rule are the prison hospital and the psychiatric units.

Information about color TVs, telephone privileges, and work requirements account for more than half of the questions posted at the frequently asked questions page of the TDCJ website. Interested readers can learn that color televisions are available in "dayrooms where 60 to 90 offenders may watch one set [showing] the basic networks, sports and education channels." The sets are purchased with profits from the commissary where prisoners buy snack foods, toiletries, and approved reading materials. Texas Defender Service attorney Jim Marcus thinks more TVs would solve some of the prison's discipline problems. "If I ran a prison I would give every single prisoner a television. Eight hours of their day would be sucked up by staring at television and you wouldn't have to worry about them attacking anyone… it's a big mental pacifier."[94]

In an era when even elementary school children have cell phones, prisoners who "demonstrate good behavior can earn one five-minute collect phone call every 90 days."[95] The PIOs also try to communicate that prisoners are not slug-a-beds; their wake-up call comes at 3:30 each morning and breakfast is at 4:30. By 6 A.M. every prisoner who is physically able reports to a nonpaid job, either in prison support areas such as cooking, cleaning, or maintenance, in the agricultural department (the prisoners grow much of their produce and raise various livestock), or in the prison industries programs, which range from computer repairs to license plates to furniture. Ironically, all of the flags displayed at state buildings in Texas are made by prisoners in the flag factory. Prisoners who refuse to work are placed on "cell restriction," which requires them to remain in their cells twenty-four hours a day.

Those on death row live under even more restrictions. "I think it is fair to say the average person has not a clue what death row is like," Thompson says. "I don't think they know the inmates get three showers a week or that they have to cuff up, or they get one hour of isolated rec time a day; I don't think people understand how grueling conditions are."[96]

The amenities prisoners do have are important incentives for acceptable behavior, according to the public information officers. Lyons says those people who don't think inmates should be able to recreate or watch television don't realize that those privileges are important from a security standpoint.

"You have to give them some incentive to be good," Lyons says. "If you didn't let them watch TV and recreate, what would you take away from them when they're bad?"[97]

"If I ran a prison I would give every prisoner a television. Eight hours of their day would be sucked up by staring at television and you wouldn't have to worry about them attacking anyone...it's a big mental pacifier."

Many taxpayers probably don't realize that the most expensive "amenity" prisoners receive is medical care. With the aging prison population, this expense promises to accelerate, but it represents one of those complex stories reporters seldom tackle. The costs vary dramatically depending on the age of the offender. According to a 1999 report by the Criminal Justice Policy Council, health care for "elderly" offenders (fifty-five and older) costs the state $14.80 per day, while younger offenders require only $4.93 per day.[98] Interestingly, food and security costs are about the same—roughly $2 a day per offender.[99] Prison produces premature aging—offenders generally have the health problems of people ten years older in the free world.[100] Prisons are problematic for diseases such as HIV/AIDS and hepatitis. "I can't tell you how many clients we've lost to disease," Marcus says. "At least five of our clients have died before they could execute them."[101]

Myth #2: Liberal Good Time Policies

Another common misconception, according to Viesca, involves the "revolving door" concept that prisoners serve only a fraction of their sentences.[102] "There is this misconception if you get life in a Texas prison it's forty years," Fitzgerald says. "That's inaccurate; it's forty years and the parole board will look at you. If you have an aggravated offense, which obviously murder one is, that first time they look at you is really just pro forma. I think it's safe to say if you receive forty years in prison for an aggravated offense, it'll be fifty years before anything really happens."[103] It would appear that the public perception that many prisoners serve a small fraction of their sentences has a solid historical basis; in 1990, according to TDCJ figures, the average inmate served only 20 percent of his or her sentence; the number had risen to 60 percent by 2004.[104] The early release figures were widely reported in the 1990s as a result of prison overcrowding, which is a topic that surfaces in Texas on a regular basis, particularly during budget discussions.

The public often believes that recidivism rates are increasing and that most parolees return to prison within a year. The PIO office tries to tell a different story. Viesca points to a reduction in recidivism rates: 28.3 percent for offenders released in 2001, compared with 49.1 percent for those released in 1992.[105] Nevertheless, an astounding one out of every twenty Texans is under the control of TDCJ, either in prison, on parole, or on probation.[106]

Parole became a focus of media attention and public controversy in 2005, when the state legislature, to the surprise of many, approved a life-without-parole bill. Now, juries have two options in capital cases: the death penalty or life with no hope of parole. The PIOs have the added job of explaining this new law, which has both avid supporters as well as outspoken opponents across the state.

In his job as an expert witness during the penalty phase of capital murder trials, Fitzgerald sees prison issues in a broader context. "I can see the benefits of a capital life sentence as opposed to a death sentence. It really boils down to an economic issue. Some of the smaller counties might have a horrible, horrible crime that would probably warrant the death penalty, but because of the cost, they can't afford to go for a capital death penalty case."[107] A number of studies support Fitzgerald's contention: One of the more recent, by the Death Penalty Information Center, found that the cost of a death penalty case in Texas averages about $2.3 million.[108] Fitzgerald points out that "most of the people who wind up on death row are indigent, so the taxpayers are paying for the initial trial on both sides of the aisle. Then in Texas if you get a capital death sentence, the appeal is automatic, so then [taxpayers] are paying for the attorney general's office as well as for appellate attorneys to walk it through the state as well as the federal appellate process."[109]

Financial considerations aside, reporters see the death penalty as a career maker for the district attorneys who prosecute the cases. "For a prosecutor, to get the death sentence in Texas is pretty much the pinnacle of their careers, so it's an ego thing as much as it's a law thing," Prew says.[110] Thompson agrees that county elected officials profit from a reputation of being tough on crime: "Your county district attorney can make a decision whether to go after a life sentence or seek capital punishment and he sees an underfinanced or inexperienced defender as an easy mark. Then he can say, 'I sought and received the death penalty, so I'm tough on crime.' It spirals."[111]

Marcus agrees that political aspirations figure into the equation. "If you ask a prosecutor why you are seeking death in this case, he or she might say, 'This is a really heinous case. If there ever was a case for the death penalty, this is it.' This is what they say to the newspaper and in the closing arguments. [But] the first question is, 'Is that D.A. up for reelection?'"[112]

Myth #3: Prisons Are Out of Control

You have guards who are selling drugs in the prison; you have prostitution; you have sex slaves in the prison; we destroy what humanity there is left in these people.[113]

In a world isolated behind prison walls, it is not surprising that tales of frightening and deviant behavior abound. When news stories report prisoner abuses, that public sentiment is reinforced, and the PIOs' job of dispelling myths becomes more difficult. They fight this firestorm of public outrage with statistics: In 2004, with a prison population of more than 150,000, there were three offender homicides, Viesca says.[114]

The lurid stories have more power in the public imagination; conversations with any number of Huntsville residents and businesspeople quickly establish that the perception of prison abuses is alive and well. The proliferation of Internet sites dealing with prison topics has, on the one hand, provided a public forum for the average citizen to speak out. On the other hand, Internet information is uncensored and often wildly partisan, so many people are unable to distinguish the credible from the biased. Online prison images range from sensitive portrayals of inmates being released and greeting family members to tasteless near-porn.

Perhaps to help counter such images of debauchery, a strict prison dress code is in place: a white cotton pullover shirt tucked into white elastic-waist pants. Shoes are state-issue or purchased from the commissary. Conservative hairstyles are de rigueur for men and women—men must be clean-shaven with closely trimmed hair. Guidelines for women are more ambiguous: "Female offenders will not have extreme haircuts."[115]

The statistics work against the PIOs on the topic of improperly supervised prisoners; for several years media reports have sporadically reported on the shortage of correctional officers in the state. In 2004 the shortfall had dropped from the 3,401 level reported in 2001, but nevertheless remained at 2,455,[116] still a significant deficit by any standard. To put this in the most positive light, the PIOs emphasize the downward trend and help promote recruitment, but the hundreds of unfilled positions give rise to public concerns about safety, both for inmates and for prison employees.

Myth #4: Prisons Are Warehouses

Is prison about punishment or is it about correction? Public opinion is divided on the underlying purpose, but a common misconception, according to the PIOs, is that prisons warehouse people. In reality, in addition to work programs, there are treatment and education opportunities for those who qualify. Viesca gives TDCJ's position: "People are given an opportunity to change. Whether they want to change is up to them."[117]

It might be truer to say that some—not all—prisoners have the opportunity. High school GED and college degree programs as well as an innovative cognitive intervention program and a variety of counseling and vocational courses do exist, but funding and prison regulations restrict who is eligible. Death row inmates are not eligible for any of these programs, and older prisoners who are serving long sentences do not get high priority. According to the TDCJ guidelines, "Offenders who are less than 35 years of age and within five years of projected release have the highest priority for placement in academic and vocational programs."[118]

Limited access to programs is due in part to budget problems. The Windham School District has taken some heavy financial hits in the past decade. In 1995 the district expanded to serve the entire state, contracting with twenty colleges for postsecondary classes, and in the same year funding was cut by 50 percent, according to Bob Evans, director of continuing education for Windham.[119] In 2002 funding was again reduced, this time by 35 percent. Nevertheless, in 2004 prisoners earned 415 associate degrees, 58 baccalaureate degrees, 22 master's degrees, and almost 4,000 junior college vocational certificates.[120]

Evans keeps a sheet of statistics at hand showing that inmates who get college educations experience significantly lower recidivism rates (5 percent after four years of college), which eventually can save taxpayers as much $59 million for every one thousand offenders who complete a four-year program.[121] Evans also cites improved behavior and decreased disciplinary rates for those attending school. "The public doesn't realize inmates have to walk a tight line and be on their best behavior to maintain their college status."[122]

Although study after study shows that prisoners who get an education seldom return to prison, public opinion is generally against tax dollars being used to educate prisoners. In fact, the PIOs point out, higher education is paid for by the prisoners themselves, and some of the participating colleges, like Sam Houston, require payment in advance. By legislative mandate, offenders must reimburse the state for college courses as a condition of parole. In 2004 inmates paid more than $253,000 to register for classes.[123] Getting this story out to the public is difficult. "We're doing a good job with the resources we have and affecting lives in a positive way—helping reduce recidivism; making those changes is hard work; we're dealing with failures of public schools," Kiser comments.[124]

Although study after study shows prisoners who get an education seldom return to prison, public opinion is generally against tax dollars being used to educate prisoners. In fact, higher education is paid for by the prisoners themselves.

On the flip side, concentrating on the punishment aspect of prison and withholding educational, vocational, or cognitive development opportunities can have far-reaching consequences. James Griffith, Windham principal at the Polunsky unit, sees a public benefit in funding cognitive intervention programs, which teach offenders self-control, anger management, and goal setting. "These people will be out some day and will be your neighbors. Do you want them to have learned ways of controlling their anger?"[125]

Aside from the financial and social benefits, Thompson comments on the humanitarian aspect of the controversy: "There are a couple of theories on warehousing people, and one is you can't take everything away from people because then you have nothing left to take away from them. At the end, if you're just going to treat me like an animal, what if I just become an animal? You've given me nothing and now I expect nothing. Is that what justice is?"[126]

Myth #5: Justice for All?

This quandary is not one that appears on the PIOs' "myth list," but it is a concern frequently voiced by reporters, public defenders, and sociologists who see glaring inequities in the state's criminal justice system. One aspect is how sentencing is applied: "It's funny to me that serial killers can be in the general population of our prisons, and people who killed once in a cracked-out drugstore robbery are going to die for it," Prew comments.[127]

Questions of fairness arise at every stage of the appellate process. "There is a very serious David and Goliath story happening every time there is a court-appointed attorney going into a capital murder trial [against] a well-financed district attorney," Thompson says. He adds that the makeup of juries is not always representative of the person on trial with respect to race or social class.[128]

Questions of fairness arise at every stage of the appellate process. "There is a very serious David and Goliath story happening every time there is a court-appointed attorney going into a capital murder trial [against] a well-financed district attorney."

Perhaps the most disturbing aspect of the justice issue is whether the convicted is indeed guilty of the crime. Brown, who chooses his words carefully even after retirement from TDCJ, voices a common concern: "The thing about executions, I'm not going to say whether I am for or against them. Just say, for some reason, after they execute a person, if they find out, without a shadow of a doubt that person is innocent, there is no way to bring them back."[129] Determining guilt or innocence "without a shadow of a doubt" is now possible, thanks to DNA testing. Or is it? Beginning in 2004, the *Houston Chronicle* began to publish investigative reports showing the Harris County police crime lab work to be shoddy beyond comprehension.

As the scandal unfolded, there were calls for a moratorium on death penalty cases involving evidence from that lab. Some convictions were overturned and the newly found innocents were set free after years behind bars. "Science gets perverted if the people doing it have an agenda," Marcus comments. It's a case of the fox watching the henhouse, Texans might say. "When you put all of your scientists in the employ of law enforcement, they are going to have a bias."[130] Stories such as these seem to have reshaped public opinion to some extent; public support for the death penalty is dropping nationwide.[131]

Such malfeasance also adds fuel to support the "Innocence Protection Act," which would guarantee death row inmates competent counsel and DNA testing. This is part of a process masterminded in Illinois by a professor of journalism at Northwestern University, David Protess, who realized the way to change American public opinion was not to appeal to notions that the death penalty is intrinsically, morally wrong, but to prove that innocent people were being executed.[132]

The media's role of looking behind the criminal justice system's facade proves its value in such situations, Blumenthal says. "It is a high calling to right a wrong by exposing a wrongful conviction, especially for someone on death row. *The New York Times* has done it on a number of occasions. I teamed up with another reporter recently to talk about some cases of people who were wrongfully convicted by fake DNA evidence, but those are very difficult."[133]

Is true justice even possible under the present criminal justice system? Marcus searches for an answer: "Can you truly create a system that reserves the death penalty for the worst of the worst? You can try and you can do a lot better than we do now, that's for sure. But it's so subjective; what is a death case in Harris County is not a death case in Dallas."[134]

Creating an Image, Setting an Agenda?

Is there an image or a public relations agenda TDCJ seeks to convey? One of the messages that crops up repeatedly is that TDCJ is carrying out the laws of the land with no malice toward the prison's inhabitants. "I had a warden tell me one time, we don't make the laws and we don't enforce the laws," Prew says. "We're like the last line of criminal justice. We baby-sit them, essentially. We get them and then we facilitate the rest of their lives."[135]

Foreign journalists see an unemotional detachment they find inexplicable.

Viesca demurs about the use of the word image: "Not so much image, but just factual information about the process itself. How things are done." He says his office gets questions about what happens when an offender goes to prison and how the execution procedure works. "It's not so much an image concern as it is just making sure people know exactly what happens." Viesca hopes his office can convey that the prison system is humane and that safety is always a concern, both for staff members and for offenders.[136]

Reporters, not surprisingly, see the image issue a bit differently. Foreign journalists see an unemotional detachment they find inexplicable. Closer to home, Thompson says he thinks TDCJ wants to project that "it's a bit Wild West tough and it's fair," particularly as the system is defined by the death penalty. "I think Texas suffers from a little micronational identity and some people hang on to the death penalty as a fleeting vestige of their Texas heritage."[137]

> *Texans have bravado and a machismo about them that other people don't. It's unique to Texas and to Texas women. We all have it; I have it, even though I try very hard not to. We're very defensive and we're very self-important sometimes. And the institutions in this state are no different than the people. TDCJ is very proud of the fact they are so strict and have all these rules. There is an image to uphold as far as Texas having the safest prisons, Texas being the biggest prison system, the best prison system. Everything is very thought out and polished and perfect.*
>
> —Kelly Prew, *Huntsville Item* reporter

―――― *Prison City Close-Up* ――――

Man on the Run:
The Escape Mystique

Perhaps due to popular media images, many people perceive prison escapes are frequent events. In reality, escapes do not happen often, but when they do, the situation can escalate into a major news story.

How do the PIOs deal with an escape crisis? A good example is the breakout of 29-year-old Martin Gurule from death row, which sparked lurid headlines and a local climate of fear during a week-long manhunt in December of 1998. Gurule, the first Texas death row prisoner to escape in 64 years, made it over the razor wire fence surrounding the Ellis Unit by wrapping his chest in cardboard.[138] Once over the prison walls, Gurule's only place to run was into the miles of dense woods surrounding the prison. The ensuing media coverage portrayed desperate dashes through the woods of East Texas, with tracking dogs and horse-mounted guards in hot pursuit. Interviews with area residents resulted in quotes such as, "We slept with a gun next to our bed."[139]

Larry Fitzgerald remembers he had an "uneasy feeling" that Thanksgiving day before he received a late-night call that a death row inmate had gone over the walls at the Ellis Unit, about 15 miles from Huntsville. In keeping with TDCJ's crisis communications plan, he immediately headed to the prison, but heavy fog stretched the 15-minute trip to half an hour. Given the nature of the crisis, the PIO office moved quickly to set up a media command post with phones and computer connections in a log cabin in front of the Ellis Unit. By daybreak, the media onslaught began; before the fugitive was found seven days later, the command post was buzzing with satellite trucks and media helicopters.

"With electronic communication being the way it is, a local story can become an international story within a matter of minutes just because of satellite trucks," Fitzgerald says.[140] Establishing a command post adjacent to the prison where a crisis is occurring is standard procedure. "When you do that, you control the situation," Fitzgerald explains. "We found as long as everyone gets the same thing they are happy. If you give an exclusive, everybody gets upset."[141]

Reporters covering the story from their home desks did not understand why TDCJ could not locate the fugitive quickly. PIO Michelle Lyons says it is difficult to explain East Texas terrain because "people in New York think in terms of blocks, not acres." The wooded areas around Huntsville are choked with dense underbrush, bisected by streambeds and swampy areas. "There's not any vehicle able to get back there. You have to use guys on horses and even then it's hard," Lyons says.[142]

> *"I went into great detail to describe wild hogs and fire ants... Also alligators and poisonous snakes. I might have been the culprit of making it sound like it was 'Deliverance'."*

Fitzgerald admits he may have contributed to some of the out-of-state reporters' backwoods images, especially during a conversation with a New York Times editor who couldn't understand why prison officials could not quickly locate the missing prisoner. "I went into great detail to describe wild hogs and fire ants, which he never heard of. Also alligators and poisonous snakes. I might have been the culprit of making it sound like it was 'Deliverance'," Fitzgerald says with a mischievous chuckle.[143]

The end of the high visibility search came when two off-duty corrections officers fishing in a creek about a mile from the prison unit found Gurule's body. Fitzgerald held a news conference where he dramatically tore up a wanted poster bearing Gurule's photo and announced, "It's all over. Gurule is no more. We have all our people back in custody."[144] ✪

Notes

[1] Monica Wolfson, "Poll: Texans Split on Gun Control," *Brownsville Herald*, September 10, 2004, online edition.

[2] Dennis Longmire (criminal justice professor and anti-capital punishment activist), interview by Melody Davison, Huntsville, Texas, June 21, 2005.

[3] Ibid.

[4] Mike Viesca (former TDCJ director of public information), interview by Ruth Massingill, Austin, Texas, March 18, 2005.

[5] Larry Todd, telephone conversation with Ruth Massingill, April 22, 2003.

[6] *TDCJ Media Relations Manual: Ideas for Working with the News Media.* Revised July 18, 1997, 2.

[7] Ibid.

[8] Mike Graczyk (Associated Press reporter), interview by Tina Baiter, Huntsville, Texas, June 7, 2005.

[9] TDCJ Public Information Website. Available at: http://www.tdcj.state.tx.us/pio/.

[10] Mike Viesca (former TDCJ director of public information), interview by Ruth Massingill, Austin, Texas, December 15, 2003.

[11] Mike Viesca, TDCJ job descriptions, email, March 22, 2005.

[12] Michelle Lyons (TDCJ public information officer), interview by Ruth Massingill, Huntsville, Texas, March 29, 2005.

[13] Michelle Lyons (TDCJ public information officer), interview by Ruth Massingill, Huntsville, Texas, February 12, 2003.

[14] Bambi Kiser (communications coordinator, Windham School District) and Marjie Haynes (director, Division of Instruction, Windham School District), interview by Ardyth Sohn, Huntsville, Texas, March 23, 2005.

[15] Frank Dobbs (Huntsville native and independent filmmaker), interview by Ruth Massingill, Huntsville, Texas, March 12, 2005.

[16] Viesca interview, 2003.

[17] Viesca interview, 2005.

[18] Lyons interview, 2005.

[19] Rodney Ellis, "Time for Leadership in the Wild, Wild West," press release, 2001. Available at: http://www.senate.state.tx.us/75r/Senate/Members/Dist13/pr01/c060701a.htm.

[20] "Governor Announces Appointments to New Texas Criminal Justice Advisory Council," *Austin American-Statesman*, June 29, 2005.

[21] Kathy Walt (spokesperson for Texas governor Rick Perry and former *Houston Chronicle* reporter), interview by Ruth Massingill, Austin, Texas, March 17, 2005.

[22] Viesca interview, 2005.

[23] Lyons interview, 2003.

[24] Longmire interview, 2005.

[25] Frank Krystyniak, telephone conversation with Ruth Massingill, May 12, 2005.

[26] Lyons interview, 2005.

[27] Offender Information—King, John, "Death Row Home Page," TDCJ website. Available at: http://www.tdcj.state.tx.us/stat/deathrow.htm.

[28] Larry Fitzgerald (former TDCJ public information manager), interview by Ruth Massingill, Austin, Texas, March 17, 2005.

[29] Walt interview, 2005.

[30] Kelly Prew (*Huntsville Item* reporter), interview by Tina Baiter, Huntsville, Texas, March 10, 2005.

[31] Lyons interview, 2005.

[32] Ibid.

[33] Larry Fitzgerald (former TDCJ public information manager), interview by Ruth Massingill, Huntsville, Texas, April 7, 2003.

[34] Fitzgerald interview, 2005.
[35] Lyons interview, 2003.
[36] Charles Brown (former TDCJ public information officer), interview by Melody Davison, Huntsville, Texas, June 23, 2005.
[37] Walt interview, 2005.
[38] Prew interview, 2005.
[39] Viesca interviw, 2005.
[40] *TDCJ Media Relations Manual*, 4.
[41] Lyons interview, 2003.
[42] Ibid.
[43] Bambi Kiser (communications coordinator, Windham School District), interview by Tina Baiter, Huntsville, Texas, March 23, 2005.
[44] Ibid.
[45] Bambi Kiser (communications coordinator, Windham School District), interview by Ruth Massingill, Huntsville, Texas, March 2005.
[46] Lyons interview, 2003.
[47] Ibid.
[48] *TDCJ Media Relations Manual*, 4.
[49] TDCJ Public Information Office website. Available at: http://www.tdcj.state.tx.us/pio.
[50] Ibid.
[51] *TDCJ Media Relations Manual*, 5.
[52] Fitzgerald interview, 2005.
[53] Brown interview, 2005.
[54] Lyons interview, 2005.
[55] Dobbs interview, 2005.
[56] Ibid.
[57] Ibid.
[58] Prew interview, 2005.
[59] Ibid.
[60] Graczyk interview, 2005.
[61] Ibid.
[62] Eric Thompson (reporter for Pacifica affiliate KPFT), interview by Ruth Massingill, Conroe, Texas, June 20, 2005.
[63] Ibid.
[64] Julie Stuart, "Judgment Day," Night and Day magazine supplement, *London Daily Mail*, June 14, 1998.
[65] Graczyk interview, 2005.
[66] Longmire interview, 2005.
[67] Kathy Walt (spokesperson for Texas governor Rick Perry and former *Houston Chronicle* reporter), interview by Ruth Massingill, Huntsville, Texas, December 14, 2003.
[68] Lyons interview, 2003.
[69] Ibid.
[70] Ibid.
[71] Graczyk interview, 2005.
[72] Jim Marcus (administrator and attorney, the Texas Defender Service), interview by Ruth Massingill, Houston, Texas, August 15, 2005.
[73] Thompson interview, 2005.
[74] Lyons interview, 2003.
[75] Ralph Blumenthal (Southwest bureau chief for the *New York Times*), interview by Ruth Massingill, Houston, Texas, May 23, 2005.
[76] Andrew Davis (TDCJ webmaster), interview by Ruth Massingill, Austin, Texas, March 18, 2005.
[77] Lyons interview, 2003.

[78] Blumenthal interview, 2005.
[79] Brown interview, 2005.
[80] Lyons interview, 2005.
[81] Viesca interview, 2003.
[82] Davis interview, 2005.
[83] Viesca interview, 2005.
[84] Ibid.
[85] Blumenthal interview, 2005.
[86] Denis Johnson, "Five Executions and a Barbecue," *Rolling Stone*, August 17, 2000, 52–62, 123–24.
[87] Viesca interview, 2005.
[88] Blumenthal interview, 2005.
[89] Ibid.
[90] TDCJ Public Information Office website. Available at: http://www.tdcj.state.tx.us.pio.
[91] Blue-collar workers in Huntsville, conversations with Melody Davison and Ruth Massingill, spring–summer 2005.
[92] Gary Crawford (former Huntsville city council member), interview by Melody Davison, Huntsville, Texas, June 21, 2005.
[93] Fitzgerald interview, 2003.
[94] Marcus interview, 2005.
[95] "Correctional Institutions Division—TDCJ FAQ." Available at: http://tdcj.state.txus/faq/faq-cid.htm.
[96] Thompson interview, 2005.
[97] Lyons interview, 2003.
[98] Tony Fabelo, "Elderly Offenders in Texas Prisons," Criminal Justice Policy Council Report, 1999.
[99] Scott Nowell, "Lite Sentences: TDCJ Cuts the Calories for Convicts, Leaving Them and Guards Grumbling," *Houston Press*, October 23, 2003; Editorial, "Prison System Will Get Attention," *Austin American Statesman*, January 2, 2005.
[100] Fabelo.
[101] Marcus interview, 2005.
[102] Viesca interview, 2005.
[103] Fitzgerald interview, 2005.
[104] TDCJ, PowerPoint presentation provided by Mike Viesca, March 18, 2005.
[105] Ibid.
[106] Jake Bernstein, "They Shot More than a Messenger," *Texas Observer*, February 18, 2005.
[107] Fitzgerald interview, 2005.
[108] G. Sasser et al., Facts and Issues—Criminal Justice: Capital Punishment," League of Women Voters of Texas Education Fund, 2002.
[109] Fitzgerald interview, 2005.
[110] Prew interview, 2005.
[111] Thompson interview, 2005.
[112] Marcus interview, 2005.
[113] George Russell (Huntsville business owner and local activist), interview by Ardyth Sohn, Huntsville, Texas, March 21, 2005.
[114] TDCJ, PowerPoint presentation.
[115] TDCJ website, FAQ page. Available at: http://www.tdcj.state.tx.us/pio.
[116] TDCJ, PowerPoint presentation.
[117] Viesca interview, 2005.
[118] "Policies and Procedures," TDCJ website. Available at: http://www.tdcj.state.tx.us/policy/policy-home.htm

[119] Bob Evans (director, Division of Continuing Education, Windham School District), interview by Ruth Massingill, Huntsville, Texas, March 9, 2005.
[120] Executive Summary, Division of Continuing Education Post-Secondary Program, Windham School District, TDCJ, December 2004.
[121] *Benefits of College Programs for Offenders*, TDCJ publication, November 19, 2004.
[122] Evans interview, 2005.
[123] *Benefits*.
[124] Kiser interview, 2005.
[125] James Griffith (Polunsky unit principal, Windham School District), interview by Tina Baiter, Livingston, Texas, March 8, 2005.
[126] Thompson interview, 2005.
[127] Prew interview, 2005.
[128] Thompson interview, 2005.
[129] Brown interview, 2005.
[130] Marcus interview, 2005.
[131] Death Penalty Information Center, *The Death Penalty in 2003: Year End Report*, December 2003. Available at: http://www.deathpenaltyinfo.org/YER-03-F.pdf.
[132] Elizabeth Brackett, "Illinois Death Penalty," PBS, February 4, 2000. Available at: http://www.pbs.org/newshour/bb/law/jan-june00/deathpenalty_2-4.html.
[133] Blumenthal interview, 2005.
[134] Marcus interview, 2005.
[135] Prew interview, 2005.
[136] Viesca interview, 2005.
[137] Thompson interview, 2005.
[138] "Medical Examiner: Texas Death Row Fugitive Drowned," CNN.com, December 4, 1998.
[139] Ibid.
[140] Fitzgerald interview, 2003.
[141] Fitzgerald interview, 2005.
[142] Lyons interview, 2005
[143] Fitzgerald interview, 2003.
[144] "Medical Examiner."

CHAPTER FOUR
DEATH ROW: TARGET OF THE PUBLIC'S MACABRE FASCINATION

There are always bizarre things, situations you would never have thought of. We had a situation where a man was about to be executed for killing a ten-year-old girl, and the girl's mother, who was his girlfriend at the time, wanted to witness the execution, but she was serving time in Gatesville for killing the girl's biological father. It's just a huge ordeal; you can't make this stuff up.
—Michelle Lyons, PIO for Texas death row

An Eye for an Eye, a Tooth for a Tooth...a Life for a Life

The Old Testament view of a just but vengeful God is not just a message delivered from Texas pulpits on Sunday mornings; it is cultural bedrock across generations, a principle as unyielding as the broiling August sun. This vision of divine justice through human-directed retribution is at the heart of the state's 150-year-old death row, a long-standing tradition in Texas, which executes more offenders than any other state.

Since 1924, death sentences for the State of Texas have been carried out in Huntsville, an East Texas town where incarceration and education are the twin pillars of the local economy. In an unguarded moment, a former mayor is said to have remarked that death row in Huntsville was good for business. That may have been a bit too blatant even for people so inured to institutional death; in the next election, Huntsville citizens selected a new mayor.

Mostly, the populace prefers not to be reminded that Huntsville is the execution capital of the state. In fact, the death ritual occurs so frequently that local citizens scarcely notice "routine" executions. Only when national or foreign media roll into town for a high-profile case does attention focus on the Huntsville Walls unit, site of more than three hundred executions in the last twenty-two years alone, an average of about fourteen souls each year. Although the prisoners' families may mourn their passing, few in Huntsville grieve for the killers who meet their fate there. For the most part, Huntsville's citizens, like Texans in general, unwaveringly support the death penalty despite recurring hints of wrongful convictions and corruption in the criminal justice system.

Beneath these outward political concerns, a wealth of lurid folk legends surrounds the death tradition; native East Texans have grown up hearing such stories. The urban legends are born of misinformation and superstition, but plenty of bizarre stories actually occurred. The best sources for these gruesome vignettes are the public information officers for the Texas Department of Criminal Justice and the veteran Texas reporters who have covered the TDCJ beat for years. These eyewitness tales are as varied as the human experience, ranging from poignant to macabre. Ultimately, each one is, as they say in East Texas, serious as a heart attack, because they all end in death, for both the convicted and their victims.

While the condemned wait for their trip to the death house, they usually spend more than a decade on death row, giving them plenty of time to court the media if they so desire. For their part, the news media are easily lured by the promise of an exclusive interview, especially with an inmate who has captured the public's interest. Reporters from near and far are eager for a new twist on a death row story to feed public curiosity. Caught in the middle, the PIOs must carefully manage the interactions between death row inmates and the media, walking a tightrope between security issues and freedom of speech.

For Condemned, All Roads Lead to Huntsville

The nerve center for the death tradition in Huntsville lies behind red brick walls only two blocks from the downtown square but a world away from the slow-paced, conservative lifestyle of this small piney woods town. The compound of prison and support services occupies about ten square blocks of prime downtown real estate. Shaded by ancient oaks, the two-story fortress constructed in 1848 and known simply as the Walls is at the center of the complex. Barbed wire tops the thirty-two-foot-high walls, scanned by armed guards in the corner towers. A hodgepodge of brick structures has been added over the years. Administration buildings, warehouses once used to gin cotton for prison garments, and living quarters for high-ranking corrections officers encircle the prison. Directly across the street from the

Walls, a graceful white-columned residence, formerly home to the warden, now serves as a conference center.

Perhaps it is telling that few residences in old Huntsville neighborhoods are constructed of red brick—for many red is the color of prison. The deep orange-red of the buildings in the prison complex is the hallmark of "Corsicana Reds," bricks made of native clay, fired in kilns in the East Texas town of Corsicana, which made them cheap and readily available. They are also solid; there are no holes in the interior, so they are heavy and sturdy, ideal for restraining prisoners.

Ironically, the first Texas inmate to be executed by electrocution in 1924, Charles Reynolds, was from Red River County, red-dirt country north of Corsicana. Three hundred and sixty inmates followed Reynolds to the Texas electric chair, nicknamed "Old Sparky," until the U.S. Supreme Court declared capital punishment "cruel and unusual" in 1972. A year later, the Texas Penal Code was revised to allow assessment of the death penalty again, and Texas soon resumed executions, using the "more humane" method of lethal injection.[1]

Public information for death row is handled from the TDCJ administrative headquarters, a three-story secure building adjacent to the Walls unit. Visitors must call for clearance from a wall-mounted phone at the front door and are escorted inside to their destination. On the second floor, a modest office suite houses the Huntsville public information staff, consisting of two public information officers and a secretary. Their director is three hours away, in an office overlooking the capitol in Austin, where the Texas legislature meets biennially and the need for additional prisons is invariably on the agenda.

Even in tight budget years, prisons are a growth industry in Texas. On average, the State of Texas houses about 150,000 prisoners, with more than 60 percent in and around Huntsville. The number of inmates in the city varies between 9,000 and 15,000; it is a much-worn joke that every third or fourth citizen is an inmate. Death row for men, once located at the Ellis 1 unit near Huntsville, is now at the Polunsky unit, near Livingston, about forty miles due east. (Women on death row are housed at the pastoral Mountain View unit in Gatesville, in the Hill Country northeast of Austin. The society of the condemned is primarily a male culture; of the approximately 420 prisoners on death row, fewer than a dozen are women.) Those 420 prisoners get the lion's share of media attention and therefore occupy an inordinate amount of the public information officers' days.

"It is really kind of unfair inasmuch as a small percentage of the Texas prison population is actually on death row," comments Larry Fitzgerald, who was a PIO from 1995 until 2003. "The PIOs spend an unbalanced amount of time dealing with death row, but it's the squeaky wheel that gets all the attention."[2]

State Executions by Time Frame

Executions that occurred under civil authority in the United States or within territory that later became the United States:

State	1607–1699	1700–1799	1800–1899	1900–1967	Pre-Furman	1976–2001	Grand Total
Alabama			395	313	708	23	731
Alaska*			4	8	12		12
Arizona			26	78	104	22	126
Arkansas			231	247	478	24	502
California		5	238	466	709	9	718
Colorado			36	65	101	1	102
Connecticut	12	16	33	65	126		126
Delaware	2	8	27	25	62	13	75
Florida			46	268	314	51	365
Georgia		18	307	625	950	27	977
Hawaii*			7	42	49		49
Idaho			17	9	26	1	27
Illinois		1	143	204	348	12	360
Indiana			59	72	131	9	140
Iowa*			13	32	45		45
Kansas			16	41	57		57
Kentucky		8	214	202	424	2	426
Louisiana		61	277	294	632	26	658
Maine*	1	7	13		21		21
Maryland	15	43	139	112	309	3	312
Massachusetts*	99	102	79	65	345		345
Michigan*	2	5	5	1	13		13
Minnesota*			59	7	66		66
Mississippi			107	244	351	4	355
Missouri			175	110	285	53	338
Montana			32	39	71	2	73
Nebraska			14	20	34	3	37
Nevada			20	41	61	9	70
New Hampshire		6	15	3	24		24

State	1607–1699	1700–1799	1800–1899	1900–1967	Pre-Furman	1976–2001	Grand Total
New Jersey	8	76	90	187	361		361
New Mexico			39	34	73	1	74
New York	8	167	311	644	1130		1130
No. Carolina		131	245	408	784	21	805
North Dakota*			3	5	8		8
Ohio		1	129	308	438	2	440
Oklahoma			39	93	132	48	180
Oregon			54	68	122	2	124
Pennsylvania	1	202	293	544	1040	3	1043
Rhode Island*	4	44	4		52		52
So. Carolina		93	270	278	641	25	666
So. Dakota			9	6	15		15
Tennessee		4	152	179	335	1	336
Texas			262	493	755	256	1011
Utah			12	31	43	6	49
Vermont*		1	17	8	26		26
Virginia	10	386	577	304	1277	83	1360
Washington			23	82	105	4	109
West Virginia*		6	58	91	155		155
Wisconsin*			1		1		1
Wyoming			6	16	22	1	23
D.C.*			40	78	118		118
Federal**						2	2
Totals	162	1391	5381	7555	14489	749	15238

*States without death penalty.
**Before 2001, federal executions took place in the state where the crime occurred.

(From Rob Gallagher's informative website, Before the Needles, based on the historic research of M. Watt Espy. Available at: http://users.bestweb.net/~rg/execution.htm. Used by permission.)

Tops in Executions:

Texas was not always the leader in executions. Prior to 1976, Virginia, New Mexico, Pennsylvania, Georgia, and North Carolina, respectively, led the country in total executions, with Texas trailing in sixth place. Since 1976, however, Texas has held a decisive lead in the body count; the state has executed more than three times the number put to death in Virginia, the distant runner up.[3]

Covering the Execution Beat, Past and Present

Although some view the death ritual as a vestige of Texas's frontier mentality, seasoned death row reporters recall when executions were less sedate by far than they are now.

"Well, in the early days there was—party is not the right word—but there was an atmosphere of this is a big event and a lot of people came to town for it," remembers Kathy Walt, who spent ten years in Huntsville covering death row, first for the *Huntsville Item* and then for the *Houston Chronicle*. "That's when they did executions at midnight." Students from the nearby college sometimes added to the revelry, congregating outside the Walls to drink beer and "cheer the execution on," Walt recalls.[4]

As recently as 1997, TDCJ changed the time for executions from midnight to 6 P.M. The reasons were primarily logistical, according to the PI office. A midnight schedule required employees who carried out the execution and other state employees, such as the attorney general's and the governor's staffs, who must be available until the process is complete, to work until the wee hours of the morning. When a stay was involved, everyone could be up until 3 or 4 A.M. "Also, prisoners can more easily get last-minute access to their attorneys during regular working hours," PIO Lyons explains.[5]

Mike Viesca, a former TV news producer, had never seen an execution when he was appointed director of public information for the Texas Department of Criminal Justice in 2003, but serving as witness to the ritual was part of his new job.

"I didn't know what to expect, but now I've seen how it's carried out in such a professional manner and with respect not only toward the victims' families but also toward the families of the condemned," Viesca comments. "I was very impressed by that; people think we're cold and we're harsh and that we don't have feelings ourselves."[6] Viesca suggests that reporters who want to write about the death penalty should attend an execution so they can write with authority. "[I say to reporters] if you are going to write about this, I would appreciate it if you would experience it first and then go from there."[7]

Some agree that more people should witness executions, but not necessarily for the same reasons Viesca expresses. George Beto, a former prison administrator for whom the SHSU criminal justice building is named, thought that if executions were to be a deterrent to crime, they should be carried out "on the courthouse square in the city where the crime was committed rather than in a dark prison in Huntsville."[8] Others have suggested that the twelve members of the jury that condemns a prisoner to death should witness the execution.

Unlike the early 1900s, when public hanging was the state's method of execution, a select group of people who serve as the public's representatives now view the death ritual. Texas allows up to five media witnesses to attend each execution. This list usually includes a reporter from the Huntsville newspaper, an Associated Press and a United Press International reporter, and media from the condemned's or the victim's hometowns. Sometimes there is not enough media interest to fill all available slots; at other times, the witness assignments are much in demand and the PIOs must choose which reporters get the death chamber positions.

> *"It was more difficult to watch an inmate be executed if it was one I had interviewed on many occasions and gotten to know. Over the years it became a very depressing issue to deal with."*

Kelly Prew of the *Huntsville Item* was reluctant to accept the assignment to cover her first execution. "I felt completely out of the loop. I was in the room and no one knew who I was and I just felt like I was watching a train wreck happen...I had a lot of anxiety about it. I swore I would never do it again."[9] After that first experience, Prew reconsidered and agreed to continue to cover executions, but decided she would take time to get to know the condemned prisoners beforehand.

Death row reporters who get to know inmates during years of interviews and then attend their executions must find ways to deal with their own emotions. Walt, a seasoned reporter who never flinched from asking tough questions and was not easily swayed by prisoners' claims of innocence, took a pragmatic approach during her years of death row coverage, but she admits it was not always easy to keep her emotions in check. "It was more difficult to watch an inmate be executed if it was one I had interviewed on many occasions and had gotten to know. Over the years it became a very depressing issue to deal with."[10]

In his compelling book, *Have a Seat, Please,* Don Reid, *Huntsville Item* reporter, editor, and publisher, chronicled thirty-five years of covering the prison system, during which he witnessed 189 executions. Reid came to

Huntsville in 1937 as a reporter for the then-weekly community newspaper and was shocked when he was contacted by the Associated Press and asked to cover an execution to report the "times" when the convicted man went into the death chamber and when he was pronounced dead. Reid candidly describes that first experience and his feelings:

"I was not much of a drinking man, but I would have gone for one had Huntsville not been the seat of a dry country," Reid said of that first evening while he waited for his eleven o'clock appointment at the warden's office. "I sat on the bed for a good half hour, my mind and emotions swinging like a tavern sign in a stiff wind."[11]

Afterward, Reid returned to his room, battling "the clammy dampness of an enveloping nausea." He dreamed of the man he had just seen die:

> There on the ceiling Albert Lee Hemphill knelt on the Death House floor as if on a movie screen, his face a chalky white. He opened his mouth and the sad blues of the old spiritual began running through my mind. I closed my eyes tightly, telling myself harshly I was overreacting; I was a fool and worse. But I was overwhelmed by the stench of his burning flesh. The bedclothes reeked of it. I fled the stinking room, but the odor accompanied me to the silent, early-morning square...I sat there holding my face in my hands, berating Albert Lee Hemphill and every murdering creature on earth until I ran out of words and anger.[12]

In the years that followed, Reid interviewed most of the men who were put to death and was instrumental in obtaining stays for several, but his book makes it clear he was always haunted by the execution experiences, even when he was convinced of the prisoner's guilt.

"As time passed, I became in effect a functionary of the Ritual of Death," Reid wrote. "Prison officials quickly learned I had a soothing effect on men who were ready to go down. So prison officials welcomed me into the official family, partly to make their job easier....[They] don't like to see a man create a wild scene by fighting his way step by step to the chair."[13]

Reid continued, "Finally, I began to see my visits to Death Row as a form of duty because I could help the inmates with my presence. And with that, I simply grew accustomed to the job. Accustomed but not calloused, for the time never came that I did not leave the Death Chamber shaken and to some degree haunted."[14]

Only a few news people have witnessed more executions than Reid. One of them is Mike Graczyk, the Associated Press reporter from Houston who has been present for more than two hundred executions since 1984.[15] Although he refuses to discuss his personal stance on the death penalty, Graczyk takes care to interview the victim's relatives after the execution. "The biggest complaint I hear from victims' rights advocates or family members of the murder victims is: 'I wish he would have died the same way my loved one died. It's too quick, too clean, and too sterile.'"[16]

Trying to give evenhanded coverage to all aspects of execution reportage is a challenge for professional news people; less scrupulous media representatives fall into the trap of sensationalizing for the sake of ratings and readership.

Public Appetite for Titillating Topics

An ongoing frustration for the PIOs is the media's overweening interest in sensational topics, to the detriment of more substantial stories. The last meal of the condemned, for example, has long been the target of morbid public curiosity and therefore the focus of numerous media stories.

For example, the *Houston Chronicle*'s City State section in April 2003 featured a sixty-four-inch story on last meals of executed prisoners. Reporter Rachel Graves collected information from the TDCJ website and included viewpoints from a variety of sources, including the prison's cook and the chaplain as well as a sociologist and a nutritionist."Facing lethal injection, death row inmates make requests ranging from the strange (a jar of dill pickles) to the ethereal ('justice, equality and world peace')," writes Graves. "But in the end, prison officials say, most simply want a cheeseburger."[17]

A popular misconception is that prisoners can order anything they wish for their last meal, but the PIOs quickly debunk that myth. No truffles or lobsters; the last meal has to be something that can be concocted from ingredients on hand in the prison kitchen, although there are stories of occasional exceptions, such as PIO Larry Fitzgerald purchasing fresh cherries to fulfill a prisoner's craving. However, prisoners who hope to delay their executions by ordering exotic cuisine are destined to be disappointed.

It is not unusual for the last meal to be uneaten. Brian Price, who prepared 171 final meals for prisoners in Huntsville, reports that Karla Faye Tucker, the first woman to be executed in Texas since the 1800s, asked for fruit and a salad with ranch dressing as her last meal in 1998, but returned her plate untouched.[18]

The last meal ritual in Texas, according to Graves, dates to the early part of the twentieth century, when prisoners requested something such as cake they could share with the handful of others on death row. Since then, the last meal has become a personal statement whereby an inmate makes a political comment, provides a media "sound bite," or just makes the inevitable more palatable with a final portion of comfort food. A list of death row meals for most of the killers executed since 1982 was the most popular feature on the official TDCJ website for years, but was removed in 2004 during a reorganization of the site.

"We had a ton of calls about that," recalls Lyons. "We took it down because we had complaints—people said it was in poor taste, we shouldn't have it, we were making a spectacle. We had it there in the first place because people always wanted to know what the last meal was."[19]

Lyons says the exclusion of the last meals listing on the website has brought some requests from the media to reinstate the feature. "We can't please everyone," she comments. Although the public information officers still distribute last meal requests in execution media kits, they do not contemplate returning the information to the website.

However, the website that publishes a national chronicle of condemned killers' last meals, www.deadmaneating.com, is still kept current by its founder, Mike Randleman, of Santa Monica, California. The site features a crude drawing of a hanging stick figure and provides plenty of fodder to fuel morbid curiosity. "Food and death are two of the most emotionally charged things in our lives," Randleman said when explaining his creation.[20] The site lists the "last ten diners" and those with the "next reservations" in addition to selling dead man–branded merchandise, ranging from T-shirts to thongs, mouse pads to mugs.

Bizarre but True Last Breath Stories

The public appetite for the odd and bizarre doesn't end with last meal stories. A couple of the more unusual true execution stories involve an errant glass eye and a missing handcuff key.

In searching through his memories, Fitzgerald recalls an execution of a nameless prisoner from San Antonio who surprised his executioners after his death.

> He committed a crime in which he took a banker and his wife hostage at their home in Alamo Heights and the plan was to get the husband, who was a bank officer, to go down and get the money out of the bank to free his wife. Well, it went awry and he wound up killing the woman and of course he got the death penalty for it.... He was probably legally blind or very close to it; he wore very thick glasses. When we put him on the gurney for some reason we didn't have his glasses on him. He was being pronounced dead by the physician, and the guard checked his pulse and looked in his eyes with a flashlight, but no one told them this guy had a glass eye.

It popped out and the guard grabbed it before it hit the ground and kind of stuffed it back in.[21]

Lyons tells the bizarre execution story she has heard most frequently:

One of the strangest was the execution of Panchai Wilkerson. He is the inmate who spit out a handcuff key—yes, he was taking his last breath and he popped this key out of his mouth and caught everybody off guard. Nobody had any idea he had a key in his mouth. The first question is "Could he have escaped?" No, he couldn't have. Inmates that are transported have two sets of handcuffs and he had a key to one of them, but he didn't have a key to the other set. So, he could not have escaped, but we never found out where he had gotten the key or how he hid it all that time.[22]

The PIOs agree that each prisoner handles the last minutes of his or her life differently and that no two executions are quite the same. Some of the condemned opt for black humor; they make jokes, even play pranks. "Some of them get in the holding cell that is adjacent to the death chamber and they act like comedians—they stand up and do one-liners—tell lawyer jokes," Fitzgerald says. "Some of them are very introspective, very quiet, very reflective; some are very prayerful."[23]

The last words of the condemned, like the last meal, are traditionally reported by the media and are posted verbatim on the TDCJ website. The privilege to utter a last dying speech to assembled witnesses is a First Amendment right. In Texas the warden is required to ask the prisoner if he or she has any last words, and the convicted must be allowed to give the entire statement—with no durational or editorial restrictions.[24]

Final statements run the gamut from tearful to unrepentant to obscure. Inmates typically direct doleful goodbyes to family members, especially their mothers. "Tell Mama I love her and tell the kids I love them, too. I'll see you all," concluded Kia Johnson (June 11, 2003).

Many convicts are converted while on death row, taking what Reid called the "Jesus route," and express faith in the hereafter. Reginald Reeves's final words had the tone of a benediction: "I know your spirit and God dwells within us and we are all one big family of humanity; we must all learn to love and live together. I will see you on the other side. Thank you for your hospitality" (May 9, 2002).

As often as the condemned admit their guilt and remorse, there are at least as many who proclaim innocence until the end. "If you think I did this, you need to think again," said William Chappell. "All I was asking for was a DNA and I could not get it....You are murdering me and I feel sorry for you" (November 20, 2002).

Some go to their death angry with their accusers, whom they blaspheme with their last breath. Edward Ellis said, "I just want everyone to know that the prosecutor and Bill Scott are sorry sons of bitches" (March 3, 1992).

> *The power of last-breath statements is considerable: "Because they emanate from a person who stands on the brink of extermination, these utterances are more likely to influence public opinion than any billboard, banner, or editorial."*

Many inmates are functionally illiterate, and their final words are somewhat cryptic, such as this statement by James Ronald: "As the ocean always returns to itself, love always returns to itself. So does consciousness, always returns to itself. And I do so with love on my lips. May God bless all mankind" (December 15, 1998).

The distinction of the shortest statement might go to Warren Bridge, who succinctly said, "I'll see you" (November 22, 1994). Charlie Livingston used his last words to point out, "You all brought me here to be executed, not to make a speech" (November 21, 1997).

Most final statements are three to four minutes long, but a few inmates have stretched out the last moments of their lives with voluminous discourses. Kathy Walt recalled an inmate who had the "gift of gab": "He loved to talk. I mean, he talked up a blue streak to the point that I had to quit visiting him because I couldn't get anything else done." This particular execution was not one of the thirty-eight Walt witnessed as a death row reporter, but the talkative inmate created his own legend, which she still remembers.

"He almost filibustered his execution past midnight he talked so much. He actually stopped and asked for a drink of water to moisten his mouth, and they gave him some and he ticked off names of reporters over the years he'd talked to; he talked about wardens and fellow inmates on death row."[25]

The power of last-breath statements is considerable, according to Kevin O'Neill, writing in the *Arizona State Law Journal*: "Because they emanate from a person who stands on the brink of extermination, these utterances are more likely to influence public opinion than any billboard, banner, or editorial."[26]

On the other hand, some inmates are ready, even eager, for the escape of death: "There was a biker Larry Fitzgerald and I talked about a lot because he was almost too excited about the execution," Lyons remembers. "He was used to being out on the road, and he could not stand being kept in a cell. So, when he was on the gurney, he was happy and he was singing the words to Robert Earl Keen's 'The road goes on forever and the party never ends.' It was just definitely memorable."[27]

Urban Legends Take on a Life of Their Own

Some legends persist through generations even though there has never been a shred of evidence to support the stories. Both the public as well as the news media are familiar with a variety of old wives' tales regarding prisoners and executions.

One of the most popular and enduring of these is the legend of the lights. When Don Reid was in the death chamber waiting to view his first execution in 1938, he asked the assistant warden if the prison's lights would dim when the executioner "threw the switch" on the electric chair. The warden gently set him straight: "The Death House has its own set of generators. That only happens in the movies—the lights of the town going dim and the townspeople hiding under their blankets so they won't know and all that tripe."[28]

More than sixty years later, the PIOs still get that same question. "Did the lights really flicker? Well, that's not so," Fitzgerald patiently explains. "It is my understanding that it is against the law to use a public utility to execute. Anyway, we had our own generator—our own setup—we did it internally."[29]

After Old Sparky was retired in 1964, the myths continued. Walt says that many envision the inmate being sedated or forced onto the gurney where the lethal injection takes place. Although there is a five-member tie-down team at hand, prisoners seldom "kick up a ruckus," according to Walt. During the three dozen executions she covered, there were no such scenes. "I always attributed that to the prison staff and to the counseling, particularly from the chaplain, who got them ready for their fate."[30]

Execution as a cost-saving measure is the basis of yet another misconception, Lyons explains. "A lot of people say we should execute them because it is a lot more expensive if we keep them alive all that time. That is not true—it's more expensive to put someone on death row because most of these inmates are indigent and therefore they have to have legal representation before the Supreme Court for filing all of those appeals—it is really costly. It would be less expensive to keep someone in prison for his whole life."[31]

The current estimated cost per day to house an offender in Texas is $61.58 according to the TDCJ website's "Death Row Facts."[32] At that rate, the accommodations are anything but luxurious; the "country club myth" is another common fiction the PIOs work to correct. (See "Prison Myths Abound" in chapter 3.) "I think people believe these prisoners have it pretty easy, and that's not the case at all," Viesca says.[33]

Death row offenders are housed in single-person cells measuring sixty square feet without air-conditioning. In Texas summers, when daytime temperatures often climb past one hundred degrees, the prisons are a miserable place to be according to both reporters and PIOs.

Prisoners must earn the smallest privileges; a few death row offenders are allowed the luxury of a radio, but none has a television and all spend twenty-three hours a day in their cells, where they can read, write, and contemplate their futures.[34]

> *"There are two types of people when it comes to prisons—those who think we are not beating the prisoners enough and those who think we are coddling them."*

Ordinary citizens, however, don't see these scenes inside the walls; public opinion is often based on hearsay and perceptions largely formed from movies and television. "There are two types of people when it comes to prisons—those who think we are not beating the prisoners enough and those who think we are coddling them," Fitzgerald says wryly.[35]

Walt speculates that part of the perception problem, at least in Huntsville, may stem from the prominent location of an exercise area for trustees along a main road on the outskirts of the town. "When the public sees the basketball court, they get the idea these inmates aren't in their cells, they are out playing basketball and having better sports facilities than a lot of schools have," Walt observes.[36]

Countering these misperceptions as well as other "tall tales" about executions and prison life is the everyday job of the public information officers, who try to pitch as many positive stories as possible when they are not busy responding to media queries or managing media relations during executions.

Prison City Close-Up

Deadly News, but Never Deadly Dull:
A Day in the Life of Michelle Lyons

In the male-dominated prison culture, where the lions' share of prisoners and administrators are men, the public information manager for TDCJ is a woman. Michelle Lyons has been disseminating both good and bad prison news for almost a decade, but her gender is still a surprise and a concern to some reporters and prison officials. "I think it's such a fascinating field I don't let it bother me," Lyons says.[37]

She began writing about TDCJ as a local reporter. In three years Lyons covered fifty-two executions for the Item. Her next career move still had her covering executions, but it also provided opportunities to discuss more positive aspects of TDCJ. In 2001 Lyons became part of the public information office for TDCJ, and when Larry Fitzgerald retired from his position in August 2003 Lyons took over as manager for the Huntsville PI office. On any typical day, Lyons spends time both inside and outside her office, primarily doing media relations.

"I never ask why they want the information because I don't want them to think I don't want to provide it," Lyons says.[38] Not surprisingly, most media requests concern death row and executions. Execution days are busy in the PI office, since Lyons or a staffer must attend every execution to escort media witnesses and to officially report what happened.

After the execution at the Walls, Lyons provides the media a sheet containing the offender's last statement and an execution recording, which gives the minute-by-minute account of each step of the execution: (1) Taken from holding cell; (2) Strapped to gurney; (3) Solution flowing; (4) Last statement; (5) Lethal dose began; (6) Lethal dose completed; (7) Pronounced dead.[39] As the reporters file their stories, Lyons phones two radio station networks, Metro Source and Texas State Network, to leave a recording of the offender's last statement and the time of death. A member of her staff is responsible for faxing the same information to Reuters and other newswire services not present for the execution.

Lyons concludes every workday by sending the director a media run, a list of all reporters and affiliates who contacted the PI office that day, plus a brief description of information provided. This list goes to the top TDCJ administrative officials, so they know what stories to expect when they open their newspapers or turn on their radios or televisions the next morning. ✪

Strict Media Guidelines Govern Access to Prisoners

Death row prisoners' physical movement is severely limited by their surroundings, but the law of the land confers two types of privileged communication on incarcerated offenders: legal and media. Within the restrictions imposed for the "safe and secure operation of the facility,"[40] prisoners are allowed to freely communicate with their attorneys and with the media. Prisoners can write letters to the media and they can choose to accept or decline interview requests from reporters. The PIOs facilitate the interaction between prisoners and reporters; TDCJ outlines specific procedures that are followed without exception, ranging from time restrictions to dress codes.

Reporters who wish to interview death row inmates must submit in advance a written request on the news organization's letterhead to the public information office. Death row interviews with male inmates are scheduled every Wednesday from 1 to 3 P.M.; women's interviews are on Tuesdays during the same time period. If the prisoner agrees to the interview, the reporter has forty-five minutes, including set-up time, to interview the inmate.[41] The inmate may initially agree and later have a change of heart.

Fitzgerald remembers that Gary Graham liked to "play games" with the media. "Sometimes he would have the media in there and it would be like he was trying to hold court one after another: boom, boom, boom, going through. Then sometimes someone would want to come from Europe to interview the guy and he would say, 'Sure, I'll do it.' I would set up the paperwork, the reporter would show up, and Graham would go back to his cell and say, 'No, I don't want to do it.'"[42] (For more about the Graham execution, see "Countdown to Death" at the end of this chapter.)

This is one of the few opportunities inmates have to be in control; they can choose whether to invoke their power of saying "no" over the opportunity to communicate beyond the walls that imprison them. Reporters, particularly those who have traveled to Huntsville for a promised interview, are frustrated with the situation and sometimes are unhappy with the messenger when the answer is "no." The PIO is caught between the role of assisting the media and maintaining credibility with the prisoners. "The reporter who had traveled all the way from Europe would say, 'Well, can't you go back and convince him?' Fitzgerald recalls. "I'd say, 'No, I'm not going to go back and beg a convict. Either he does it or he doesn't do it. I am not going to get in a position of being a person who has to 'cow down' to a convict."[43]

As a convict's execution date nears, the media requests for face-to-face interviews increase. "The execution list is pretty stacked right now and when that happens, we have a lot of reporters who apply to interview death row inmates," Lyons explains.[44] With Texas's annual execution rate, there are often "stacked" times, months when several prisoners are slated for death. TDCJ's Death Row Information site has a page for upcoming executions, which chronologically lists the offenders by their scheduled execution dates. It is not unusual to have four or five executions slated for a given month. It is simply a matter of when a convict's appeals have been exhausted.

Reporters who want to talk to convicts cannot conduct telephone interviews; they must travel to the prison unit where the condemned inmates are housed and meet with the prisoners in person.

Reporters who want to talk to convicts cannot conduct telephone interviews; they must travel to the prison unit where the condemned inmates are housed and meet with the prisoners in person. For men's death row, that means driving to the Polunsky unit in Livingston, a town of about 6,400 near Lake Livingston, where the unincarcerated bring their ski boats and bass rigs to take advantage of the miles of recreational waterways. Livingston lakefront property, increasingly in demand as the supply dwindles, is expensive despite proximity to the prison. A waterfront home in the area can easily cost $300,000 or more.

Since the prison was built in the late 1990s and death row moved to Polunsky in 2000, local businesses have enjoyed an uptick in customers. Most residents are not concerned about the source of the increased traffic. "All the bad guys are locked up here," says a local convenience store employee. "In the city, they're all out running loose."[45]

There is no public transportation to Polunsky; Livingston's airport is too small to accommodate commercial aircraft. Foreign reporters—to many Texans, this is anyone who does not live in Texas—would most likely fly into Houston's Intercontinental Airport and then drive a rental car sixty miles north into the heart of rural East Texas. Some even hire taxis from the Houston airport, not realizing the distance and the fares involved.

Reporters may take still photos and television crews can shoot footage inside the unit, with restrictions. "We are very limited in the footage and the photos they can take inside because we don't want to compromise security," Lyons explains. "We don't want to show all the checkpoints."[46] For TDCJ's legal protection, prisoners sign release forms for photos or film footage in addition to the consent forms required for interviews.

When reporters arrive at the Polunsky unit they must abandon many of the trappings of life "in the free." Cellular phones, pagers, briefcases and purses, paper money, magazines, and tobacco products cannot be brought inside.[47] The TDCJ Media Policies for Inmate Interviews advise reporters to bring with them "only the equipment they need to conduct the interview and a valid form of identification."[48] Reporters can expect to be searched with a hand-held metal detector at the first checkpoint.

Security remains high throughout the media visit. *Item* reporter Prew describes the interview process: "When the inmates walk in, they sit in the cage area and put their hands through a little slot to have their handcuffs removed. Then they sign a release. There's a glass wall between us, where the phones are, but the wall goes all the way down to the cinder blocks, so there is no way to pass business cards or pens or anything through. It's kind of intimidating for a reporter the first time just because it's so distant."[49]

Media representatives visiting the prison for the first time are sometimes surprised to learn there is a dress code for interviews. As might be expected, visitors to this rural conservative area are expected to don inconspicuous attire. The dress code, published on the public information office's website, states:

> Shorts/cutoffs, open-toe shoes, tank tops, t-shirts (underwear type), fishnet shirts, see-through fabrics, and shirts or blouses with an open midriff are prohibited. Men must wear long pants and women may wear dresses, skirts or long pants. Shirts or other articles of clothing with pictures or language which may be considered profane or offensive by current public standards will not be allowed. Dresses or skirts must be no more than three (3) inches above the middle of the knee.[50]

Walt says she considered the dress code "absolutely appropriate." She explains that her goal was always to present herself in as neutral a way as possible and use common sense about her manner of dress. "When I was in an older prison where there were open grates, I didn't wear a skirt. I don't think I wore perfume."[51] Prew believes the media tries to be considerate. "I've never seen anyone wear hot pink. Usually, I wear a suit, just out of respect—no low-cut things, no open-toed shoes."[52]

Janet Parker Dial, who covered the death row beat for the *Huntsville Item* after she graduated from the journalism program at Sam Houston State University, remembers that she always dressed "demurely," in conservative pants or dresses that fell below her knees when visiting the cell blocks. "You wouldn't want to tempt the prisoners to get agitated," Dial explains.[53] Even scented soap is not a good idea, Walt warns. "The inmates can tell if there is someone different on the blocks, either by the sound of their shoes or they can smell the difference."[54]

> *"I have had a lot of phone calls from overseas, especially. I have had people call me a murderer for being at executions, which is absurd. The State of Texas executes its citizens. If the media is not there, there is no record of what's happening. I sure as heck want to know what's going on inside the death chamber."*

Once the interview begins, convicts' conversations with the media are not censored. "I don't monitor what they are talking about. I don't care; that's not my business," Lyons says. "I guess, having been a reporter, I'm very adamant that I don't want to infringe on their lives whatsoever. So, I don't listen in on them at all. I just monitor. I give them a five-minute warning."[55]

Many local and state reporters who work with the PIOs on a regular basis are complimentary of the job the public information officers do in their role of helping carry out the orders of the Texas courts. Some reporters, particularly those from other countries, are more combative and tend to see the PIOs—and the Texas media—as complicit in the execution process.

"I have had a lot of phone calls from overseas, especially," Prew says. "I have had people call me a murderer for being at executions, which is absurd. The State of Texas executes its citizens. If the media is not there, there is no record of what's happening. I sure as heck want to know what's going on inside the death chamber. If it weren't for us, there wouldn't be any protocol."[56]

Walt thinks the death row prisoners consciously project a rational image and discourage flamboyant or extreme comments during interviews. "So I have no doubt they saw themselves as using the media and we saw ourselves as using them to get a story; both sides knew the other was using them."[5]

Prison City Close-Up

Women in Prison: A Growing Demographic

Women are the fastest-growing segment of the prison population nationwide, largely as a result of mandatory drug sentencing laws.[58] From 1990 to 2000, the number of women in state and federal prisons more than doubled, jumping from approximately 40,000 to over 87,000.[59] Although women are a fraction of the prison population—7 percent nationally—incarceration has a different and more intensely negative effect on women than it does on men.[60]

Nevertheless, the number of women in state or federal prisons, which exceeded 107,500 in 2005, is expected to continue to rise. The Bureau of Justice Statistics estimates that about eleven women out of one thousand will be incarcerated at some time in their lives. Broken down by ethnicity, thirty-six out of one thousand black women are likely to serve sentences, compared to fifteen out of one thousand Hispanic women and five out of one thousand white women. Of these, only a very few will reside on death row—nationally women account for 1.5 percent of the condemned.[61]

In Texas women make up less than 3 percent of the death row population, but media and public interest in them is strong. Prison staff agree that women are different from male inmates in adjusting to prison life, in enhancing their appearance and surroundings, and in responding to the media. On average, they are also better educated than their male counterparts; the majority have at least a high school diploma.

On a more personal level, women tend to be more emotional and less physical in dealing with frustrations, and they are especially concerned about their children and grandchildren. More than 60 percent of women in state or federal prisons have young children, which translates into "more than 1.3 million minor children who are the offspring of women under correctional sanction."[62]

Brian Cox, a school psychologist for TDCJ, says that men in prison usually must deal with feelings of anger and aggression, but women tend to suffer from bouts of depression and victimization, which can result in a higher recidivism rate. "The men are involved, but the women are committed," Cox says. "It's a very intense thing." He adds that women and men view prison sentences with a different mindset. "The guys perceive their lives are on hold, but the women feel they give up their lives when they come to prison. For women, it is all about family."[63]

For the handful of women on Texas's death row, their fellow prisoners become their family unit. A sisterhood of ten among the 1,600 females imprisoned in the state, the condemned women are reluctant to grant media interviews, perhaps because they are apprehensive of how publicity might affect their cases.

Item reporter Prew sees a double standard for women inmates just as in free society. Citing as an example Frances Newton, who was convicted of murder in 1987 and given a 120-day stay in 2004, Prew says women are more likely to be granted reprieves than men, "so they try to distance themselves" from public attention. "They really don't want to do anything to hurt their case. The media can do great things and they can do horrible things, even if it's unintentional."[64]

The handful of women on Texas's death row are reluctant to grant media interviews, perhaps because they are apprehensive of how publicity might affect their cases.

PIO Lyons says that women prisoners usually decline interviews unless they get to know the reporter through extensive correspondence. "I've noticed women on death row only grant interviews to men; they think the men are going to be more sympathetic. They dress for the interview, and they fix their hair and makeup. I think they're hoping to use feminine wiles to persuade the reporter to write something favorable."[65]

Carla Faye Tucker, the pickax murderer who became a born-again Christian in the fifteen years between her arrest and execution, drew sympathy from many quarters, ranging from former PIO Larry Fitzgerald, who describes her as a "very spiritual person,"[66] to anti–death penalty activist Dennis Longmire, who says, "Everybody associated with [Karla Faye] acknowledged she was not the monster who was convicted."[67]

Despite latent sympathy for some condemned women, the executions go forward. When appeals from a host of supporters failed, Frances Newton was put to death in September 2005, the first African-American woman to be executed in Texas since the Civil War. Coincidentally, her court-appointed attorney was Ron Mock, who lost numerous capital cases and is notorious for falling asleep in court while defending Gary Graham.[68] ✪

East Texas Town Draws Media from Near and Far

By executive directive, the TDCJ public information office has a clear set of priorities for dealing with media access. The home state reporters are first, followed by national and then by international media outlets. Not surprisingly, the PIOs feel that Texas media are more likely to view executions as a state-mandated function that is generally supported by the citizens. In general, the farther reporters must travel to reach Huntsville, the more likely they are to arrive with an anti–death penalty agenda, or, at the very least, with some preconceived notions about the frontier nature of Texans.

In Texas, executions have taken place so often—more than 350 times—since they were reinstated in 1976 that they have lost much of their news appeal. Walt notes, "When the death penalty was started up again, all those details became a fascination—this is what he said, this is what he ate—now, the stories that run in the paper are three or four paragraphs; it's not front-page news anymore."[69] The majority of the men on Texas's death row are black or Hispanic, many with impoverished and illiterate backgrounds. The horror of their crimes may bring them to the public's attention for a short time, but usually by the time of their scheduled executions only the convicts' and victims' families are still involved with the story. Usually, their executions are barely noted by the media or by the citizens of Huntsville.

To some, this translates as cold-heartedness on the part of the PIOs as well as the residents of Huntsville. The public information officers must absorb these criticisms and try to explain that they are state employees who are responsible to the taxpayers and are obligated to communicate with those taxpayers through the media but have no control over the death penalty process. Fitzgerald remembers that he sometimes received calls from anti–death penalty advocates. "We're like shooting fish in a barrel; people recognize us and call us and say, 'Please tell the governor to stop this execution'—like we really can—it just doesn't happen."[70]

Reporters also must separate their own principles from their jobs as media witnesses to executions. Dial, who personally is against the death penalty, clearly remembers the first execution she covered for the *Item*. "I kept having these Walter Mitty kinds of thoughts: 'I'll just stand up, say this is wrong and stop the execution,'" Dial recalls fantasizing. She did not sleep the night before the execution, and because the sentence was carried out at midnight did not sleep on execution night, either. Instead of trying to stop the death ritual, she focused on practicalities: "I reminded myself not to lock my knees and to take deep breaths." Her editor had told her to pay close attention to the convict's final words, which she still remembers: "I can feel the poison running down," although she no longer recalls the prisoner's name.[71]

The bizarre civility of the execution process gives reporters new to the beat pause. Special etiquette questions arise: Are the rules of comportment similar to those for attending a funeral? What does one wear to an execution? In the Old South tradition of falling back on convention under difficult circumstances, most witnesses attending executions adopt somber attitudes. Dial wryly recalls her dilemma over what to wear to her first execution.

Reporters from other parts of the country sometimes misinterpret this stiff upper lip attitude as callousness and view Texas as part of the Old West's "life is cheap" mentality.

"I usually dressed casually at work, but that didn't seem appropriate, so I went shopping and bought a dark green dress."[72] Some create rituals for the occasion; Walt remembers a reporter who always purchased a new outfit—not necessarily in a dark color—to wear to an execution.[73] Humor—dark or otherwise—is frowned upon, but the surreal nature of the situation is unsettling. "It is a cold, clinical setting; it looks like an emergency room with the prisoner strapped to the gurney. The witnesses stand around and make polite conversation while someone dies," Dial says.[74]

Reporters from other parts of the country sometimes misinterpret this stiff upper lip attitude as callousness and view Texas as part of the Old West's "life is cheap" mentality. Even in the twenty-first century, Huntsville, like most small Texas towns, is essentially a closed society that treats outsiders politely but holds them at arm's length. National reporters sometimes complain that the PIOs block them from attending executions. Denis Johnson, a *Rolling Stone* reporter who spent several weeks in Huntsville trying to view one of the five executions scheduled for May 2000, categorized Texas as "grandly and profoundly Southern, reclusively and myopically Southern."[75]

Johnson spent considerable time with Fitzgerald and criticized him roundly in his ten-page published article. Johnson's premise was that TDCJ tries to block media coverage of "justice Texas-style," and Fitzgerald's job was "to protect the [death] machine from non-Texan scrutiny."[76] Johnson portrayed Fitzgerald as a "boob," a liar, and a "good old boy" who thwarted the *Rolling Stone* writer's every effort to be added to the witness list for one of the executions. It is true that Johnson did not witness an execution; at the end of May, he left Huntsville without achieving that objective, although he interviewed several of the condemned prisoners, toured the prison museum, and talked to dozens of people on both sides of the issue. In frustration that he was not allowed to be an execution witness, Johnson declared, "It's vendetta journalism now, the tale of Stonewall Fitzgerald, the Hero of Huntsville."[77]

Not surprisingly, Fitzgerald has not forgotten Johnson: "He hated me. Boy, did that guy hate me, but that's okay. I did my job. And I was told by somebody high up in the governor's office they recognized I took a hit for the governor."[78] Texas governor George W. Bush was recognized in the same issue of *Rolling Stone* as the "American governor [who] has put more people to death"—about one every two weeks since he took office.[79]

International media, officially specified as the public information office's lowest priority, represent the proverbial thorn in the side for the PIOs because they usually arrive in Huntsville with an agenda. The European media in particular are predisposed against the death penalty, Fitzgerald and Lyons agree. The PIOs say they frequently find themselves defending the State of Texas, the judicial system, or the criminal justice system to European reporters.[80] "A lot of foreign journalists just don't understand that the governor does not have the power to commute a sentence without the parole board's approval," Lyons points out.[81]

The prisoners recognize that foreign media will likely be sympathetic. "A lot of inmates keep in close contact with Amnesty International and then AI drums up media support abroad," Lyons says. "There are inmates who won't agree to interviews from someone in Texas, but they will accept any interview with someone from Belgium or France. They know they'll have a shot at getting some public support."[82] The public information officers do make arrangements for foreign journalists to interview prisoners, but reluctantly. An exception is Mexican media, since many of the convicted are Mexican nationals, and the proximity of the two countries facilitates cooperation.

No matter how much or how little media attention a particular case attracts, on execution day the PIOs prepare a press kit, which is essentially the same each time: a double-pocket folder containing a page of death row facts, a synopsis of the crime, the last meal request, a list of scheduled executions, and a "death watch" summary, which is a snapshot of some of the inmate's activities during the past three days. Typical is the death watch list for Douglas Alan Roberts, #999218, who was sentenced to die for the kidnapping and murder of a San Antonio man in 1996.[83] This one-page litany of the inmate's activities during his last days on earth hints at the "quiet kind of terror" Pacifica reporter Thompson says permeates death row, where prisoners "say goodbye to their mom and their friends on death row and pack up all their things—their bags of law books and their tennis shoes and their Bibles—and leave Polunsky and come on over here" to the Walls, hoping for a last-minute stay, "like spinning Russian roulette."[84] Roberts's three-day death watch report shows he lost the spin; his sentence was carried out as scheduled:

April 18, 2005
    12:04 a.m.   Inmate sleeping
    6:02 a.m.   Inmate standing at cell door
    8:22 a.m.   Inmate arrived at visitation
    11:37 a.m.   Inmate visiting and eating
    5:06 p.m.   Inmate escorted back to the cell from
                          visitation
    8:31 p.m.   Inmate showering
    10:57 p.m.   Inmate sleeping

April 19, 2005
    12:04 a.m.   Inmate sleeping
    3:29 a.m.   Inmate eating breakfast
    7:26 a.m.   Inmate standing at cell door talking
    8:05 a.m.   Inmate escorted to visitation
    12:38 p.m.   Inmate visiting
    4:40 p.m.   Inmate visiting
    6:46 p.m.   Inmate standing at cell door
    8:30 p.m.   Inmate reading and opening small mail
    11:30 p.m.   Inmate sleeping

April 20, 2005
    12:02 a.m.   Inmate sleeping
    2:44 a.m.   Inmate sorting mail
    4:30 a.m.   Inmate reading mail
    8:01 a.m.   Inmate is packing property
    8:25 a.m.   Inmate escorted to visitation
    9:06 a.m.   Inmate eating and visiting
    12:00 p.m.   Inmate visitation terminated
                  (Media Kit, Douglas Alan Roberts, 4/20/05)

The Final Word

After an execution, the witnesses are escorted outside, where the PIO answers any questions the media representatives may have. Reporters usually take this opportunity to collect comments from families of both the executed and the victim. "Talking to the family members at this point is not as tough as talking to the victim's families where the death is still fresh, and they are still reeling," Dial says. "By the time of the execution, they have come to terms with the death in their family." She believes the victim's families see the media as a "tool to get their message out," while the condemned's relatives often view the media "as part of the problem."[85]

For his part, the bottom line, according to Viesca, is that the PI office must work to keep an open relationship with all media. "You know you are not always going to agree with what they write or what they air about you, but they're doing their jobs. Your job as a communicator for any agency like this is to give them what they need, be timely with it, be responsive, and treat everyone the same."[86]

When all is said and written, most reporters as well as the PIOs agree that media portrayals, with some exceptions, are largely accurate although sometimes oversimplified or overstated for dramatic purposes. All media play to their readers, whether it be Texas media writing for a population where the majority supports the death penalty, national media that see the Texas culture from an outsider's perspective, or foreign reporters who find the idea of execution inexplicable.

> *For a long time, I ran death row as far as media goes. So I got to know a bunch of the death row inmates—you learn what their problems are, about their families, the nature of their crimes—it was a strange relationship. I wouldn't say it was a friendship; you just gain knowledge of their likes and dislikes, [then] you would see them on a gurney...if I never see another execution, it won't be too soon.*
> —Larry Fitzgerald, who witnessed 219 executions

> *If we followed the "eye for an eye and a tooth for a tooth" law, we would all be blind and gumming our food.*
> —Eric Thompson, Pacifica Radio reporter

Prison City Close-Up

Countdown to Death:
The Ultimate Reality Show

A high-profile execution takes on many of the trappings of macabre entertainment; all of the elements of high drama are concentrated in the death ritual: fear, loss, sorrow, courage, and vindication, climaxing in the moment when the ultimate price is paid. If the condemned has no public visibility, the execution is reported—if the media notes it at all—in a brief news story. But if the killer's story has captured the public interest, reporters swarm to Huntsville and the media spotlight shines brightly on the small town, where a line of more than a dozen vehicles at the downtown stoplight is usually considered a traffic jam. Once the lethal injection has done its work, the satellite trucks and convoys of reporters move on and residents resume life as usual.

After the inmate's appeals are exhausted and the fateful date is set, the execution is usually orderly and methodical, moving like clockwork from one step to the next until the ritual is complete. Most executions attract little if any attention beyond that of the families of the victims and the condemned. However, high public interest, which translates to high media interest, can complicate the PIO's job and sometimes can derail the systematic process.

One such high-profile case involved the execution of a black man from Houston who was arrested in 1981 and later convicted for the robbery and shooting of a customer outside an area supermarket. Gary Graham was twenty when he was arrested, and his conviction rested on the testimony of an eyewitness who said she saw Graham reach into the victim's pockets and then shoot him as they scuffled. During Graham's trial, testimony revealed that he had been charged in ten robberies and was a suspect in two shootings, ten car thefts, and eight other robberies.[87]

Over the course of the nineteen years Graham spent on death row, his case became internationally known and reporters from around the world came to Huntsville for interviews. Media reports questioned the veracity of the lone witness and explored the world of violence and neglect in which Graham grew up. As national celebrities and organizations such as Amnesty International took up Graham's cause, media interest grew exponentially. The Hollywood-like climate of the media coverage became even more pronounced when Graham's twenty-one-year-old son was arrested for murder and robbery. (Gary Lee Hawkins did not join his father on death row but was found guilty and assessed a life sentence.) With the years of accumulated sensationalism, in the last day of Graham's life Huntsville became the focus for a "media circus" from the PIOs' standpoint.

The Final Fortnight

Here's how the countdown to the 6 P.M. execution usually progresses and how it varied for Gary Graham in June 2000:

Day 14—Time to order the last meal. No alcohol or cigarettes are permitted, but the prison chef tries to accommodate all reasonable requests. The long-honored custom of executing well-fed prisoners is grist for the media mill that churns out stories about the killer's final hours. A criminal justice professor at the nearby Sam Houston State University suggests that there is a practical consideration for the last meal: "If you can provide creature comforts, you're going to have a more malleable individual to strap down and to execute," says James Marquart.[88]

Graham declines a last meal, explaining that he does not wish to accept food from those who intend to kill him.

Graham declines a last meal, explaining that he does not wish to accept food from those who intend to kill him.

Day 12—Time to select attire and name witnesses. Most inmates are indifferent to their dress for their last day on earth, electing to die in their "prison whites," but give more attention to naming the last people they will see. The inmate can name up to five people to witness his execution, but many die without family or friends present.

Graham is dressed in a white "hospital-style" paper robe so he cannot use his clothing to hang himself, according to Fitzgerald. For witnesses, Graham asks that Jesse Jackson, a member of Amnesty International, the Reverend Al Sharpton, and Texas governor George W. Bush, Jr., attend his execution.

Day 10—Most inmates receive little public support. But members of the New Black Panthers and the Nation of Islam take to the streets in

Houston to protest Graham's scheduled execution.[89]

Day 7—At this point, legal efforts on behalf of the convict are usually over, but in Graham's case his lawyers continue to file appeal after appeal to the state's pardons and parole board until hours before the execution. The attorneys also field interviews from all the major news networks; the media feeding frenzy is in full cry.

The case becomes a major issue in Bush's presidential campaign. Media reports point out that Graham will be the 135th person to be executed under Bush's watch as governor. Some articles begin to talk about "Texacutions," and hecklers disrupt several campaign events. Bush responds that his job is to uphold the laws of the state.[90]

"[The] media are a lot like lemmings; if you put up a compound and rope it off and say, 'You stay in here and we'll come out and address you and you'll get everything everyone else gets,' they'll stay there. If you don't, they'll just run everywhere."

Mindful of the growing media interest, the PIOs prepare for the onslaught. Based on experience gleaned during previous high-profile executions, such as that of pickax murderer Karla Faye Tucker, the public information officers prepare a media compound to corral the reporters. PIO Fitzgerald says the key to successful media relations is to see that each reporter gets the same information:

"[Members of the] media are a lot like lemmings; if you put up a compound and rope it off and say, 'You stay in here and we'll come out and address you and you'll get everything everyone else gets,' they'll stay there. If you don't, they'll just run everywhere."[91] Anticipating an influx of TV reporters, the public information office even constructs camera platforms for the news crews.

24 hours—Most convicts are transferred to the holding cell at the Walls on the day of their execution, but Graham's high media profile prompts transfer a day early for security purposes. Graham promises to resist transfer and urges his supporters to protest what he terms his legal "lynching and assassination."[92]

Fitzgerald issues a media statement that Graham briefly resisted the transfer but was subdued by guards and placed in shackles. "He always said from the outset he would resist; [I didn't expect] a change of heart," Fitzgerald says.[93]

12 hours—Witnesses and media begin to arrive. Media witnesses for Graham's execution will be AP reporter Mike Graczyk, *Huntsville Item* reporter Michelle Lyons, UPI representative Wayne Sorge, *Houston Chronicle* reporter Salatheia Bryant, and Lloyd Gite, of Fox 26 News. Many members of the media circus arrive well before the day of the scheduled execution.

7 hours—Trays of sandwiches are laid out for the guards and chaplains. The PIOs try to avoid any indication that this is a festive occasion; in a much-regretted slip of the tongue, Fitzgerald once referred to the snack plates as "party platters" with unfavorable public relations repercussions.

5 hours—The PIO makes one last visit. Fitzgerald leaves his office and walks across the street to the Walls to visit the inmate. "I [talk] to him about what his final statement will be, what he can expect in the way of witnesses who will be coming in, which members of the media will be there," Fitzgerald says.[94]

On Graham's execution day, about two hundred anti-death penalty advocates march, wave signs, and chant, "Let Gary Graham live."

4 hours—The PIO reports to the media on the prisoner's "demeanor." Fitzgerald addresses the media compound, which in Graham's case is filled with print and broadcast reporters from across the world. He reports that Graham met with his spiritual adviser and paced in his cell adjacent to the death chamber.[95]

2 hours—The last meal is delivered to the holding cell. The prison chaplain often sits with the inmate while he eats. Graham refuses all food, asking only for coffee.

1 hour—Protesters gather outside the Walls. Usually, this is a small group; sometimes the sole protester is Dennis Longmire, a criminal justice professor at nearby Sam Houston State University. (See "A Constant Witness" at the end of chapter 2.)

On Graham's execution day, about two hundred anti–death penalty advocates march, wave signs, and chant, "Let Gary Graham live." Death penalty advocates also show up, including a handful of Ku Klux Klan members bearing Confederate flags. About two hundred law enforcement officers are on hand to ensure peaceful protests. Fitzgerald recalls that Jesse Jackson wanted to speak to the crowd from the podium, but Fitzgerald denied the request. "My dilemma was if I had let him do that, then I would've had to give the podium to the KKK too, and I did not want someone in full KKK drag standing in front of a state seal."[96]

Some inmates hold out hope until the end that a reprieve will stop the execution process, and occasionally the much-awaited stay has materialized. In Graham's case, the 6 P.M. execution time is delayed due to a last-minute appeal to the U.S. Supreme Court and a civil suit against the Texas Board of Pardons and Paroles. The high court declines to hear the case, and Fitzgerald reports to the media that the board has denied a reprieve or a pardon, paving the way for the execution to take place.[97] Fitzgerald thinks the delay avoided a "full-blown riot" that day. By the time the execution occurs, temperatures have cooled and a lot of the protestors have drifted away.[98]

30 minutes—Witnesses are escorted to the viewing area in the death chamber. Since 1996, close relatives and friends of the victim as well as family members of the convicted have been allowed to witness executions. Witnesses for the victim and for the inmate have separate viewing rooms. The PIO serves as an escort for the media representatives, who accompany either the victim's or the inmate's witnesses. Correctional officers search everyone who enters the prison, a standard security procedure.

10 minutes—Time to leave the holding cell and take the "last walk." A five-man tie-down team straps the inmate to the steel gurney that will be his deathbed.

Graham has stated repeatedly that he will resist at every point. Fitzgerald has assured the media, "We have an extraction team at the ready….They'll be ready for it."[99] Despite his struggles, Graham, like the hundreds of condemned who came before him, is secured to his deathbed with the standard eight leather straps, plus additional restraints.

5 minutes—Time for the final statement. With saline solution already flowing into their arms and a microphone dangling overhead, prisoners have an opportunity to speak their last words. If an offender prefers to write rather than speak a final statement, the PIO transcribes it and hands it out to the media after the execution.

Graham's rambling final statement is much longer than usual—1,268 words. He affirms his innocence and thanks his many supporters, including the Reverend Al Sharpton and Jesse Jackson as well as international figures such as Bianca Jagger, who is also a witness to the execution. Struggling to the last, Graham says, "I'm being lynched. The death penalty is a holocaust for black Americans."[100]

1 minute—The warden signals the execution to begin. The presiding warden for Graham is Jim Willett, who was the senior warden during forty executions that year alone. When Willett began as the "Death House Warden" in 1998, he removed his glasses as the signal for executions to begin, but later got an electronic device when he realized prisoners knew about the glasses ploy.[101] Once Willett gives the go-ahead, a cocktail of drugs sedates the body, collapses the lungs, and stops the heart in short order. A medical examiner declares the official time of death. For Graham, death comes at 8:49 P.M., almost three hours behind schedule.[102]

Afterward—Witnesses exit and the warden draws a white sheet over the dead face. If the body is unclaimed, it is buried by the state in Joe Byrd Cemetery, the prisoners' graveyard sited on a knoll nicknamed Peckerwood Hill, and marked with a simple headstone. Graham does not lie with the abandoned; his family claims the body and buries him in his hometown of Houston.

The PIO reports the "official times" to the media, then the long workday is over. Fitzgerald, who has witnessed close to two hundred executions, deals with the unique pressure of his position by not taking the job home. "It's just my job to be there as a witness and report what I see," Fitzgerald says. "There were some executions that stand out in my mind and I'll never forget. However, a majority of them are just a blur, and I have trouble the next day even remembering the guy's name." He has no difficulty remembering this inmate. "Actually, Graham and I got along very well."[103]

Gary Graham has gone to his final rest, but the media coverage of his story is very much alive; in cyberspace, the Graham media trail remains to this day; an Internet search for articles about Graham yields more than a million "hits" on Google's search engine. ✪

Notes

[1] "Death Row Facts," TDCJ website. Available at: http://www.tdcj.state.tx.us/stat/drowfacts.htm.
[2] Larry Fitzgerald (former TDCJ public information manager), interview by Ruth Massingill, Huntsville, Texas, April 7, 2003.
[3] "State Execution Totals." Before the Needles website. Available at: http://users.bestweb.net/~rg/execution.htm.
[4] Kathy Walt (spokesperson for Texas governor Rick Perry and former *Houston Chronicle* reporter), interview by Ruth Massingill, Huntsville, Texas, December 13, 2003.
[5] Michelle Lyons (TDCJ public information officer), interview by Ruth Massingill, Huntsville, Texas, April 23, 2004.
[6] Mike Viesca (former TDCJ director of public information), interview by Ruth Massingill, Austin, Texas, December 15, 2003.
[7] Ibid.
[8] Frank Krystyniak, telephone conversation with Ruth Massingill, May 12, 2005.
[9] Kelly Prew (*Huntsville Item* reporter), interview by Tina Baiter, Huntsville, Texas, March 10, 2005.
[10] Walt interview, 2003.
[11] Don Reid, *Have a Seat, Please* (Huntsville: Texas Review Press, 2001), 23.
[12] Ibid., 24–29.
[13] Ibid., 31–32.
[14] Ibid., 32.
[15] Rachel Graves, "Houston Chronicle Reporter Thinks, 'Stop, You're Killing Him,'" *Houston Chronicle*, July 4, 2003. Available at: http://texasmoratorium.org/article.
[16] Stefano Esposito, "Kennewick Murderer's Execution Draws Closer," *Tri-City Herald*, September 2, 1998. Available at: http://www.tri-cityherald.com/news/oldnews/1998/0902.html.
[17] Rachel Graves, "Ordinary or Odd, Last Meal Can Tell Inmate's Story," *Houston Chronicle*, April 6, 2003, 33A.
[18] Ibid.
[19] Michelle Lyons (TDCJ public information officer), interview by Ruth Massingill, Huntsville, Texas, March 29, 2005.
[20] Graves, 33A.
[21] Fitzgerald interview, 2003.
[22] Michelle Lyons (TDCJ public information officer), interview by Ruth Massingill, Huntsville, Texas, December 2, 2003.
[23] Fitzgerald interview, 2003.
[24] Kevin Francis O'Neill, "Muzzling Death Row Inmates: Applying the First Amendment to Regulations That Restrict a Condemned Prisoner's Last Words," *Arizona State Law Journal* 2 (winter 2001). Available at: http://www.web.lexis-nexis.com/universe/document?_m=8ddfe74ccb00a5417f0841ffd8d91b2&_doc.
[25] Walt interview, 2003.
[26] O'Neill, 7.
[27] Lyons interview, 2003.
[28] Reid, 25.
[29] Fitzgerald interview, 2003.
[30] Walt interview, 2003.
[31] Lyons interview, 2003.
[32] "Death Row Facts," TDCJ website. Available at: http://www.tdcj.state.tx.us/stat/drowfacts.htm.
[33] Viesca interview, 2003.

34 "Out-of-Cell Time Requirements," *Offender Orientation Handbook*, 32. Available at: http://www.tdcj.state.tx.us/publications/cid/OffendOrientHbkNov04.pdf.
35 Fitzgerald interview, 2003.
36 Walt interview, 2003.
37 Michelle Lyons (TDCJ public information officer), interview by Tina Baiter, Huntsville, Texas, May 19, 2005.
38 Ibid.
39 Ibid.
40 "Offender Visitation Rules," *Offender Orientation Handbook*, 81. Available at: http://www.tdcj.state.tx.us/publications/cid/OffendOrientHbkNov04.pdf.
41 "Media Policies for Inmate Interviews," TDCJ Public Information Office website. Available at: http://www.tdcj.state.tx.us/pio/page16.html.
42 Fitzgerald interview, 2003.
43 Ibid.
44 Lyons interview, 2005.
45 Alexis Grant, "Livingston Residents Undaunted by Prison," *Houston Chronicle,* April 17, 2006, B5.
46 Lyons interview, 2003.
47 "Additional Information for News Media Concerning Visitation," TDCJ Public Information Office website. Available at: http://www.tdcj.state.tx.us/pio/page4.html.
48 "Media Policies for Inmate Interviews."
49 Prew interview, 2005.
50 "Additional Information for News Media Concerning Visitation."
51 Walt interview, 2003.
52 Prew interview, 2005.
53 Janet Parker Dial (former death row reporter), interview by Ruth Massingill, Willis, Texas, March 17, 2004.
54 Walt interview, 2003.
55 Lyons interview, 2003.
56 Prew interview, 2005.
57 Walt interview, 2003.
58 Women in Prison project. Available at: http://prisonactivist.org/women/women-in-prison.html.
59 "Human Rights Watch: United States." Available at: http://www.hrw.org/wr2k1/usa/.
60 "Prison Statistics," Bureau of Justice Statistics. Available at: http://www.ojp.usdoj.gov/bjs/prisons.htm.
61 Ibid.
62 "Women in Prison," Bureau of Justic Statistics Special Report. Available at: http://www.ojp.usdoj.gov/bjs/abstract/wopris.,htm.
63 Brian Cox (TDCJ psychologist, Windham School District), interview by Tina Baiter, Huntsville, Texas, March 2005.
64 Prew interview, 2005.
65 Lyons interview, 2005.
66 Fitzgerald interview, 2005.
67 Dennis Longmire (criminal justice professor and anti-capital punishment activist), interview by Melody Davison, Huntsville, Texas, June 21, 2005.
68 "From Death Row: Texas Set to Execute First African-American Woman since Civil War," *Democracy Now,* August 25, 2005. Available at: http://www.indybay.org/news/2005/08/1762183.php.
69 Walt interview, 2005.
70 Fitzgerald interview, 2003.
71 Dial interview, 2004.
72 Ibid.

[73] Walt interview, 2003.
[74] Dial interview, 2004.
[75] Denis Johnson, "Five Executions and a Barbeque," *Rollling Stone*, August 17, 2005, 53.
[76] Ibid., 54.
[77] Ibid.
[78] Fitzgerald interview, 2003.
[79] Johnson, 29.
[80] Fitzgerald interview, 2003.
[81] Lyons interview, 2003.
[82] Ibid.
[83] Media Kit, Douglas Alan Roberts, April 20, 2005.
[84] Thompson interview, 2005.
[85] Dial interview, 2004.
[86] Viesca interview, 2003.
[87] Gary Graham, Offender Information, "Executed Offenders," TDCJ Death Row Information website. Available at: http://www.tdcj.state.tx.us/stat/000696.jpg.
[88] Graves, 33A.
[89] Salatheia Bryant, "Graham Executed after Struggle," CNN.com Transcripts, June 23, 2000. Available at: http://archives.cnn.com/2000/LOCAL/southwest/06/23/hci.graham.execution/index.html.
[90] "Countdown to Gary Graham's Execution in Texas," CNN.com Transcripts, June 22, 2000. Available at: http://transcripts.cnn.com/TRANSCRIPTS/0006/22/bn.05.html
[91] Fitzgerald interview, 2003.
[92] Bryant.
[93] Ibid.
[94] Fitzgerald interview, 2003.
[95] Bryant.
[96] Fitzgerald interview, 2005.
[97] "The Execution," PBS, *Frontline*. Available at: http://www.pbs.org/wgbh/pages/frontline/shows/execution/.
[98] Fitzgerald interview, 2005.
[99] Bryant.
[100] Gary Graham, Last Statement, "Executed Offenders," TDCJ Death Row Information website. Available at: http://www.tdcj.state.tx.us/stat/grahamgarylast.htm.
[101] Sara Rimer, "In The Busiest Death Chamber, Duty Carries Its Own Burdens," *New York Times*, December 17, 2000. Available at: http://www.deathpenaltyinfo.org/article.php?scid=17&did=354.
[102] Kate Randall, "In Cold Blood: The State Murder of Gary Graham," World Socialist website, June 23, 2000. Available at: http://www.wsws.org/articles/2000/jun2000/grah-j23.shtml.
[103] Fitzgerald interview, 2003.

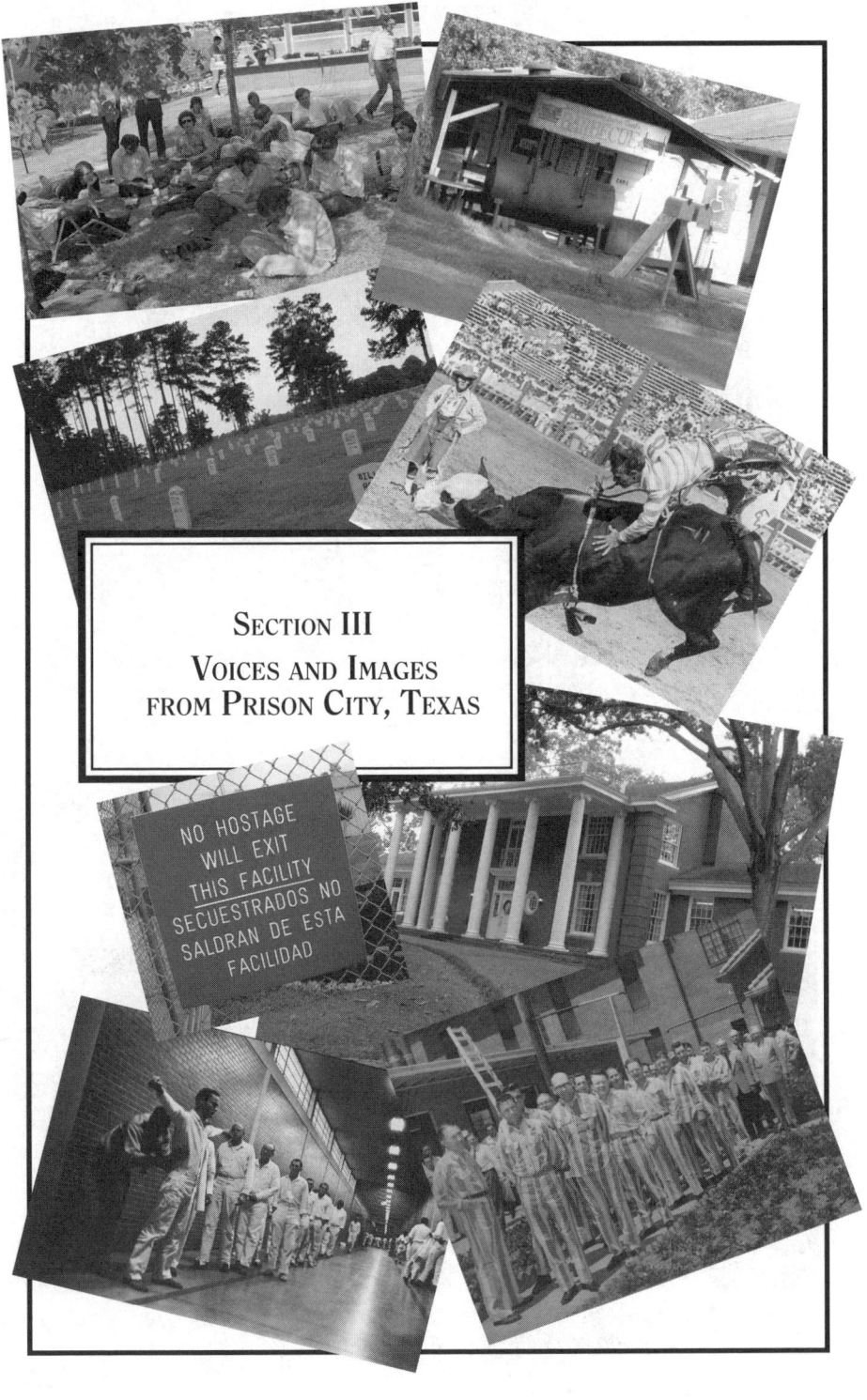

Section III
Voices and Images from Prison City, Texas

Sometimes laughingly called the "Church of the Holy Barbeque" by locals, the New Zion Missionary Baptist Church offers acclaimed brisket and fixings.

Simple headstones in "Peckerwood Cemetery" mark the final resting place for executed prisoners with no one to collect their bodies.

What's Going on Here?

This scrapbook of current and historic photos offers a glimpse of Huntsville, past and present. From the prison museum's prize exhibits of Old Sparky and handmade weapons to portraits of long-dead prisoners performing at the prison rodeo, the juxtaposition of old and new documents the prison's evolving role in the community.

Four ethnographic mini-case studies delve beneath the surface of Prison City, beginning with the story of a local family in which every member is connected to the prison in this twenty-first-century company town. Next, local tattoo artists create body art for a prison guard, who explains why she wants a tat. Then, a traditional college commencement is celebrated, but the graduates are prisoners who receive their diplomas and return to their cells. Finally, deep inside the prison, a death row inmate shares the daily tedium of his existence behind bars.

Welcome to Huntsville!

The prison museum draws thousands of visitors a year, just down the street from the high school Hornets' football stadium.

The community and the prison have always been inextricably linked. From bankers to college professors, Kiwanis members dressed in zebra-striped prison garb in this 1953 photo and held their luncheon meeting in the Walls dining room, with music by the inmate orchestra.

Prison labor has always helped grease the wheels of commerce in Huntsville. New construction and public maintenance often are the handiwork of prisoners.

Architectural twins: *Huntsville buildings often mirror those in the prison compound, and vice versa. The warden's home (top) across from the Walls closely resembles the circa-1851 Austin Hall (bottom), which houses special receptions on the SHSU campus.*

Constructed in 2005, the SHSU bell tower (bottom) is a dead ringer for the tower in this 1895 photo (top) of the entrance to the Walls unit.

Prison City Close-Up

The Family Business:
Working for the Prisons but Not Incarcerated—Yet

In Huntsville, just like in an early-twentieth-century company town, whole families work for TDCJ in one capacity or another, mostly as guards. "Earl" is typical. He has been a prison employee four different times, each time for about a year. The pay and benefits kept drawing him back for yet another stint. "Hey, I had a friend worked there five times." He pauses for a beat before delivering the punch line, "Now he works at Wal-Mart!" At one time Earl and his eldest daughter, "Amy," both worked at the Ellis unit. "She worked security," Earl says. Security is a euphemism for guard. "She worked the second shift (2 P.M. to 10 P.M.), and I worked the third (10 P.M. to 6 A.M.)." According to Amy, the only way to get assigned first shift is if someone retires. Employees in parts of the system now work on two twelve-hour shifts, a move Earl believes is not a good idea because workers get "too tired."

Earl, four of his five children, and three of their spouses are, or have been, TDCJ employees. Earl's youngest daughter works in the commissary at the Estelle unit, and her husband is a bus driver at the Ellis unit. Amy understands her sister's contentment with her desk job. "She just works with two inmates." For Amy, though, being on the front lines as a female guard in a men's unit meant "seeing more of the male anatomy than I ever wanted."

Amy grew tired of the constant disrespect, "tired of not being a lady." The job also had an effect on her relationship with her husband: "I was talking to my husband like an inmate," she said, and the last thing she wanted to see when she got home was a man. Amy now works for the county tax appraisal district and is happy to have a job without the innate stress of working as a guard. Amy reasons that no woman would work in security at a prison if there were other more viable options.

When Amy's husband lost his job as a car salesman, he went to work for TDCJ because the young family needed the benefits. He worked so much overtime when he first started that Amy thought he was going to collapse. "If he had a better option he would not be there," Amy says. She is always concerned about him because one time a prisoner tried to slit his throat with a makeshift knife. He survived the attack, but Amy still worries. She points out that prisoners are not incarcerated for "skipping Sunday school." But like others in town who choose the TDCJ job option, Amy just shrugs off her worries. What else can you do in Huntsville?

Working for TDCJ is attractive to single parents. Although on a statewide level the pay scale is not high, TDCJ offers state benefits, most notably health insurance.

Amy admits that her family is making do with less since she quit TDCJ, but she is more content and feels that the financial sacrifices are worth the stress reduction. Amy remembers too well the tensions when she was growing up and her dad came home from his job as a guard to three daughters hogging the bathroom. Her dad never expressed his frustration, but it was obvious he brought stress home from his job.

Earl tends to recount his experiences working in the prison system with the anecdotal recollections typical of a native Texan storyteller. He refers to Huntsville as "Prison City," its CB moniker for the last thirty years, but "I don't think about it too much," he says. Years ago when work as a union painter ran out down on the coast, Earl found himself in Huntsville and got hired the first time at TDCJ supervising a paint crew of convicts. Earl speaks with obvious pride when talking about his crew. "Most of them had been 'free world' painters," he says, adding slyly, "You know painters are carpenters with their brains beat out?"

The next three times he was hired back, Earl worked in "security." He admits he did not like being locked in. "You know you can't get out unless they let you out." Of course, Earl always was let out, but one of his sons eventually found himself trapped inside.

"My youngest son worked at Estelle. Then he quit, and went and got locked up in TDC in Brownwood. Now he's in county jail for parole violation." Earl explains that his son had gotten involved with drugs.

The final time Earl hired on in security, seven prisoners attempted an escape from death row, one successfully. (See "Man on the Run" at the end of chapter 3.) Although Earl had previously worked on death row, he was not assigned to it that evening. "No, that wasn't mine that night," he chuckles, relating with some relish how only one convict "got over the fence" and his body was found about a week later by two off-duty guards who were fishing in the Trinity River. The night of the breakout, all the guards were ordered to stand along the roadside for sixteen hours to watch for the escapees. During the watch, Earl was annoyed that the guards did not have access to drinking water for the double shift, so he quit the next day.

Amy remembers the night of the escape too and, like her father, she was unhappy with TDCJ. She did not appreciate standing guard armed with only a flashlight.

Another of Earl's daughters and her husband both recently quit their jobs at TDCJ. She started a day care center, while her husband began working for a landscape business. Only one of Earl's five children has never worked for TDCJ in Huntsville. Earl's oldest boy graduated from SHSU and moved to Harris County, where he has worked for the past fifteen years as a probation officer.

Earl now has an out-of-state job inspecting and painting pipelines. He jokes that if he went back to TDCJ he would be wearing prisoners' whites instead of the gray uniforms worn by guards.

Many who work for TDCJ admit that there is a big stress toll to pay. Divorce, alcoholism, and domestic violence rates all are higher in Huntsville than residents would like, and many attribute those numbers to working for "the company." A career with the prison is a life sentence of sorts, and many who work there feel as trapped as those serving time. Most locals still use the old acronym, TDC (Texas Department of Corrections), although it has been TDCJ (Texas Department of Criminal Justice) since 1973. The guards are still called correctional officers although some say punishment, not corrections, is the goal at TDCJ. For most denizens of Huntsville, TDC is simply a lot easier to say than TDCJ. Whichever acronym is used, working for the prison system is the family business for many who live in Huntsville. ✪

—Melody Davison

The more things change: The armed guard in the watchtower of the Walls has been a fixture near downtown for decades. The top picture shows a current guard standing watch, while the bottom photo is from the 1960s.

Ruta Reproductions photo

TDCJ Media Services photo

TDCJ Media Services photo

TDCJ Media Services photo

The prison rodeo was a wildly popular fund-raiser for decades, ending in 1986. The Goree Prison Girls chased greased pigs, and convicts rode raging bulls, often to the detriment of life and limb.

Voices and Images from Prison City, Texas

Ruta Reproductions photo

City of Huntsville Walker County Treasurers photo

SHSU's new student apartment complex, with its central clock and guard tower look-alikes on each corner (top), bears a striking resemblance to the Walls, shown here after an unusual 1947 snowfall in Huntsville.

— Prison City Close-Up —

Voodoo Tattoo:
Body Art in the Heart of Huntsville

Traveling south on Sam Houston Avenue, a visitor will see the kind of businesses typical to a small university town: on the square, the historic Methodist church, full every Sunday morning with the faithful, the Texan restaurant where students and judges lunch, the Sam Houston Museum with its shaded park, the newly built university welcome center for SHSU, its doors to open to incoming Bearkats...and the Voodoo Tattoo shop.

Directly across from the university's art department and sharing a parking lot with the town's popular snow cone stand sits a metal building with the word Voodoo emblazoned in giant letters across its roof. Proudly pronouncing, "We're so clean, your momma loves us," the purveyors of the "number one tattoo business in Huntsville," Jamie and Jody, practice their art throughout the day and late into the night. Jamie, an attractive woman in her mid-twenties, has extensive tattooing. Colorful flowers and butterflies adorn her upper arms and neck. She has been doing tattoos and piercings for five years. It is hard to miss her partner Jody, a large man with light green hair and extensive tattooing covering his arms and neck. Both are personable, extending an offer to sit and watch as a tattoo is applied. This Southern hospitality, mixed with quick wit and a glint of mischievousness, makes it easy to see why these two are so popular in this conservative town where churches easily outnumber pizza parlors.

While parking my car outside Voodoo, I gave little thought to a white fifteen-seat state van with a "Back the Blue" bumper sticker. State vehicles are a common sight in Huntsville. When I ask about TDCJ guards or police personnel who are clients of the Voodoo, the group laughs heartily and gestures toward a short blonde woman having a frog tattooed on her lower back and right butt cheek. She is a guard who is willing to talk as long as I do not use her real name or where she works.

"Most of my clients are guards or with the police," Jody says in a matter-of-fact way. "We have the reputation for being the best and being able to freehand any design. Unlike other places in town, we check IDs, so security people feel safe shopping here."

Jamie shows me a picture she is working on for a female client scheduled later that evening. It's a picture of three little fairies surrounded by flowers, which represent the woman's children. Jamie tells me it is the woman's Mother's Day gift. Jodie is paying a lot of attention to the shading because the woman's dark skin requires a perfect touch or the definition will be lost and the image ruined. I am interested in what happens when the artist makes a mistake while applying a tattoo. This is also a concern of "Shelley," the guard. Jamie is quick to respond, "We practice a lot before beginning the tat because once it is there it doesn't move." Jody adds, "Well, you can have it removed, but that hurts and costs a lot of money and makes a really ugly scar. If we wanted to do something that could be wiped away, then we would work with sand or oils. This is permanent, which makes it special. I like the idea that my work will be with that person until death. Even if they remove it or alter it, there will always be something showing I was there. Plus, I don't make mistakes." Shelley looks relieved, but Jamie rolls her eyes and comments, "You wish."

> **"This is permanent, which makes it special. I like the idea that my work will be with that person until death."**

To intercede, as the two seem to be headed to a "tat-off," I ask why so many guards have tattoos. The different meanings inmates assign to images is well documented, but it would seem logical that guards would avoid this practice since it is embraced by prisoners. Shelley quickly points out, "It shows our personalities. If you wear a gray uniform that looks like every other gray TDC uniform, then you want something that makes you different and we cannot wear jewelry, so the only way to dress up is with tattoos." Like the prisoners, "some guards get them to show they are tough," Shelly says. A reflective Jamie adds, "It's also a class thing. Some guards think just because their tattoo came from a professional, it is better than the home-made jobs the prisoners do to each other. They use them to show they have more money and class. "Since

Ruta Reproductions photo

so many guards have tattoos, it would seem that a newly applied tat would not incite much interest from the prisoners, but according to Shelley that is far from the truth. "They notice everything, and most will ask you about it, but there are always the assholes who take the opportunity to bump you 'cause they know it hurts at first." She points out, "mine is so low, I hope they don't see it. If they do, I have bigger problems than a sore tattoo."

While Shelley's atomic frog is cute, it is not one of the most popular designs for prison personnel; that honor goes instead to either the interlocked handcuff or rebel flags. Jamie claims they do rebel flags daily, but the handcuff design is "primarily for guys graduating from the academy." These tattoos are considered basic, take about two hours to apply, and cost around fifty dollars. There are large designs that take up to twelve hours to apply and cost between five hundred and a thousand dollars. While these are not nearly as popular, Jamie says they do one or two a month.

Many police departments, including Houston's, recently adopted a controversial policy requiring officers to cover their tattoos while on the job. Shelley says that "the prison's COs don't like it when you get a tattoo that can be seen, but they all have them so they will say something stupid and you may get to walk the runs all night, but they get over it."

"If you ain't heard of anyone breaking out lately, then you shouldn't be worried about a prisoner getting a tattoo. We don't care."

Applying tattoos in prison is considered illegal, and if inmates are caught applying or receiving tattoos they are placed in administrative segregation. Still, the practice is very popular among the prisoners, and Shelley remarks, "We can't watch 'em like a hawk. How do you think gang rapes happen? You turn your back to check on another problem and the next thing you know someone has been raped, or killed or tattooed. We are outnumbered, and it ain't our job to protect 'em. Our job is to make sure they don't get out, so we are protecting you. If you ain't heard of anyone breaking out lately, then you shouldn't be worried about a prisoner getting a tattoo. We don't care." Everyone agrees that this is pretty much how they all feel, and they turn their attention back to bringing the atomic frog to life. Just another night at Voodoo Tattoo, on Sam Houston Avenue in Huntsville, Texas. ✪

—Debbi Hatton

Security measures inside the prison are unyielding. Convicts use the pathways against the walls; visitors are allowed to stroll down the center of the hall.

Reporters still come in droves to Huntsville to cover breaking news such as escapes or riots, then wait for updates from the public information officers, as shown in this 1960s photo.

Prison City Close-Up

Graduation behind Bars:
"No Hostage Will Exit This Facility"

Usually, college graduations are ready-made PR events, with heartwarming photo opportunities and excited, happy quotes—lots of warm and fuzzy moments for the media to record. In Huntsville, two very different kinds of graduations are held several times a year. Everyone in Huntsville knows about the commencement ceremonies at the local high school and the fifteen-thousand-student state university, but far fewer realize that high school and college graduations also occur in the prisons. The ceremonies share some common themes, but the differences are profound.

Although Huntsville high school and college graduates may experience nervous jitters as they cross the stage and walk toward futures in which careers, travel, marriage, and children are all possible, their overall mood is exuberant. For the prison graduates, however, it is undoubtedly a bittersweet experience: a glimpse of the potential a "normal" life might offer combined with the knowledge that the four walls of a cell await when the all-too-brief celebration concludes.

For parents, spouses, and friends who attend the Sam Houston State graduation, happy tears and broad smiles speak volumes. Those who come to prison to witness a loved one's commencement exhibit a contradictory mixture of pride and bone-deep sorrow that it has taken so many years and such unhappy circumstances to reach this milestone.

For SHSU faculty and administrators, participating in graduation is a ritual send-off—another flock of youngsters sent into the world, a cycle to be repeated the following semester with the next group of students. Some faculty have seen this process for decades and bring books to read while hundreds of students receive their diplomas. For those who work in the prison's education system, however, graduation is a "battery charger" where they see results and dare to hope this group of inmates will eventually leave prison life behind forever.

Whereas the Sam Houston graduations are promoted with the ubiquitous "hometown releases"—news releases sent to the hometown newspapers of every graduating senior, prison graduations are kept low-key. This is because the events have both positive and negative PR ramifications, according to Bambi Kiser, the communications coordinator for the prison's Windham School District, which serves more than eighty thousand students across the state. Kiser is well aware that many members of the public do not support providing education for prisoners who are serving time for serious crimes.

To fully understand the depth of the chasm between these ceremonies, one must attend both. So, on a sunny and slightly crisp mid-April day, I go to prison to attend a college commencement for fifty men, criminals all, who have earned college diplomas from Lee College in Baytown or from SHSU.

After fifteen years of teaching at the university level, I'm a commencement veteran of graduations at Sam Houston, where the students are as free as the proverbial birds, to attend class or not, to stay in Huntsville or transfer to another institution, to eat and study and sleep as they see fit. Although they frequently complain of too much "busy" work and too little leisure time, and describe the stresses of their lives as almost unbearable, they are blithe spirits by comparison with the student-convicts I see today.

Graduation is scheduled for 9 A.M on a Saturday morning at the Wynne unit, on the outskirts of Huntsville. I am accompanied by Kiser, who has warned me that I cannot bring my cell phone, pager, or camera into the prison. I am also not allowed to bring in my purse, so I arrive at the gates with only my ID, a pen, and a notepad.

The prison's facade is forbidding—looming red brick walls topped with silver loops of concertina wire bisected by a twenty-foot steel gate.

The prison's facade is forbidding—looming red brick walls topped with silver loops of concertina wire bisected by a twenty-foot steel gate and overseen by a serious-faced female guard in a watchtower. Visitors are showing their identification and being checked against the list of those with permission to attend the ceremonies. Each graduate can invite two adults and as many children under sixteen as he wishes. Kiser and I hold our IDs up to a camera, the gate swings open, and we enter the prison grounds. The area is immaculate: a wide concrete walk bordered by flowers and manicured lawn leads to a red brick structure. Incongruously, pink hollyhocks stand at attention on either side of the prison's dark, heavy door.

Once inside, we navigate through a series of locked doors, showing our IDs at each checkpoint. We pass a secured "day room," where privileged inmates are allowed to watch television. My initial impression of the prison is one of orderliness: no stray trash, no smudges on the walls—it is much cleaner than the communications building where I teach. The hallway's concrete floors are divided into three sections with a central path designated by rows of three-inch yellow dots. The central area between the dots is polished; the outside aisles are clean but dull. Kiser explains that people from "the free" walk in the center, and inmates must use the outer paths. Rules are posted on the walls: "No talking. Silenco. Please keep feet off wall." Kiser says some of the units have signs prohibiting spitting. "That would never occur to me," she says wonderingly. All is interior space with artificial lighting; there are no windows.

Deep in the heart of the prison, we enter the chapel, where the commencement will take place. Surprisingly large and airy, this building within a building is about two hundred feet long with a center aisle flanked by long oak benches on each side. Gothic-style arches stretch to a roof probably sixty feet overhead, and dozens of narrow stained-glass windows allow filtered light to spotlight the tops of heads throughout the sanctuary. It is a peaceful oasis where it is almost possible to forget the layers of security between this spot and the sunny day outside. But the half dozen prison guards in their standard gray uniforms who are stationed along the outside walls are reminders that this is not just any church. Kiser explains that the chapel is nondenominational; services range from traditional Baptist to Muslim.

This morning, however, the feeling is traditional East Texas Christianity; the Rockwell Chapel Band is performing old-style gospel music. The band consists of four men—three black and one white—playing drums, keyboard, guitar, and sax while creating complex harmonies for the lead vocalist. They might be any church band except for their prison whites and their somewhat diffident air. Kiser says there have been no music or art classes in the prisons since the early 1970s. The arts require too much money and time. Now classes concentrate on more marketable white- and blue-collar skills such as business and plumbing.

The guests file in from a side door and are seated on the left side of the chapel. According to Rey Zuniga, the principal for the Wynne unit and the man in charge of counting—making sure those who enter the building are approved and then making certain only today's ninety-seven visitors leave—a pair of disappointed parents have been turned back because their son is not graduating today. "That's why we handle the invitations," Zuniga says. The group consists of more women than men and a smattering of children. Many of the adults are gray-haired and most are casually attired in jeans or pants, although a few women are wearing their "Sunday go-to-meeting dresses."

The traditional processional music begins and the college faculty file in, dressed in academic regalia, just like my colleagues at Sam Houston. Then the line of students begins to come down the aisle. They, too, are dressed in traditional black gowns and mortarboards, but the pant legs of their prison whites show below their robes. They are a diverse group—black, white, brown. Most appear to be middle-aged. Many have weathered, scarred faces; there are some badly healed broken noses and some mouths that clearly need dental work. Most wear glasses. But today these faces wear pleased expressions and everyone in the chapel stands as the students walk by to take their seats near the front. An observer would never guess that these men have been up since three in the morning and have been transported in full body chains to the Wynne unit. After all, they have committed every kind of crime you can imagine, says prison administrator Bill Nowlin. Now, however, they walk with pride in their borrowed gowns and smile and nod as they pass family or faculty.

The Wynne chaplain gives an invocation, asking for God's blessing for those "who have achieved what they thought was impossible." Not every unit has a chaplain these days, so some units are served by traveling chaplains, akin to old-time country circuit preachers.

The Wynne chaplain gives an invocation, asking for God's blessing for those "who have achieved what they thought was impossible." Not every unit has a chaplain these days, a consequence of budget cuts, so some units are served by traveling chaplains, akin to old-time country circuit preachers. A string of recognitions follows: principals from the various units, faculty, wardens, and educational and correctional officers. These sound much like the stultifying introductions given during a Sam Houston graduation.

But, unlike graduation at Sam Houston, there is no scurrying about of media or camera flashes. Kiser uses a small digital camera to take photos for her office's archives, to send to media as requested, or for the *Echo*, the prison newspaper. She is not allowed to give copies of any of the photos to prisoners; "that would be contraband." A photo studio has already taken individual pictures of each graduate, and Lee College will provide a copy to each inmate. Having a photographic memento of the day is a "big deal."

Commencement speaker today is Dr. Harry Hoge, a former Lee College faculty member and a geologist by profession. Hoge says he is not a motivational speaker and has chosen a topic he knows—plateaus. He develops the concept of plateaus as a metaphor for life, exhorting the graduates to start looking for their next challenge now that they have realized that "learning is something you cannot stop doing." Hoge admits that the graduates are "somewhat inhibited" in their choices, but assures them there are "still many possibilities." This is a definite departure from the typical Sam Houston speakers who urge graduates to charge headfirst into careers, family life, and community service. But many of these graduates have anticipated this advice; they are already registered for the master's program.

The ones who do attend receive a measure of respect and accolades that will have to last them for some time to come. Several are receiving two, three, or even four degrees, and many are graduating with honors.

The conferring of degrees begins with the standard language: "By the authority invested in me..." With fifteen years of practice, I automatically tune out until the familiar recitation is complete. Then each graduate comes forward to receive a red leatherette bound diploma and a handshake. The list of candidates on the program is much longer than the number in attendance; three dozen men listed on the program are not present. There are several possible reasons, explains Nowlin. Any inmate who has "had a disciplinary" in the past three weeks will receive his degree but is not allowed to attend the ceremony. And some inmates choose not to walk. "Some of them don't want the public to know where they are; they might be here under an alias and someone in Arkansas would like to find them," Nowlin says wryly. Also, some have no one to invite to the event and choose not to attend.

The ones who do attend receive a measure of respect and accolades that must last them for some time to come. They've worked hard for today; several are receiving two, three, or even four degrees, and many are graduating with honors. When their names are called, they receive the cursory title of "Mister." "Many were never successful at any time in their lives," Kiser says. "They never walked the stage to receive any sort of award or degree. This is their first experience with that."

What is missing is the happy clamor that usually accompanies graduations at Sam Houston; here everyone is subdued. There are no catcalls, spontaneous cheers, or noisemakers from the audience. The graduates beam with pleasure, but they do not make any sudden moves. None of their mortarboards is decorated with slogans such as "hell froze" and no hats are launched into the air at the end of the ceremony.

The Rockwell Chapel Band provides a final performance, prefaced by congratulatory remarks from the lead vocalist. "A lot of people come to prison and give up. Looks to me like you made a decision to go forward. I encourage you to reach out to someone else and remember, God's love is most important."

God is also called upon in the benediction to "strengthen us as we go forth from this place." Some people will be going farther than others, at least in the near future. When the grads do leave prison, however, it is statistically unlikely they will ever return; the recidivism rate for college graduates is almost nonexistent, Nowlin says. "They are virtually not coming back to prison."

Finally, the recessional music begins and, in a reversal of the prison's hallway code, the faculty line each side of the center aisle while the graduates walk down the center, gold tassels swinging from their hats as they hug, shake hands, and repeatedly say "thank you." This looks like any college graduation where students and teachers have bonded. The highlight of the event is still to come: the forty-five-minute contact visit that is almost an unheard of privilege for inmates, who usually are separated from visitors by a glass wall. Today in the cafeteria, there are no walls. Inmates, who have shed their black robes and are again in prison whites, sit at small tables with family members. A few have children or wives or girlfriends on their laps. The parents in particular put on happy faces, but their eyes are wells of sadness. Refreshments consist of punch, cake, and cookies—served on Styrofoam and eaten with with plasticware, but no

The Windham School District photo

one seems to notice. Prisoners seldom get sweets, so this also is a special treat. I think of the aftermath of SHSU graduations, when grads and their families fill every restaurant in the small town, ordering as their fancy dictates.

The prison scene is heartwarming. "You would have to be a rock not to respond," Kiser says, but there are no media people on hand to record the emotional moments. "This is not one of the things the big media finds particularly interesting," Nowlin comments. A group of about ten men, their faces carefully noncommittal, sit together in a corner; no visitors have come to celebrate their big day. Kiser roams the room taking photos, being careful to frame her shots so visitors' faces are obscured, especially if they are children. Any photos she takes must have prisoners' signed releases to be used for publication. The photos may end up on the Windham website, in in-house publications, or in the archives. Kiser is always sensitive to the public perceptions about prisoners and education. Although prisoners must pay for their college educations, many Texans perceive that state funds are providing this privilege and are resentful. So the public information staff has an unusual conundrum—promoting commencements could actually jeopardize the prison's public image.

Finally, we step through the heavy door and into the sunlight, which seems blinding. Although I have only been "inside" for two and a half hours, I am momentarily surprised it is still daylight.

Smooth is the watchword of the day—the staff members compliment each other on how "smoothly" everything went. Big bubbles, no troubles. There is reason for this care; the level of freedom the inmates are enjoying today could be exploited. If a security problem ever arose during a commencement, it is likely that the privileges graduates enjoy would be lost for all future graduations throughout the state. So the staff and principals work hard to make everything "smooth."

And smooth it is. At the end of the forty-five minutes of almost frenzied conversations—a veritable babble of sound—the teachers and staff leave, and I go with them. This means we do not have to witness the parting of graduates and family, which staff members tell me is heartrending. We retrace our steps through the various checkpoints, submitting IDs as instructed. We keep on the path between the yellow dots, passing a line of inmates along the wall. The day room is still occupied by TV watchers, who look up as we pass but make no sound.

Finally, we step through the heavy door and into the sunlight, which seems blinding. The hollyhocks still stand sentinel, and their brilliant color seems garish after the artificial light, the gray concrete, and the gray uniforms inside. Although I have only been "inside" for two and a half hours, I am momentarily surprised it is still daylight.

As we show our IDs to the camera and the tower guard releases the gate for us to leave, I notice a sign that states, "No hostage will exit this facility." Kiser explains: "That means we are all expendable—prisoners have been put on notice that taking hostages won't get them released; hostages will be sacrificed if necessary." A sobering thought for the employees of the Wynne Unit, who see this sign every time they leave work.

It is also a reminder for me that despite the surface similarities, and despite the fact that commencement at the Wynne unit may be only five actual miles from the one to be held at Sam Houston next month, the border of the prison walls sets the two ceremonies worlds apart. And the next time one of my students jokingly compares being in college to being in prison, I'll be tempted to reply, "No hostage will exit this facility." ✪

—Ruth Massingill

Photo by Bambi Kiser, courtesy of the Windham School District

Prison graduations are bittersweet events, but all the trappings of a free world commencement are in evidence, including traditional regalia, which inmates wear over prison whites.

Everyone who visits the prison museum wants to see Old Sparky, the final seat for 361 condemned prisoners between 1924 and 1972. The control panel for Old Sparky (right) is now owned by local resident George Russell.

Ruta Reproductions photos

A deadly trio (below): the holding cell for the condemned, the walkway to the death chamber, and the gurney where the lethal injection is made. "Unlike you or me, they know exactly when they are going to die. They've had a long time to think about it and prepare, as best they can."

—PIO Michelle Lyons

Texas Department of Criminal Justice photos

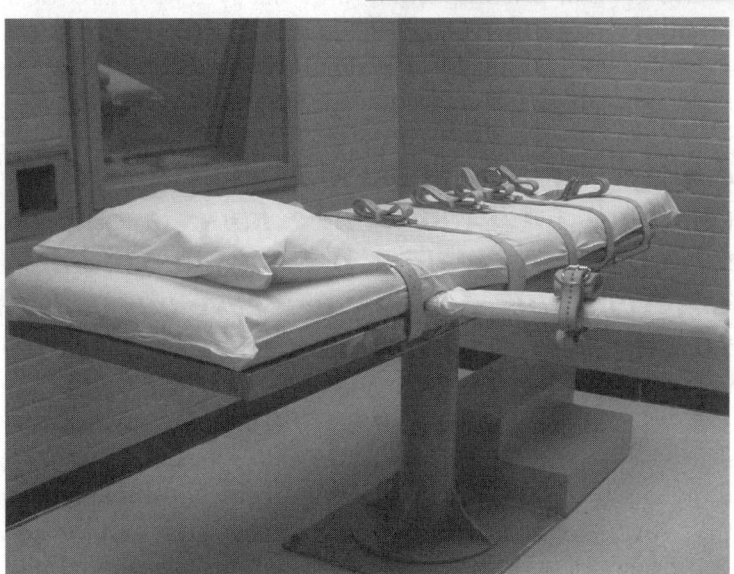

Prison City Close-Up

Living on Death Row: Groundhog Day Syndrome

Robert Pruett is on death row after being convicted of killing a male correctional officer at the McConnell unit. Pruett has an eighth-grade formal education.

Those of us living on Texas's death row are presented with many challenges and obstacles in our everyday lives. We expend an enormous amount of energy fighting for our lives and constantly struggle to cope with the stress involved with being separated from our loved ones, not to mention the loss of our freedom. There are officers who seem to think their job is to punish us rather than maintain the security of the institution; suffice it to say that these rogues are a constant reminder of exactly where we are.... These are the obvious challenges we face here on the row. I'd like to expose a problem that is more subtle, yet can be equally detrimental to our psychological well-being.

Living conditions on death row in Texas are virtually identical to those of TDCJ administrative segregation (ad. seg.), which was designed by a team of criminal psychologists. The objective was to create a behavioral modification system that punished recalcitrant inmates with the harshest living conditions (level 3). Eventually the inmate would be reintegrated back into the general prison population. This system wasn't designed to house inmates long-term, yet TDCJ has misused it by keeping people in ad. seg. for decades and forcing death row inmates to live under its guidelines as long as we have a death sentence.

We are locked in single-man cells (ten feet by seven feet) for twenty-three hours a day, with one hour of recreation per day depending on your level status. Anytime we leave our cells, we must be restrained with handcuffs and escorted by two officers.

For those who aren't familiar with the environment in which we live, please allow me to briefly elaborate: We are locked in single-man cells (ten feet by seven feet) for twenty-three hours a day, with one hour of recreation per day depending on your level status. Anytime we leave our cells, we must be restrained with handcuffs and escorted by two officers.

All visits are noncontact, and recreation occurs in a single-man cage, alone. All physical contact is strictly prohibited.... If you are level 1 status, you can utilize the commissary to purchase an AM/FM radio, shoes, fan, coffee pot, typewriter, hygiene and writing supplies, and various food items. Levels 2 and 3 aren't allowed any electrical appliances (except a fan) or any food items. We aren't allowed televisions, microwaves, access to swimming pools, or any other absurd things like that, as the media would have the general public believe.

If there is an official name for the debilitating disease that often arises out of these living conditions, I am unaware of it. I like to refer to what torments many of us as Groundhog Day Syndrome. How many of you have seen the movie *Groundhog Day*, in which Bill Murray's character keeps waking up on Groundhog Day only to relive that day over and over again? In a sense, this is basically what most of us are experiencing, in that we find ourselves repeating the same old things, day after day. While the movie is highly entertaining and absolutely hilarious, those of us on the row (or ad. seg.) who fall victim to Groundhog Day Syndrome are in danger of developing severe psychological disorders.

Life becomes a blur, creativity diminishes, depression can creep in, some fall prey to psychotic behavior, and others attempt suicide (dropping your appeals is suicide). The adverse effects of Groundhog Day Syndrome are often lethal.

The environment is geared toward sensory deprivation. The scenery never changes for us: cold steel bars, imposing white walls, dirty concrete floors, and whatever view we have from our four-foot-by-three-inch windows, which usually isn't anything to write home about. Our options for action each day are limited to recreating, writing, reading, creating art, listening to the radio, and talking with each other through our doors, which only contributes to our diminishing social skills since we aren't face-to-face. We can also play such games as chess or Dungeons and Dragons by calling out our plays through the door.

It is so easy to find yourself trapped by a fixed schedule best described as tediously monotonous, simply because we are restricted as to what we can do. We're lulled into a routine that repeats itself for months and even years at a time. Our every action soon becomes mechanical, and our behavior becomes more reflective of a robot than of a human being. I sometimes get my days mixed up, thinking I did something on a certain day when in fact it was a week before. Life becomes a blur, creativity diminishes, depression can creep in, some fall prey to psychotic behavior, and others attempt suicide (dropping your appeals is suicide). The adverse effects of Groundhog Day Syndrome are often lethal.

The other day, I asked someone I hadn't seen in a while how he was doing. He just stared at me somberly and replied, "Dude, it's the same fucking thing every day. I wake up, go to rec., eat chow, write a little, read a little, talk shit, go to sleep, then wake up and repeat the same damn thing. I'm burnt out!" Most of us here can truly empathize with that.

Peering through the window in my cell last night, I watched an electrical storm bring light and life to an open field just beyond the prison grounds. It was an awe-inspiring spectacle to behold, and it filled me with a sense of tranquility that has eluded me for quite some time.

To further illustrate just how destructive Groundhog Day Syndrome can be, I'd like to share a very personal story with you: Before coming to death row, I spent a couple of years in ad. seg. A close friend of mine, who I'd spent some time with in general population, was moved into a cell next to me. We passed the time by reminiscing about old days, and we even shared our dreams, hopes, and aspirations. Then one day, my friend came to his door and told everyone he didn't want to talk to any of us and we should leave him alone. Huh? He rejected every attempt I made to communicate with him by ignoring me. He refused to accept his mail, didn't go to rec. or shower, and once they called him for a visit and he refused. Maybe a month or so of this went on, and he began talking to himself. Finally, he covered himself in his own feces and started slashing his arms with a razor....As I watched them carry my old friend away, covered in feces and blood, I felt a profound sense of sorrow and loss. It was very difficult for me to comprehend what had transpired right before my very eyes. This was my first experience with how psychologically damaging this environment can be. I'm positive that what happened to my friend was the result of Groundhog Day Syndrome evolving into psychosis.

Peering through the window in my cell last night, I watched an electrical storm bring light and life to an open field just beyond the prison grounds. It was an awe-inspiring spectacle to behold, and it filled me with a sense of tranquility that has eluded me for quite some time. As I watched the breathtaking bright flashes of light streak across the sky, I found myself reminiscing of a time when I was just a small boy. My mother, brother, sister, and I were all living in Houston when a major storm rolled in. We were all huddled close together, watching the violent winds whip the tall pines around like mere twigs. We were dirt poor (my mother being a single parent at the time, trying to raise three kids on welfare), and I'd already experienced much adversity in my short five-year life, but I felt a strong sense of security with my family that night, despite the storms in our lives. My mother never let my siblings and me forget she loved us.

As I fondly reflected on the innocence of my youth, the lightning illuminating the razor-wired fences brought me back from my reverie. It's usually quite noisy on this cellblock at that time of night, but as I watched the storm I noticed it was peacefully quiet.

Maybe I wasn't the only one gazing out the window, remembering a time long past? Every now and then Mother Nature does her part in helping us combat the tedium of death row. ✪

—Robert Pruett

Texas Department of Criminal Justice photo

The border that separates the incarcerated and the free is emotional, political, and real. This double fence at the Ellis unit on the outskirts of Huntsville effectively divides the convicted from the world outside.

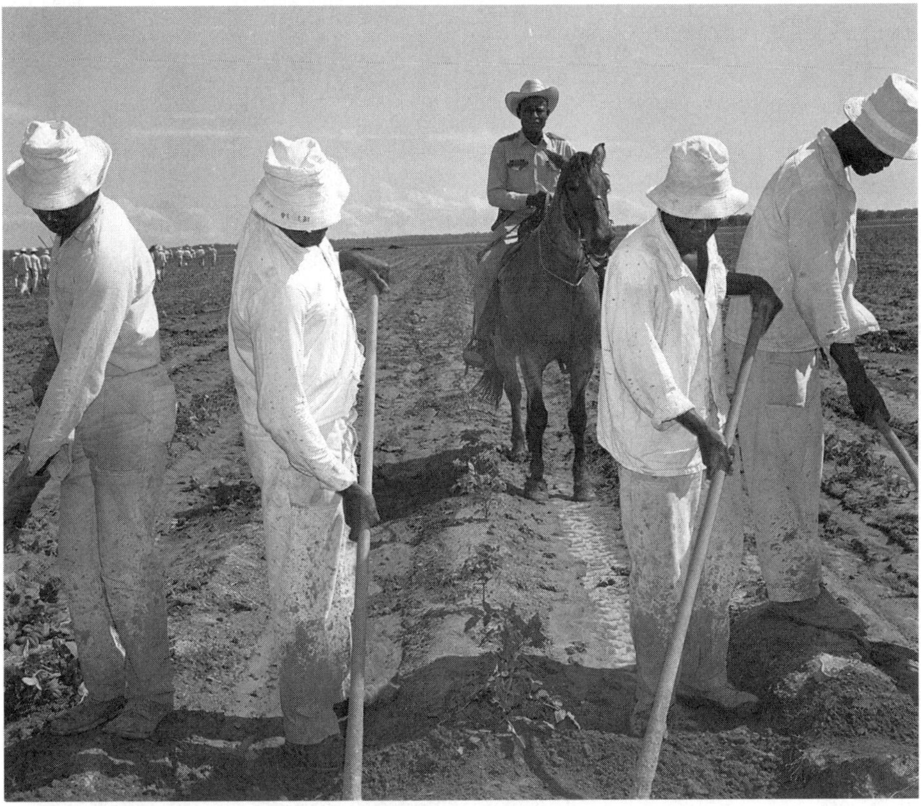

Prisoner-to-prisoner communication is always strictly regulated by guards, even when inmates work shoulder to shoulder, as in this vintage photo of a prison work squad using long-handled hoes, called "aggies."

TDCJ Media Services photos

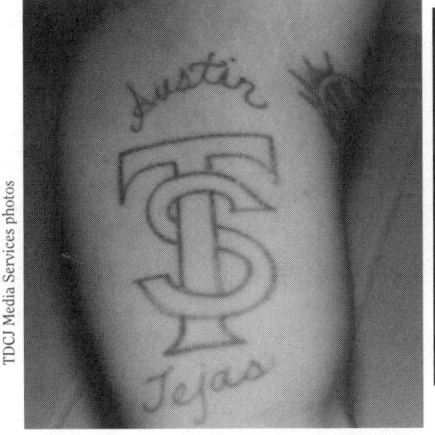

Despite restrictions of prison walls, the incarcerated communicate using traditional as well as "underground" methods such as tattoos.

Section IV
Voices from Within: *Balancing Guaranteed Rights and Protection of the Innocent*

Chapter Five
Communication Inside the Walls

Everybody has the right to adhere to his faith of choice, whether it be a popular one or not. TDCJ is committed to uphold the First Amendment, within reason, but it has to work within the security boundaries 'cause...well, they are in prison, so they can't sacrifice goats or anything.

—Jim Brazzil, retired chaplain, TDCJ

Free to Pray...Required to Stay

Of all the freedoms U.S. citizens enjoy, arguably the freedom to practice religion is the most prized. After all, it was the holy grail of religious choice that inspired shiploads of refugees to relinquish life in their home countries centuries ago and forge futures in the New World. Ironically, some of those same countries found it expedient to relieve prison overcrowding by sending thousands of convicts to the same shores.

Today, in "the land of the free," descendents of both voluntary and involuntary immigrants are at liberty to follow their religious convictions—even behind prison walls. For some felons, religion is the rock to which they cling, the tie that binds them to eternal hope. Religious choice is probably the most unadulterated freedom that endures behind the walls, but the public is often surprised to learn that prisoners are not completely denied other constitutional rights.

Once their sentences are meted out and prisoners cross into the land of the incarcerated, many of the freedoms they enjoyed as citizens are stripped away or greatly curtailed. Basic First Amendment rights—freedom of religion, speech, assembly, and the press, in addition to the right to petition for grievances[1]—all exist behind bars, but often in very limited contexts. In the country at large, court decisions continually redefine citizen rights and sometimes focus specifically on inmates. Since 1945 the Supreme Court has made a number of decisions applied to all forms of communication in the criminal justice system. Those decisions create a framework through which to understand the complexities associated with balancing security concerns and guaranteed freedoms. Many argue that prison inmates should forfeit their constitutional protection, and while this remains true in many instances legal precedence paints a somewhat different view where the First Amendment is concerned.

A storm of litigation surrounding questions of prisoners' rights emerged across the nation in the 1960s, and the ultimate result was expansion of basic rights to prisoners.

Prisoner rights, however, usually take a back seat to safety concerns. In general, prison officials and judges see security of paramount importance over and above the availability of an alternative means of expression by prisoners.[2] But the legal landscape constantly shifts, due in part to prisoner advocates and "jailhouse lawyers" who study the law and file appeals for their own cases as well as for broader issues affecting prisoner rights and conditions. A storm of litigation surrounding questions of prisoners' rights emerged across the nation in the 1960s, and the ultimate result was expansion of basic rights to prisoners. This legal legacy is evident in the Texas Department of Criminal Justice, manifesting in venues such as the monthly inmate newspaper, the *Echo*, and faith-based programs tailored for convicts.

Regardless of legal decisions, prisoners, like their counterparts on the "outside," crave spiritual succor, social interaction, companionship, and ego gratification. Where legitimate channels are unavailable to fulfill those needs, prisoners bypass the law with innovative "underground" methods of communication.

Respecting Religion

Huntsville, securely entrenched in the Texas "Bible Belt," has a diverse religious population, both inside and outside the Walls. The transient nature of those associated with the university as well as growing Asian and Hispanic communities add to the international flavor of the town. Unlike small East Texas towns of some fifty years ago, Huntsville's citizens hold a wide range of religious views: from Mormon to Buddhist, Baptist to Catholic, Methodist to Islamic, among others. Still, Sunday morning in Huntsville has a timeless quality.

Around the central square, carefully dressed families exchange greetings as they make their way to one of the stately churches that anchors downtown, where religion and criminal justice rub elbows. First Methodist Church, with a wealth of stained-glass windows, holds a prime spot on the west corner of the square. When the church's parking spaces are taken, parishioners often use the Huntsville police department's parking lot next door. East of the boxlike county courthouse, silent for the Sabbath, stands the First Baptist Church with its massive entrance columns and the Walls compound in its backyard. Other denominations, including the block-size charismatic Family Faith Church, are scattered around the town and environs. Inmates cannot enter these places of worship, of course, but there is plenty of religion behind the prison bars nevertheless.

As a prison chaplain for years, Jim Brazzil provided religious ministry to TDCJ inmates in Huntsville. He thinks the state offers adequate spiritual support for convicts: "We make sure they have the right kinds of material, and we put them in touch with the right organizations," Brazzil says. "The prisoners have a right to their literature and to the particular stuff they need to do their worship."[3]

By respecting religious freedoms, the prison system assists inmates in turning their lives around because "religion is very important as far as rehabilitation is concerned," Brazzil explains. "A lot of times before a person can be rehabilitated, he has to be habilitated. I believe if a man has an opportunity to pursue his faith and does so honestly and legitimately, it's important."[4] Expanding on the idea of faith-based initiatives widely heralded by politicians, Brazzil says,

> The peace and calmness that comes with faith, the attitudes of cooperation and giving, of learning to live and love and forgive, all play an important part. A good faith-based program will teach all of that: accountability, responsibility, the practice of not just hearing the Word, but doing the Word; it makes a huge success. I would like to say we have a whole lot of stats that back that up. The problem is most chaplaincy programs are so overwhelmed by the task at hand there aren't a lot of scientific stats to support what we're trying to do. But you watch these guys and it does make a difference.[5]

They Said What? Prison Argot as Free Speech

Beyond accommodating spiritual needs, the law allows prisons to enforce significant restrictions on other constitutional rights. In 1945 in *Coffin v. Reichard*,[6] the high court ruled, "A prisoner retains all rights of an ordinary citizen except those expressly, or by necessary implication taken from him by law."[7] But the more traditional view that prisoners' rights are limited was emphasized four years later by the high court, which said, "Lawful incarceration brings about necessary withdrawal...of many privileges and rights, a restriction justified by the considerations underlying our prison system."[8]

Prison expressions are terse but convey strong emotions that reflect the inmates' experiences, frustrations, cynicism, and desperation. Many terms have made their way into popular culture through musicians and writers.

To this day, prisoners' freedom of speech is restricted—both for external and internal communications—ranging from telephone calls outside the prison to conversations with other inmates. One response to these regulations has been to create a specialized language: prison argot.

Distinctive prison argot, often peppered with Spanish phrases and full of double entendres, is spoken not only by inmates, but also by guards. Like all slang, inmate argot is continually evolving. Prison expressions are terse but convey strong emotions that reflect the inmates' experiences, frustrations, cynicism, and desperation. Many terms, such as rack (an inmate's bunk) and shank (a homemade stabbing weapon) have made their way into general usage outside the prisons. (See excerpts from "Argot for the Incarcerated" in this chapter.) According to Laurence Horn, professor of linguistics at Yale University,

> Criminal argot has been studied for hundreds of years as a means to breaking the code of criminal activity. Much like the outside world, an in-group develops terms that are opaque and enable members to communicate without their messages being interpreted. These vernaculars have a sort of covert prestige because they involve a macho image young men seek to emulate. [Prison] inmates...are not only separated from society, but society is also separated from them, which facilitates forms of expressions that never can be fully understood by the outside world.[9]

Prison jargon may begin behind bars, but the free flow of language to the outside is clearly evident as the words and phrases frequently make their way into popular culture through musicians and writers.

Prison City Close-Up

PrisonSpeak: Argot for the Incarcerated

Some of the more common terms found in Texas prisons include:[10]

- *Aggie*: A long-handled hoe
- *All day and a night*: Life without parole
- *Bean chute*: Slot in cell door used to insert food and handcuff prisoners
- *Beat your feet*: Order by guards to move out of an area
- *Buck Rogers time*: A parole date too far in the future to imagine release
- *Chester*: Child molester
- *Deck* or *square*: Pack of cigarettes
- *Dirt nap*: To die
- *Donkey dick*: Sliced cold cuts used on a sandwich
- *Gangster*: HIV
- *Getting buzzed*: Receiving a tattoo
- *Hard candy*: To kill a fellow prisoner
- *Head running*: Talking
- *High rider*: An armed guard assigned to watch prisoners work outside the security perimeters
- *In the car*: Inmates who lift weights together, a tight circle of friends
- *Jigger*: One who watches for guards while an illegal act takes place
- *Johnny L*: A sandwich of stale bread and peanut butter served to prisoners in lockdown or segregation
- *Kitty kitty*: Female guard
- *Little bitch*: A sentence of more than fifty years
- *Ninja Turtles* or *goon squad*: A team of five officers in riot gear prepared to forcibly remove an inmate from his cell
- *On the cool*: Something done without the knowledge of the guards
- *Rack*: An inmate's bunk
- *Robocop*: A guard who reports every minor rule infraction
- *Runs* or *bowling alleys*: The walkways between the cells in a unit
- *Shank*: Homemade stabbing weapon made by sharpening any hard object
- *Shitter*: Punitive segregation or solitary confinement for one to fifteen days due to a major disciplinary infraction
- *Tac*, *ink*, or *tat*: A tattoo
- *Yoke*: Choke to death
- *Zip fool*: An inmate who is considered a hopeless case because he continues to act foolish after being corrected ✪

Tattoo My Soul: Free Expression in Prison

For thousands of years, humans have deliberately permanently marked their skin for a variety of purposes: rites of passage, protection from evil, group identity, proof of status or wealth, medical therapy, beautification, or to ensure entry into the afterlife. The nonverbal communication of tattoos is a profound type of symbolic expression because of their placement on the skin and their permanence.[11] Known as "tats," "tacs," or "inks," the tattoo is a core communication channel in the prison system.

Historically created by rubbing ashes into cuts on the skin, tattoos have evolved into intricate designs known today as body art. Even as tattoos gain popularity with musicians, professional athletes, and college students, many still associate the practice with sailors, gang members, and prison inmates. Tattoos allow the duality of identifying with a particular group while retaining a sense of individuality through selection or placement of the art. Studies show that the number of tattoos on an inmate increases with length of time incarcerated,[12] and record significantly more tattoos among inmates doing time for felonies than those sentenced for misdemeanors.[13]

Tattoos have long represented nonverbal communication of anti-authoritarianism and rebellion. While many inmates had tattoos prior to incarceration, jailhouse tattoos are distinctive. Prison tattoos are created in one of two ways: the original Polynesian technique or through the use of a homemade gun. The primitive Polynesian method employs a sharpened object to cut the skin and then forces ink or ash under the skin.[14] These tattoos often appear sloppy and crude in appearance. A tattoo gun created with a simple motor, a hollowed-out ballpoint pen, a guitar string, and a battery creates a much more professional and elaborate design. An inmate with a tattoo gun and a skilled hand is held in high regard.

Wanda Mayes, who teaches inmates basic reading and writing skills at the Windham School in Huntsville, has students write papers on how tattoo guns are made. "They use broomsticks to make the needles because they can get a fine tip and they find motors wherever they can," she explains. "When I first started teaching here, I was using machines that would read a passage and then the prisoner would read it—they are common in elementary schools. Not long afterward, I noticed the machines were getting lighter. That's when I discovered the guys were removing the motors. They knew they couldn't take the entire machine because the guards would notice, but the motor was small enough to stick in their pants and take back to their cells."[15]

Inmates would not mention that their machines were not working properly during class, Mayes says. "They wouldn't tell you anything because then they would have gotten strip searched. Plus, they all want tats, so they kept their mouths shut. I just stopped bringing the machines. They knew I had caught on but wasn't going to say anything. You've got to earn their trust or you will get nowhere in there."[16]

Once a prisoner has purchased a tattoo by paying the artist with postage stamps (the most common currency in the prison system), the tattoos must be applied quickly since guards conduct walk-throughs every thirty minutes. If an inmate is discovered with a tattoo gun, he faces strict punishment and loss of the device. Most prison tattoos lack the color and definition found in those applied by a professional tattoo artist and do not retain their colors. But a prison tat garners respect because it indicates that the prisoner "got one over on the system." According to "Shelley," a prison guard, inmates are recruited to run "jiggers" (stand watch) while the inmate artist applies the design. Tapping on bars, running water, or singing gospel songs are common methods to conceal the hum of the tattoo gun's motor. Inmates who are skilled tattoo artists are held in high regard and allotted a level of protection not available to other inmates.[17]

A tattoo indicates three important aspects of the inmate: who he is, what he has done, and where he has been. Prisoners may have their names, nicknames, or the names of their loved ones applied to their fingers or upper arms. Mayes describes two student-inmates with memorable tattoos: "One of the guys in my class had the most beautiful tat I had ever seen across his back. It was a skeleton riding a motorcycle, and it was so detailed you could see the bones in the skeleton's hands. It took him almost two years to have it completed, and I do not know how he stood the pain, but it was nice. Another student had a son who died while [the inmate] was in prison, and they tattooed that baby's picture on his arm. It was nearly perfect."[18]

Racial images or the names of places where the inmate has served time are common among prison designs. If an inmate has killed someone, it is common to display the weapon used in the murder pointed away from the body. In the movie *Cry Baby*, the actor Johnny Depp portrayed an ex-con sporting a teardrop tattoo under his eye, indicating that he was responsible for a death. According to photojournalist Andrew Lichtenstein, who obtained TDCJ clearance to document prison tattoos, today the teardrop tat is a remembrance of a family or gang member who died during the prisoner's incarceration.[19]

Prison City Close-Up

Graphic Communication:
The Significance of Body Art

While tattoo designs vary by state and prison unit, some of the most common include:[20]

- The biohazard symbol means that the wearer is a hazard to humans. It is popular because its basic design is easily applied.

- Brick walls are symbols of time spent in prison. Each brick indicates a year of incarceration. Other designs symbolizing time imprisoned include hourglasses and clock faces. It is common for an inmate to get an hourglass tattoo while serving in prison, then add wings to the image upon release.

- The theater masks of comedy and drama are common symbols prisoners use to symbolize the idea of "play now, pay later."

- A dagger through a skull is the symbol of a killer.

- Thirteen and a half is a prison tattoo that stands for the judge (1), the jury (12), and the "half-assed" sentence.

The tattoo artist at Voodoo Tattoo in Huntsville indicates how easy it is to disguise meaning in popular prison images:[21]

- A tattoo with the number 13 encircled indicates the Aryan Circle, a vicious branch of the white gang.

- A clown or joker denotes a member of the Mexican Mafia.

- The phrase "Only God Can Judge Me" is very popular for its defiant manner.

- MOB is the acronym for Money Over Bitches, rather than for the crime syndicate.

Sometimes customers request a repulsive combination of images. The Voodoo artist remembers a potential client who wanted a brutal image on each arm—a woman being raped and a woman having her throat cut—along with numbers beside the images for "bragging rights." The artist was relieved when the customer balked at the quoted price. ✪

Signs of Association

The right of association, not in itself a specific First Amendment freedom, has been repeatedly recognized as a way of safeguarding guarantees of speech, assembly, and petition.[22] Freedom of association is a privilege the courts have restricted in prisons, but many inmates nevertheless find a sense of community by joining a prison gang and adopting that group's special symbols to demonstrate their allegiance. Gang tattoos are an intricate part of the prison culture because they provide a sense of empowerment and inclusion.

Gang members play essential family roles inside and outside prisons, which might account for the sharp rise in the number of Hispanic gangs. With a language barrier preventing them from communicating with other inmates, many Hispanic inmates feel isolated, Mayes explains. "Most of the Mexican prisoners do not speak English very well, so they need to be part of the gang; otherwise, they can't communicate. The Mexican gangs usually speak only to their own [members], so if you see a Texas Syndicate member speaking to a Mafia member, something bad is about to happen."[23] Most gangs are protective of the emblem that indicates membership, and permit only the group's official tattoo artist to apply the tat. Smaller, less organized gangs will allow the prison's resident body artist to affix the gang symbols.

One of the most notorious groups is the Mexican Mafia, which began as a street gang in Los Angeles but, as members were arrested and sentenced to long prison terms, the organization expanded throughout the penal system, including in Texas. Members of the gang are either tattooed with the Mexican flag's symbol of an eagle with a snake and the initials "EME," or with a single black handprint. Another Hispanic gang, the Texas Syndicate, originated in the California prison system after a turf battle for drug territory. Its members sport intricately designed patterns with the initials "TS" on the back of their right forearms.

Amy Brush, who holds an advanced criminal justice degree from SHSU and worked for TDCJ, recalls a Texas Syndicate member who spent his time in solitary applying the gang's initials in an unauthorized location. "He worked in the cap shop over at the Ferguson unit where he was sewing tiny little TSs in each hat. Hundreds of caps had to be recalled because guards were walking around wearing the Texas Syndicate's gang symbol."[24]

Although outnumbered by Hispanic and black inmates, white gangs are also active. The Dirty White Boys and the Aryan Brotherhood (AB) are the best known. AB members cover their bodies with tattoos incorporating their initials with ribbons and hearts, shamrocks, double lighting bolts, and neo-Nazi symbols. Gaelic symbols and phrases are also popular. The swastika, used by all white gangs, is considered to be one of the most heinous and offensive symbols. Jody, a body artist at Voodoo Tattoo in Huntsville, observes that most people cannot easily identify the swastika when it is integrated into beautifully elaborate symbols. "We tell people who select a Celtic flower pattern they may want to pick something else because of the hidden symbol. It is very popular with girls, so I can't imagine how many are walking around with Nazi symbols on their navels or lower backs."[25]

Mayes explains how the Aryans acquire respect in prison:

> No one messes with the Aryans. Period. They are the politicians. Most guards are white, and they trust the white prisoners more. The prisoners will tell the guards what is going down, and the guards handle it. In return the Aryans control how the prison is run. If someone pisses one of them off, they tell the guard. The next thing you know, the guy is lying face down in the dirt getting the shit kicked out of him by the guards. The Aryans didn't raise a finger, but everyone knows what happened.[26]

Not all gangs are formed to intimidate their fellow prisoners. For instance, a former Black Panther member began the Black Guerrilla Family with the objectives of eradicating racism, maintaining dignity for the black inmates, and overthrowing the United States government. The most typical symbol is a black dragon overtaking a prison tower or the letters BGF over a crossed saber and shotgun.[27] In light of recent terrorist attacks, the gang culture has attracted the attention of U.S. government officials, who consider these well-organized groups a serious threat to homeland security.[28]

On a more mainstream and legitimate front, prisoners have tested the legal waters for the right to associate through labor unions. In *Jones v. North Carolina Prisoners' Union, Inc.* (1977),[29] the Supreme Court heard a case examining the right of association, wherein inmates claimed that their constitutional right to association was infringed when the prison administration refused to allow a prison labor union. Prison officials feared that a union might organize a work stoppage "or other undesirable concerted activity," and the Court agreed that a union had the potential to disrupt the prison's order and security. The penal system's arguments were recognized as speculative since no union had been organized, but the precedent of recognizing a potential threat to prison security was established in deference to the superior experience of prison administrators and "legitimate policies and goals of the corrections system."[30]

The (Somewhat) Free Press

Even behind prison walls, the news business flourishes, within carefully prescribed boundaries delineated by a succession of court decisions. In Texas the prison newspaper is the seventy-eight-year-old *Echo*, with a circulation of more than 150,000 and a history of testing the right of free speech.

When publication began in 1928 the *Echo* was offered in limited release and contained little more than the warden's mandates to prisoners, but now the monthly newspaper includes stories by inmates from each unit, pictures celebrating achievements, recipes, "Dear Darby" (an advice column), and a Crime Watchers report. Lyndol Wilkinson, self-described as the "original square one, little Southern Baptist girl who has been married to the same man for thirty-nine years," is the associate publisher for the paper. Aided by an assistant and a staff of inmates in Huntsville, Wilkinson is charged with publishing an informative and entertaining newspaper that avoids material likely to be censored.

Wilkinson joined the *Echo* more than twenty years ago, following Justice William Wayne Justice's ruling against the Texas prison system in *Ruiz v. Estelle*,[31] the longest-litigated prisoner rights case in U.S. history. Ruiz was a jailhouse lawyer who wrote his civil rights complaint on toilet paper in 1972.[32] His case was combined with other suits to become a class action on behalf of all Texas prisoners.

After extensive prisoner testimony about substandard medical care, overcrowding, lack of legal access, and guard brutality, Justice found that the state's prisons violated the U.S. Constitution's Eighth Amendment against "cruel and unusual punishment," and Texas was instructed to make sweeping changes in its prison system.[33] As part of that overhaul, TDCJ administrators were required to disseminate information to inmates about the results of the court's ruling, so they hired Wilkinson to change the *Echo*'s format accordingly.

Wilkinson knew she needed an experienced managing editor for the paper. She went to the Coffield unit, near Palestine in northeast Texas, and asked Guy Marble if he would take the job. Prior to his conviction for burglary and intended rape, Marble had been the managing editor at several well-respected newspapers in northeast Texas. It took a lot of convincing to get Marble to agree to move to Huntsville, but Wilkinson says her tenacity finally won him over.

She soon learned one of the unwritten rules of TDCJ. "I found out how much I was in the dark about the prison world. The administrators were infuriated I would ask Marble if he wanted to come to Huntsville. You [are supposed to] tell the inmate what he is going to do. It even became worse when it was discovered I asked if he wanted to speak to me." They said, 'Do you want to speak to him? 'Cause if you do, he damn well will speak to you.'"[34]

Wilkinson thinks one of the best stories to ever appear in the Echo *focused on legendary singer and songwriter David Crosby, who spent time in Huntsville on a drug conviction.*

Wilkinson's in-laws are from northeast Texas, so she was familiar with Marble's earlier work and respected him as an intelligent man. The idea of forcing him to speak to her was distasteful. Her approach led to what she calls "the first really big mistake I made working for TDCJ. I asked, 'Why?' My boss said, 'You don't ask why!' and I said, 'Well, yeah, I do, because I don't want to make that mistake again.'" Luckily, all turned out well. "They thought I was challenging their decision, when in fact I was trying to clarify what the parameters were," she explains. "I am still learning quirky things about TDCJ because there are a lot of them."[35]

Wilkinson thinks one of the best stories to ever appear in the *Echo* focused on legendary singer and songwriter David Crosby, who spent time in Huntsville on a drug conviction. "We didn't know if he would talk to us because he had a block on all press interviews. Eventually, he agreed to talk to me, and I turned my notes over to Marble to write the story. I knew it was good because Crosby loved it so much. David Crosby was one of the all-time nicest guys."[36] Such above-average content was recognized; under Marble's direction, the *Echo* was named the best prison newspaper in the U.S.

In 1989 Texas's financial straits led to a series of layoffs at TDCJ, and Wilkinson was one of many casualties. Soon after, the *Echo* became "an outlaw publication" that was shut down by prison administrators. Wilkinson reflects, "The [inmate staff members] were brilliant ... they did exceptional work. Remember the men who broke out of the Connally unit and ended up killing a guard? They all got the death penalty. The *Echo* wrote a comprehensive report on the anatomy of a breakout and hammered TDCJ from one end to the other, which wasn't welcomed."[37]

Managing editor inmate Jorge Renaud, formerly a journalism major at SHSU, argued that the prison administrators were violating guaranteed rights provided by *Burke v. Levi* (Virginia, 1975)[38] and *The Lupar v. Stoneman* (Vermont, 1974),[39] but the prison administrators' decision stood. Renaud's arguments were understandable, since in *Burke v. Levi* the courts limited prior restraint by authorities and ruled that only the materials prison officials felt might specifically lead to violence within the prison could be suppressed. At that time, the court said that inmate editors should have the right to comment freely and critically upon all aspects of prison life, including prison administration.[40]

Similarly, *The Lupar v. Stoneman* focused on inmates' claims that prison officials had rejected a newspaper article because it challenged their administrative methods. In that Vermont case, the court found that "prison officials may unilaterally enact regulations pertaining to publication of a newspaper by prison inmates, but such regulations must be no broader than is necessary to protect the legitimate government interests of prison security, prison order and prisoner rehabilitation."[41]

Further, the Court cautioned prison officials to be mindful that even if an article is "critical, attacks personalities or is even defamatory, [that] is not a sufficient reason to suppress the publication in which it appears"[42] and "although inmates do not have a constitutional right to distribute a newspaper within the prison, they do have the right to be free of discriminatory punishment because of their beliefs."[43]

However, these cases, which had provided a glimmer of hope that certain First Amendment rights were recognized for prisoner publications, were outweighed by the "reasonable belief standard" set by *Jones*[44] in 1977. That decision provided the basis for Virginia's Fourth Circuit Court of Appeals to find in *Pittman v. Hutto*[45] that prison officials could suppress publication and distribution of an inmate-edited newspaper if they believed the newspaper's content threatened the state's legitimate penological interest. In *Pittman* the courts focused on a magazine, *FYSK (Facts You Should Know)*, published by inmates at the Virginia State Penitentiary. *FYSK* was a "forum for inmate discussion and for communication between inmates and the staff of the penitentiary."[46]

In 1977 a dispute arose when inmate editors accused officials of censorship and refused to remove a disputed article, claiming First Amendment protection. The officials declined to print the edition, saying the article could disrupt prison stability and interfere with the penological objective of the institution. The court found in favor of the prison officials because "publication of inflammatory articles in a newspaper with wide circulation among inmates, like union activity, could lead to disturbances."[47]

While district court decisions in other states are not binding in Texas, the U.S. Supreme Court finding in *Jones* uses very similar language and arguments as the earlier Virginia cases, but emphasizes the importance of deferring to the expertise of prison administrators, which would seem to predict a similar result if raised later in Texas, or any other state, unless content-based censorship or punishment for disagreeable beliefs was shown to have taken place.

Using these legal precedents as ammunition, prison administrators closed the *Echo*. Wilkinson summarizes, "What happened was a band of inmates reprimanded the criminal justice system and humiliated the administration. In the process of exercising First Amendment rights [the *Echo*] damaged reputations, so the criminal justice board shut it down."[48]

While it is apparent that Wilkinson supports free speech protection for the prison reporters she once again oversees, she also accepts the parameters of her position. "We put a statement in the masthead that clearly says the *Echo* is a Texas Department of Criminal Justice publication, but that doesn't protect us from the anger." She reels off complaints as if reading from inmates' letters: "'You are keeping things from us. You need to talk more about mental health problems caused by the prisons and inmate-on-inmate rape.' It is just endless, but we are here to help inmates."[49]

Wilkinson has an outside staff of two, plus an inmate managing editor and an inmate reporter for each unit—not nearly enough staff to do the in-depth reporting the requested stories would require. "We get thirty or forty letters a day," she says, "and we just can't handle all of the inmate correspondence." Wilkinson's penchant for looking at the positive comes through in stories that are published. "I want to tell about the thousands of inmates who got their GEDs this past year. I want to tell about the men who walk out of here and straight into state-licensed jobs. I want the readers' poems and recipes to be published."[50]

She points to the diverse coverage in recent issues. "The last edition focused on methamphetamines. Most do not know over half of the newly reported AIDS cases involve meth, so we did a big thing on that. The month before, we did one on spiders, especially the brown recluse that will eat your face off if you don't get something done."[51] (See the close-up of the current

Echo editor at the end of this chapter.)

One problem the *Echo* shares with newspapers in the free world is unwelcome requests to purchase questionable advertisements. Wilkinson describes an all-too-common occurrence: companies wanting to advertise a packet "guaranteed" to get an inmate paroled. "I will not allow that type of advertisement to be placed in the *Echo* because ninety-nine times out of a hundred it is just screwing his family out of their money. I am not going to promise a mother that paying fifteen hundred dollars will get her son back home by Christmas, because it will not happen! So, we try never to print anything that will victimize the inmates' families anymore. They are already the most victimized people of anyone associated with the prison system." To avoid such problems, the *Echo* does not accept any advertising. All publication costs are paid by TDCJ, but budget restrictions limit the paper to 10 issues a year of 12-16 pages.

"Kites," Walkie-talkies, and Envelopes

The courts have often recognized that family ties have special weight when it comes to inmate communication issues. For example, in *Turner v. Safley*,[52] the Court heard claims that a Missouri law relating to inmate-to-inmate correspondence was unconstitutional. At that time, Missouri prison officials only allowed prisoners to correspond with incarcerated inmates if they were family members.

To enforce this policy, administrators relied on the security test set up in *Jones v. North Carolina Prisoners Labor Union, Inc.*[53] and the earlier decision of *Procunier v. Martinez*[54] in 1974, which repeated the traditional view that state prison officials had the power to preserve internal order and discipline, maintain institutional security against escape or unauthorized entry, and were charged with prisoner rehabilitation.[55] However, the *Procunier* decision also invalidated blanket mail censorship regulations that had allowed prison systems to unilaterally censor prisoner mail if officials thought the letters were inappropriate.[56]

Nevertheless, *Procunier v. Martinez* helped set the standards lower courts still use in First Amendment cases. Prison officials and judges see security concerns of paramount importance over and above the availability of an alternative means of expression by prisoners.[57] The issues were further clarified in *Turner v. Safley*[58] in 1987, when Justice O'Conner stated for the Court, "When a prison regulation impinges on inmates' constitutional rights, the regulation is valid if it is reasonably related to legitimate penological interests. In our view, such a standard is necessary if prison administrators...and not the courts, [are] to make the difficult judgments concerning institutional operations."[59]

This provided the lower courts with a new standard to weigh prisoners' rights: governmental interest need only be legitimate to be deemed reasonable. Many believe that the *Turner* decision is still causing First Amendment cases to be denied. The change in the standard shifted the policy from simply monitoring internal inmate correspondence to full prohibition of such correspondence because the level of monitoring required would place undue hardship on the prison and would not be entirely successful. The courts determined that inmates could plan assaults, murders, riots, and other activities detrimental to the security of the prison.[60]

Once prisoner-to-prisoner correspondence was curtailed, inmates developed innovative communication alternatives, including "kite-stringing," "fishing poles," and decorative envelopes.

Once prisoner-to-prisoner correspondence was curtailed, inmates began to develop innovative communication alternatives, including "kite-stringing," "fishing poles," and decorative envelopes. Kites (letters between inmates) are sent through a complex network called kite stringing. Inmates unravel bed linens to create a thin chain of multiple twisted threads up to sixty feet long. Correspondence is attached to the end of the string with a paper clip and is "flown" (tossed) out into the "run" (the walkway separating prison cells). An inmate retrieves it by throwing a weighted string across the kite and pulling it into the cell. The process is repeated until the message reaches the intended recipient. Using this method, letters can travel a few feet or down halls, across units, and even to inmates in solitary confinement.

Bulkier items such as parcels containing food products, magazines, books, and articles of clothing are also transported through the prison unit. Inmates bundle the items they want to send, attach a tag with the intended recipient's name and cell number, then pass the bundles between the cells with so-called fishing poles. These devices are made by rolling newspapers or magazines into long stiff poles and attaching a hook (several paper clips or a fork) at the end to catch the item as it is passed along.

Offenders create primitive telephones by connecting two cans with twine or wire and alter their radios to make prison walkie-talkies. Transforming a radio into a vocal transmitter/receiver requires only a basic knowledge of electronics, a skill readily found within prisons. According to one prisoner, many inmates begin their criminal careers stealing car radios before advancing to hotwiring cars, so it is child's play to rewire a radio to create a cellblock "party line."

Until recently, prisoners also used their artistic talents to communicate with their peers through hand-drawn images on envelopes that were being sent outside the prison. Impressive to look at, this artwork was more than decoration—much of the design was code. Hidden inside the artwork were messages to other inmates who saw the envelopes before they were mailed. By glimpsing a familiar crest on an envelope, a new inmate could learn that members of his gang were also incarcerated within the unit. Coded envelopes could alert inmates to problems brewing in the unit or might advertise wares available from a prisoner's underground shop. To curtail this covert communication, prison officials passed rules against decorating the outside of envelopes. No doubt inmates will soon devise new methods to communicate these kinds of messages, if they have not already done so.

Petitioning the Government for Redress

While most people know that prisoners can challenge their incarcerations, few realize that the freedom to petition for a redress of grievances also includes the right to protest deprivation of inmates' rights by prison officials. This protection is seldom sought because prisoners who want to petition the court are often unable to write the writ or get proper legal assistance.[61]

Jim Marcus, director of Texas Defender Service, an organization that assists inmates in legal appeals, says people often have misconceptions about inmates abusing the judicial system. "There is this myth that lawyers come up with technicalities to win cases and guilty people get off, but the reality is just the opposite. We lose cases on technicalities all the time: the lawyer didn't file the right thing at the right time; the lawyer didn't make the objection at the trial; the lawyer didn't put the issue in the right pleading; the lawyer didn't cite the right case in his or her brief."[62]

The federal review process for filing grievances or appeals can easily be mishandled, with dire consequences for prisoners. "If you look at the path of appellate review in criminal cases, federal review is limited to issues raised or litigated in state court, so it's not a clean slate," Marcus explains. "You don't get to start over. If the lawyers miss something in state court, that issue is waived forever." The cost of such negligence may be extreme. "There have been four people executed with no federal review of their cases whatsoever and all four of them were here in Texas—and there are several more in the pipeline," Marcus observes.[63]

Legal aid to prisoners is provided either by state-paid licensed attorneys or by fellow prisoners, referred to as "writ writers" or "jailhouse lawyers."

While the courts have had few opportunities to hear First Amendment grievances concerning inmates' right to petition, the cases of *Gibbs v. King*[64] and *Hadden v. Howard*[65] established that even though prisoners were allowed to file grievances they should not expect protection from retribution for their actions. In *Gibbs v. King* the U.S. Court of Appeals for the Fifth Circuit upheld a prison regulation prohibiting prisoners from making or writing "derogatory or degrading remarks about an employee" so as to "prevent the escalation of tension" and to allow guards to work without "challenges to their authority." The U.S. Court of Appeals for the Third Circuit went one step further in *Hadden* by permitting internal prison discipline for "insolence, disrespect," and "lying to an employee,"[66] even when such conduct took place in the form of an official grievance filed by a prisoner.

The extent of legal assistance available to prisoners has not been completely clarified by the courts. Legal aid to prisoners is normally provided either by state-paid licensed attorneys or by fellow prisoners, referred to as "writ writers" or "jailhouse lawyers." The 1969 decision in *Johnson v. Avery*[67] paved the way for fellow inmates to write writs for illiterate peers to ensure their opportunity to petition. Prison administrators argued that the practice of jailhouse lawyers was undesirable because it allowed inmates to subvert prison security by creating a group of powerful, educated inmates who required loyalty as payment. Marcus, familiar with the writ writers' work, explains the limitations of the assistance his office can provide. "I receive letters every day saying, 'Will you take my case?' But out of ten cases, we can only accept two or three because we do not have the resources."[68]

Inside TDCJ, incidents are handled by the Administrative Review and Risk Management Division, which houses the Offender Grievance program, headquartered in Huntsville. The program's mission is to help inmates interact responsibly with legitimate authority, avoid conflicts, and accept rules as a necessary part of participation in society. All inmates have access to the grievance program to file written complaints related to their classification, personal property, disciplinary status, or other confinement issues. Each unit has a grievance investigator responsible for processing offender complaints and assisting during the process. If the grievance cannot be resolved within the unit, prisoners receive legal assistance through the State Counsel for Offenders (SCFO), which processes between 4,500 and 10,000 pieces of mail per month from inmates seeking redress.[69]

Inmate grievances play an important role in disseminating concerns and issues facing prisoners. Marcus says, "Because federal judges are appointed for life, they do what is right without worrying about any reprisal. Our state system doesn't work that way; our state judges are all elected, so they all think about reelection. If you are running for election, you're going to be tough on crime. You're not going to say, 'I'm running because I feel the constitutional rights of these people in the criminal justice system are getting short shrift.'"[70]

He tells a poignant story to illustrate how important federal appeals can be. "George McFarland's case may be one of the worst examples of a miscarriage of justice—his lawyer was sleeping. There was no dispute about whether he was sleeping. The *Houston Chronicle* covered the 1992 trial, and the courtroom reporter described how the lawyer was nodding off. Each time he woke up, there would be a different witness on the stand. The reporter asked the lawyer, 'You looked like you were sleeping. Were you really sleeping?' And the lawyer said, 'Well, it's boring.' The reporter asked the judge about it, and the judge said, 'The Constitution says you have a right to a lawyer. It doesn't say he has to be awake.' So, access to the federal courts is critical; if you're going to have constitutionally fair trials in this state, you need access to a court that is going to enforce the Constitution."[71]

Life in a correctional institution is definitely different from life as a free citizen in several aspects, but it's like a small community. Each person has a role and a job that is integral to the operation of that society.

—Lt. Ann Avery, TDCJ guard

Prison City Close-Up

Time to Change:
From Teenage Murderer to *Echo* Editor

"I was a thug. Now I'm a nerd."[72]

At thirty-four, Derek Ian Hilla has served about one third of a forty-five-year prison sentence for a gang-related murder. Since then, he has become an artist, a college graduate three times over, and the editor of the largest prison newspaper in the United States.

Hilla is a large man, articulate but modest, who wears the requisite prison whites and close-cropped hair. His forearms are decorated with tattoos reminiscent of his teenage gang years. Since entering prison at eighteen, Hilla says he has lived through the cycle of anger, introspection, and positive change prison is intended to inspire. Now he talks excitedly about a recidivism awareness and retention program to prepare convicts who are "going home" for the world outside.

"We're ex-cons; we can't do anything to change the system, so we decided to work on our own attitudes and beliefs," Hilla explains. "We think things are going to be rosy when we get out, but we have to find jobs, we have to find a place to stay. The world's going 110 miles an hour. How do you fix that?"[73] To look for answers, Hilla has recruited about twenty inmates incarcerated for various offenses, from different economic and racial backgrounds. The group members appointed him their leader, a vote of confidence that obviously pleases him.

It wasn't a quick or easy trip from thug to role model, Hilla admits. "I've been on the worst units possible; I've been among the worst offenders, but I've also been among the best offenders. I've seen people leave and come back and leave and come back and leave again. The same people. Why do some people leave and make it, and some people don't?" Hilla's personal interest in this question prompted him to enroll in Sam Houston State University's sociology program, from which he graduated with top honors. The subject fascinates him: "The most important thing you can have is a sociological imagination—look at who you are in an historical context, an economic context. How do you live to the best of your ability?"[74]

Hilla sees his position with the prison newspaper as an opportunity to distribute information that helps prisoners grow and prepare for life outside the walls. He was reluctant to take on the job as *Echo* editor when first approached by associate publisher Lyndol Wilkinson and Windham School District communications coordinator Bambi Kiser. "They kidnapped me on the cool," Hilla jokes.

Becoming editor posed significant risks to both his life and lifestyle, Hilla explains. After beginning his sentence in 1990, Hilla gradually made huge changes in his situation and his attitude. Ten years later, he had managed to snag the coveted artist job for the media center at the Walls unit in downtown Huntsville and had earned an associate's degree in art. He transferred his artistic ability to the digital world—doing graphic design and layout on the computer using Publisher, Excel, PageMaker, Corel, and Illustrator. He was earning enough money to pay for college classes, and he was established as a model prisoner.

Leaving all of that and moving across town to the newspaper office at the Wynne unit was not a pleasant prospect. Hilla knew about the *Echo*'s "outlaw editor" of the 1990s—Jorge Renaud—who had published articles critical of the TDCJ administration that resulted in the paper being shut down. "I was afraid of writing something [that made someone mad] and spending the next six years on a chain bus," Hilla says. "What they have is chain bus therapy; if somebody gets upset with you, they can put you on a bus and ship you from unit to unit to unit, effectively destroying any plans for trying to do something with your time." Hilla says he also was at personal risk since some members of a rival gang from his thug days were housed at Wynne. But the new, non-thug Hilla resolved those differences in a peaceful fashion. "I talked it out with them."

Now, with several years of editorship under his belt, Hilla says the job has been a "real blessing." He still is not completely comfortable with the line he must walk between prisoners' expectations and administrative censorship, but he sees the *Echo* as the best way to distribute helpful information to over 150,000 Texas inmates. Hilla points out that many readers remember what the *Echo* once was and see the "defanged" publication as a PR tool of the agency.

When the paper was resurrected in 2001 TDCJ was careful to put a three-tiered approval process in place. Before the *Echo* goes to press, all copy is edited by Wilkinson and Hilla, then it is read by Kiser, and, finally, it must be vetted by legal counsel. Nothing negative about TDCJ or any elected official is published.[75]

Some inmates have told Hilla the paper is not even good enough to "wrap fish in." But Hilla estimates that 60 to 70 percent of the inmates read the prison rag. Content includes letters, poems, and questions submitted by inmates, material filed by volunteer reporters from the various units, and stories written or assigned by Hilla. His information-gathering abilities are closely circumscribed since he has no access to email, the Internet, or telephones. He certainly can't travel around the state to conduct interviews or take photos. Even though he has earned the "minimum custody" designation, Hilla points out, "I am stuck on this unit."[76]

The *Echo* is the seventh-largest paper in the state,[77] but its production is primitive by modern media standards. However, some of its rules are the same as for papers outside the walls. For example, Hilla tries to have a variety of content so there is something for everyone, from short-termers to lifers; he uses his graphic skills to make the layouts aesthetically pleasing, and he puts "photos of girls on the front page as often as possible." But his foremost goal for the publication is to spread the word about resources the system offers inmates and to publicly recognize their achievements. "I see that the majority of people in here have the same goals, the same dreams I do," Hilla says.[78]

> **Hilla uses his graphic skills to make the layouts aesthetically pleasing, and he puts "photos of girls on the front page as often as possible."**

Beyond his aspirations for the *Echo*, Hilla has hopes for his own future. "I would love to get out. I'm looking seriously at going into teaching sociology because I think I have something valuable to give back to the community. It's well and good to analyze what happens in here, [and] it's easy to sit up there in the ivory tower and say, 'This is the way it works.' A large majority of what I've read on criminology and gangs and delinquency hits the target, but it's not even close to the bull's eye. They're missing a lot of important issues because they haven't had to live it."[79]

Hilla is looking toward an upcoming parole hearing that might give him an opportunity to pursue his dream. But he is realistic: "I've been up for parole four times already."[80] In the meantime, he has a newspaper to publish; he has just completed an associate's degree in applied science, and he is busy trying to find ways to teach inmates how to leave and not return. That's a lot of responsibility for a thug turned nerd. ✪

Notes

[1] U.S. Constitution, Amendment I.
[2] *Jones v. North Carolina Prisoners' Union, Inc.*, 433 U.S. 119 (1977).
[3] Jim Brazzil (former prison chaplain), interview by Tina Baiter, Huntsville, Texas, August 18, 2005.
[4] Ibid.
[5] Ibid.
[6] *Coffin v. Reichard*, 142 F. 2d 443 (6th Cir. 1944), cert. denied, 325 U.S. 887 (1945).
[7] Ibid.
[8] *Price v. Johnson*, 334 U.S. 226 (1948).
[9] Laurence R. Horn, *Descriptions in Context* (New York: Garland, 1997).
[10] Sources of terms: "A Prisoner's Dictionary" at www.prisonwall.org/dict.htm, compiled by Arnold Erickson, and "The Correctional Officers Guide to Prison Slang," compiled by Lt. Avery and P. Anderson CO III, members of the Institutional Division of TDCJ.
[11] Terisa Green, *The Tattoo Encyclopedia: A Guide to Choosing Your Tattoo* (New York: Fireside, 2003).
[12] Bill Valentine, *Gang Intelligence Manual: Identifying and Understanding Modern-Day Violent Gangs in the United States* (Boulder, Colorado: Paladin, 1995).
[13] B. Britt, E. Panepento, and I. Wilson, "The Incidence of Tattooing in a Male Criminal Population," *Behavioral Neuropsychiatry* 4 (1972): 13–16.
[14] Green.
[15] Wanda Mayes (teacher, Windham School District), interview by Debbi Hatton, Athens, Texas, July 2, 2005.
[16] Ibid.
[17] Jamie Winn (local body artist), interview by Debbi Hatton, Huntsville, Texas, July 6, 2005.
[18] Mayes interview, 2005.
[19] Andrew Lichtenstein, "Foto 8." Available at: http://www.foto8.com/issue01/dprisontattoos/prisontattoos1.html.
[20] Green.
[21] Winn interview, 2005.
[22] *Bates v. City of Little Rock*, 361 U.S. 516, 522–23 (1960); *United Transportation Union v. State Bar of Michigan*, 401 U.S. 576, 578–79 (1971); *Healy v. James*, 408 U.S. 169, 181 (1972).
[23] Mayes interview, 2005.
[24] Amy Brush (TDCJ employee), interview by Debbi Hatton, Huntsville, Texas, July 6, 2005.
[25] Winn interview, 2005.
[26] Mayes interview, 2005.
[27] Green.
[28] Ibid.
[29] *Jones v. North Carolina Prisoners' Union, Inc.*
[30] Ibid.
[31] *Ruiz v. Estelle*, 503 F.Supp. 1265 (S.D. Tex. 1980), rev'd in part, 679 F.2d 1115 (5th Cir. 1992), modified in part , 688 F.2d 266 (5th Cir. 1982), cert. denied, 103 S.Ct. 1438 (1983).
[32] Gloria Rubac, "Historic Prison Activist David Ruiz Dies," *Workers World,* November 27, 2005. Available at: http://www.workers.org/2005/us/david-ruiz-1201/.
[33] *Ruiz v. Estelle.*
[34] Lyndol Wilkinson (associate publisher of the *Echo*), interview by Melody Davison, Huntsville, Texas, June 26, 2005.
[35] Ibid.
[36] Ibid.

37 Ibid.
38 *Burke v. Levi*, 391 F. Supp. 186 (E.D. Va) vacated and remanded mem. 530 F. 2d 967 (4th Cir. 1975).
39 *The Lupar v. Stoneman*, 382 F Supp. 495 (D.Vt. 1974), appeal dismissed, 517 F. 2d 1395 (2d Cir. 1975).
40 *Burke v. Levi*.
41 *The Lupar v. Stoneman*.
42 Ibid.
43 Ibid.
44 *Jones v. North Carolina Prisoners' Union, Inc.*
45 *Pittman v. Hutto*, 594 F.2nd 407 (4th Cir. 1979).
46 Ibid.
47 Ibid.
48 Wilkinson interview, 2005.
49 Ibid.
50 Ibid.
51 Ibid.
52 *Turner v. Safley*, 107 S. Ct. 2254 (1987).
53 *Jones v. North Carolina Prisoners' Union, Inc.* 433 U.S. 119 (1977).
54 *Procunier v. Martinez*, 416 U.S. 396 (1974).
55 Ibid.
56 One of the most significant roles played by *Procunier v. Martinez* was at the beginning of the "probable consequences" standard, which allowed prison officials to determine the potential peril that correspondence could produce. No longer was it necessary to show absolute danger or consequences after *Procunier v. Martinez*; the Court provided the prison administration leeway in determining the possible detriment and thus prevent it from occurring. However, while the courts were allowed to place limits on correspondence containing inmate complaints to retain order, the Justices indicated that the administration had not explained how a letter being sent to an individual outside the prison would cause such unrest. L. S. Branham, *The Law of Sentencing, Corrections, and Prisoners' Rights*, 5th ed. (St. Paul: West Group, 1998), 151. In *Procunier v. Martinez* it was decided that inmates had not been afforded due process in the handling of their mail. The Justices then established the following guidelines for prisons to follow when censoring the mail: (1) an inmate must be notified if his or her mail has been censored; (2) the inmate must be provided an opportunity to defend the correspondence; and (3) the final decision must be made by someone other than the initial reviewer.
57 *Jones v. North Carolina Prisoners' Union, Inc.*
58 *Turner v. Safley*, 482 U.S. 78 (1987).
59 Fred Cohen, "The Laws of Prisoners' Rights: An Overview," *Criminal Law Bulletin* (1997): 321–49.
60 According to Cohen, during recent history the Supreme Court has repeatedly found against prisoners' rights and has adopted a nonactivist approach to prisons. He also points out that by handling cases in such a manner the real or presumed expertise of the prison officials has been widely accepted as establishing the rule of thumb for order and security. There may not be any hierarchy of constitutional rights held by inmates.
61 Rabun C. Sanders, "Prisoners' First Amendment Rights within the Institution," master's thesis, Sam Houston State University, December 1970.
62 Jim Marcus (director, Texas Defender Service), interview by Ruth Massingill, Houston, Texas, August 15, 2005.
63 Ibid.
64 *Gibbs v. King*, 779 F.2d 1040, 1045 (5th Cir. 1986) cert. denied, 476 U.S.1117 (1986).
65 *Hadden v. Howard*, 713 F.2d 1003, 1006 (3d Cir. 1983).

[66] Ronald L. Kuby and William M. Kunstler, "Silencing the Oppressed: No Freedom of Speech for Those behind the Walls," 26 *Creighton Law Review* 1005 (1993).
[67] *Johnson v. Avery*, 393 U.S. 483 (1969).
[68] Marcus interview, 2005.
[69] George Coleman, *Criminal Justice Connections Newsletter,* September–October 2004.
[70] Marcus interview, 2005.
[71] Ibid.
[72] Derek Ian Hilla (TDCJ inmate and editor of the *Echo*), interview by Ruth Massingill, Huntsville, Texas, October 4, 2006.
[73] Ibid.
[74] Ibid.
[75] Lyndol Wilkinson (associate publisher of the *Echo*), interview by Ruth Massingill, Huntsville, Texas, September 22, 2006.
[76] Hilla interview, 2006.
[77] Wilkinson interview, 2006.
[78] Hilla interview, 2006.
[79] Ibid.
[80] Ibid.

Chapter Six
Communication Beyond the Walls

It's nice to know there is a voice heard deep inside those walls.
No matter how many doors they lock,
Well, they can't keep you away.
It's nice to know you're out there,
The Prison Show and Ray.
—Lyrics from the Ray Hill Prison Show song

When Time Stands Still

In prison the ephemeral commodity that is time loses meaning for those doing time as well as for their keepers, who sometimes say they too are serving life sentences, shackled by their "addiction to a paycheck."[1] Behind the walls time is both endless and all too finite. On the one hand, each day in prison is carefully divided and apportioned so there are no awkward leftover minutes. There is a time for every daily task and activity, forcing a sameness that tends to make the days flow seamlessly into weeks, months, years, without distinction.

For those under sentence of death, time hangs heavy while awaiting appeals to wind through the legal system. Once those petitions are exhausted, however, time is fleeting. For those who enter prison under Texas's new life-without-parole mandate the tedium of prison is forever—life means life. Even for those with hope of eventual freedom once their time is served, the challenge is finding ways to maintain a connection with the outside world in preparation for that day when the inmates rejoin the free.

Within the prison culture, inmates use their allotments of discretionary time in the limited ways open to them. They often choose to breach the prison walls by sending messages to family, friends, enemies, or advocates. Correspondence—via handwritten letters or websites constructed by outsiders—provides a means for inmates to rail at their captors, plead for assistance, or woo women into marriage.

Although media messages from outside the walls pass freely through barriers of brick and steel, the instant interactivity of modern technology eludes inmates, who cannot "surf the Net" or call in to radio talk shows.

The accelerated life that instant communication brings to the business and personal world of free citizens does not exist for the incarcerated. If time doesn't exactly stand still in prison, it certainly moves more deliberately, stoically unaffected by the busy, multitasking outside world.

Nevertheless, decisions from outside make a world of difference in the way the guards and the guarded spend their days. Legal verdicts designed to balance prisoners' human rights against security measures required by incarceration circumscribe the pattern of inmates' days. This continual tug-of-war between conflicting agendas—prisoner rights versus safety concerns—forms the basis of daily prison life.

Locked away, Forever and a Day

In the 2005 Texas legislative session, Senator Rodney Ellis of Houston presented a bill that would allow juries to sentence a convicted felon to life without parole in lieu of the death penalty.[2] Given the state's large population of death row inmates and public support for the death penalty, the bill represented a major shift in Texas's political environment. The proposed legislation seemed destined to die as the end of the session loomed, but when Ellis agreed to an amendment changing the official cause of death from "homicide" to "state-ordered execution" for inmates who were put to death, Governor Rick Perry immediately signed it into law, much to the surprise of many.

This signaled the first major, statewide modification in the penal system since wide-ranging prison reforms mandated by *Ruiz v. Estelle*.[3] When he heard that his bill had been approved, Ellis said, "For too long, the Texas criminal justice system has tilted toward the 'hang 'em high' mentality. This will take a little of the wild out of the Wild, Wild West."[4]

While detractors believe that allowing juries to choose life without parole will create disciplinary problems in the prisons and make the state appear soft on crime, Jim Marcus, administrator of the nonprofit Texas Defender Service, disagrees. "The argument that people serving life have no incentive to behave is exactly the opposite of what is true, based on Louisiana, which has life without parole. They report the lifers are some of the best behaved. Granted, if inmates are never going to get out, there is a series of privileges they want: jobs within the system and commissary access, to begin with."[5]

Marcus has harsh words for people who oppose the new law, saying,

"There is an assumption if we have life without parole, the number of inmates condemned to death will go down, so I assume if you want to kill people you would be against life without parole."[6]

> *"For too long, the Texas criminal justice system has tilted toward the 'hang 'em high' mentality. This will take a little of the wild out of the Wild, Wild West."*

From his research, Marcus concludes, "It's certainly going to change the way juries are instructed. I've probably interviewed between one and two hundred capital jurors in Texas personally, and I asked, 'When you were thinking about punishment, what did you think?' They all said, 'We thought he would get out in ten years.' But when I asked, 'What if you had known it would be thirty-five or forty years?' they said, 'Oh, we would have given him life.'" Marcus is unsure if Texans will embrace the option of life without parole, but he's pleased that jurors now know that "life means life. At least there will be truth in that part of the jury instructions. There's still a lot of very misleading—actually downright untruthful—instructions jurors are given by statute that mislead them and push them toward death, but at least that will be fixed."[7]

As Marcus notes, the psychological climate in Texas prisons is certain to be affected as more inmates enter under this new sentencing option. With a lifetime of incarceration in their future, those "lifers" may be more insistent in demanding access to modern communication technologies.

Letters from Prison: Sentimental, Profane, and Censored

One of the oldest means of communication—the handwritten letter—may be a virtual anachronism in the fast-track world of today, but it is still the most common way for prisoners to convey messages to those outside the walls. Unlike the confidentiality afforded personal mail in the free world, prisoners' correspondence is subject to close scrutiny. This is an area where First Amendment rights are substantially curtailed.

Both the Constitution (in its explicit protection of the right to privacy) and federal statutes[8] that outlaw tampering ensure citizens' right to confidential communication. In the 1967 case of *McCowan v. United States*,[9] the federal government confirmed protection of mail from the time it enters the postal system until it is delivered. Some argue that prisoners have the same privilege and prison personnel who open and read an inmate's mail without permission from the postmaster general, a court order, or the inmate violate federally protected rights and should be held liable.[10]

While Americans expect mail to be protected, federal cases in the District Court of Tennessee, *Jackson v. Norris*,[11] and in the Court of Appeals for the Seventh Circuit, *Gaines v. Lane*,[12] made it clear that prisoners in those jurisdictions should not expect privacy in their incoming (Jackson) or outgoing (Gaines) correspondence. Prison officials in several states contend that all mail must be reviewed to prevent derogatory remarks concerning prison personnel and other officials, thwart introduction of escape plans and codes, restrict inflammatory letters to news media, screen out pornography, prevent introduction of contraband, and ensure prison discipline and security.[13] To date, the courts have agreed when litigation arose.

In the cases of *Whalen v. Roe*,[14] *Houchin v. KQED, Inc*,[15] and *Bieregu v. Reno*[16] the courts examined a prisoner's right to correspond with his attorney under the constitutional right to petition for redress of a grievance. While the judiciary has uniformly upheld a prisoner's First Amendment right to free speech through confidential correspondence with attorneys and governmental officials, the protection is not extended to other correspondence.

Before any piece of mail leaves the prison, an employee reviews the contents, and documents the sender and receiver, then seals the envelope and forwards it to the U.S. Postal Service. To receive mail, inmates must sign an authorization to let prison officials open and examine their correspondence. While in *Palmigiano v. Travisono*[17] the courts found that this waiver was not voluntary if signed under coercion, threats to prohibit inmates from exchanging correspondence were not considered oppressive.

Employees in the Texas Department of Criminal Justice mailroom, mostly SHSU students, process thousands of pieces of mail daily. One of those readers is Amy Brush, a newly married graduate student who has lived in Huntsville all her life. Her father and brother both worked for the prison system, and she was "determined not to go there," she says, "but it was a job, and where else are you going to work in this town?"[18] There is plenty of work for the readers: for example, in a six-month period in 2003, the mailroom processed about 9.8 million pieces of outgoing correspondence and almost 10 million pieces of incoming mail at all 105 TDCJ units.[19]

Every day, Brush and other Huntsville mailroom workers remove the contents of every envelope, read and document each piece of correspondence, then either attach a denial code or seal it for mailing. Only letters to legal counsel are exempt from inspection. Due to the contents of some letters, readers "suit up" with gloves and keep bottles of disinfectant close at hand. According to Brush, many letters resemble what one would expect if reading college students' mail—questions about family members, pleas for money, and sentiments about missing loved ones. But some, she says, contain "drawings of dirty pictures, X-rated fantasies, scenarios from the inmate's dreams, and, of course, the standard bitch that it ain't like home."[20]

Although Brush finds these letters trying, another group she finds utterly disgusting. "Every day there are these guys who take a dump and then use the letter as toilet paper. When we see a letter addressed to Governor Perry or President Bush, it is saved until last because we know what we will find."[21] According to Brush, "If the letter contains things it shouldn't, we code it with a number 6, and send it back to the unit."[22] The often-used 6 code indicates an illegal substance, which can run the gamut of bodily functions. Brush laughs about a man who signed all correspondence with a drop of semen, saying, "It was just his special touch."[23] Inmates can receive reprimands, including being placed in lock-down, for such conduct.

Sometimes a prisoner chooses a more creative approach to protest his living conditions. Brush remembers opening a suspiciously heavy parcel and finding a peanut butter and jelly sandwich with a bite missing, along with a letter about the inhumanity of feeding inmates sandwiches daily. The prisoner wanted to file a grievance against the state, so wrapped the letter around the sandwich and sent it to the governor."[24]

As to how the parcel was coded, Brush, smiling, says, "The letter was fine; it is not illegal to send food through the mail, so we taped it up and dropped it in the box to be mailed. We are looking for illegal or harmful substances, and since the prison had provided the sandwich, it would have proven his point if we coded it as harmful. I am sure Governor Perry never saw it, but we gave [the prisoner] points for creativity."[25]

Brush's team only handles flat mail such as letters and magazines, but another group of readers sorts and catalogues parcels sent to inmates from family and friends on the outside. Items mailroom employees examine include food, clothes, watches, photo albums, and, once, a typewriter—all had to be returned to the senders.[26] A friendly rivalry exists between the two staffs for the most unusual contraband. "The box crew usually wins because there are only so many pictures of naked people [in letters]," Brush says, "and those don't hold a candle to the crazy packages people send."[27]

Still, the number of letters containing pictures the prison system deems inappropriate is staggering, according to Brush. The images are removed and the correspondence is coded with the number *8* and forwarded to the addressee. Unacceptable images include pictures of people or animals in graphic or irreverent poses (such as "flipping off the camera"), drug usage, criminal acts, and nudity in any form.[28]

> **"So, every day he would write her ten letters saying the same thing: 'I am coming after you.' I know letters are merely paper, but those were evil and they frightened me."**

A record of this correspondence is kept on file throughout the prisoner's stay. Occasionally, an inmate attempts contact with a victim or the victim's family, and the archives can be helpful in court cases and parole hearings. In one instance, the prisoner's file provided the mailroom staff with a reprieve from the monotony of their jobs. "One guy told the women he wrote he needed stuff, but that his family was too poor to buy it for him," Brush recalls. "He said it wasn't safe to send money into the prison because it might be stolen, so he would have them send money via his 'mother.' But his 'mother' was actually his wife. This guy had women from all over the world sending his wife money while he was in prison."[29]

Another incident, not as humorous, changes Brush's demeanor completely. "A convicted serial killer decided the only reason he got caught was an author had written a book about him. So, every day he would write her ten letters saying the same thing: 'I am coming after you.' Of course, he was never going to get out, but if she got the letters it would have scared her to death. We would just tag them and send them back. But his writing was perfect; everything was in blocks as if typewritten. The paper was always the same size and always perfectly white—not a smudge on it—and his grammar was perfect. I know letters are merely paper, but those were evil and they frightened me."[30]

Free Americans have the choice of purchasing magazines and books from newsstands or bookstores or through the mail, but prisoners' subscriptions and books are closely monitored to intercept material deemed unsuitable. Typically, the mailroom might review as many as 4,500 publications over the course of a year to determine if they should be denied under agency rules that outlaw sexually explicit images.[31] In *Bell v. Wolfish*[32] the Supreme Court determined that the difficulty of detecting contraband required that hard- or softbound reading materials must be mailed directly from publishers or distributors. Ten years later, in *Thornburgh v. Abbott*,[33] the Court upheld the decision to exclude entire publications that contained one censorable passage or image. Relying on the standards established in *Turner v. Safley*,[34] the Court decided that the amount of time required for officials to extract censored materials would be overwhelming.

Additionally, the Court felt that prisoners' negative reactions to publications with missing pages or images would endanger the civility of the prison environment.[35] According to Brush, "Before I started working here, [readers] went through each magazine and cut out offensive pictures... less of the magazines were being sent to the inmates than what was thrown in the trash. This made a lot of people angry because they personally paid for the magazines. Today, it is the mailroom's job to make sure the magazines come in plastic wrap from the company and not from someone's home. We also verify they are on the approved subscription list. Another office verifies the content is acceptable."[36]

To determine the structure needed for inmates' rehabilitation and prison security, the prison administration relied on federal guidelines when faced with the cases of *Wagner v. Thomas*[37] and *Espinoza v. Wilson*.[38] *Wagner*, a case out of Dallas, Texas, approved a ban on all publications depicting "nudity, pandering to sexual interest or advocating racial prejudice" unless approved by the warden. Ronald Kuby and William Kunstler reported in *Prison Legal News* that the warden testified that magazines such as *Playboy* and *Penthouse* should be banned, but he was unsure about the *National Enquirer* or *Rolling Stone* because he was "not familiar with them."[39] The warden said he was "no ignorant peckerwood and could determine what materials with nudie photographs might cause prisoners to fight over the magazines."[40]

There were no recorded incidents of fights breaking out over magazines with nude photographs, yet the courts still upheld the ban.[41] Supporters praise the prisons' attempt to clean up their reputation with the pornography ban, while detractors claim that the law creates a hypocrites' prison. Due to legal appeals, plus time to notify inmates of the ban, it was not until June 2005 that the full impact of the Court's decision became apparent. Now fully in place, the ban may cause more uprisings.

Wanda Mayes, who teaches for the Windham School District, fears that the *Wagner* decision could shatter prison security. "They [the inmates] are raising hell about losing their 'release,' as they call it," she says. "I think it is the worst move the prisons could have made, and it really concerns me. I have already heard the men make comments about the female guards, so I am a bit uneasy. I had one guy write a paper about how he fantasized about the female guards, and it was pretty graphic. I really hope they change that rule quickly or it could get bad."[42]

The warden said he was "no ignorant peckerwood and could determine what materials with nudie photographs might cause prisoners to fight over the magazines."

In the second case, *Espinoza v. Wilson*,[43] the federal district court for the northern district of Texas allowed a ban on gay rights publications, including the *Advocate*. The court found such publications to be a security risk and a detriment to rehabilitation efforts. In their article "Silencing the Oppressed: No Freedom of Speech for Those behind the Walls," Ronald Kuby and William Kunstler explain that the stated justification was that "specific publications which advocated or legitimized a homosexual lifestyle should be barred because...prisoners possessing such materials might suffer physical assaults."[44] The wardens contended that "tolerating a homosexual lifestyle could lead to more homosexuality, which would threaten the security of the prison."[45]

Tuning in to the Airwaves

Some states permit private television sets in cells, but Texas is not among them. Typically, each unit has one color TV for prisoners. TDCJ limits the channels allowed and follows a strict viewing policy—the meanest inmate gets to select the channel, and the others watch without complaint.

A common public misconception is that Texas inmates have television sets in their cells. "I know people think they have TVs, but they don't," Mayes remarks. "There is usually one TV at the end of the run, and I think it stays on sports most of the time, because my students never know any news but they can tell you what is happening in every sport."[46]

Prisoners who can afford the purchase are allowed to keep one AM/FM radio in their cell. For many prisoners these radios are the only connection to the outside world. In the 1990s National Pubic Radio contracted with

Mumia Abu-Jamal, an inmate on New York's death row, for a live weekly radio broadcast from his cell about the hard-hitting reality of life on death row. Mumia was an award-winning journalist prior to his conviction for killing a NYC police officer.[47]

In one episode, Mumia mimicked the successful *Saturday Night Live* format: "Perhaps we can shrug off and shed some of the dangerous myths laid on our minds like a second skin—such as the right to a fair trial even. They're not rights—they're privileges of the powerful and rich. Don't expect the media network to tell you; they can't because of the incestuousness with government and big business, but I can. Even if I must do so from the valley of the shadow of death, I WILL. Live From Death Row, this is Mumia Abu-Jamal."[48]

> *"Death row inmates are not 'doing time.' "Freedom does not shine at the end of the tunnel. Rather the end of the tunnel brings extinction. Thus, for many here, there is no hope."*

After intense political pressure on NPR, the contract was canceled for "editorial reasons." The commentaries were later published in book form. In one notable commentary, Mumia pointed out, "New York prisons permit inmates to have TVs, which numb the mind, but not typewriters, which could be tools for legal liberations. Death row inmates are not 'doing time,'" Mumia said. "Freedom does not shine at the end of the tunnel. Rather the end of the tunnel brings extinction. Thus, for many here, there is no hope."[49]

A much less controversial prison radio show blankets the airwaves in southeast Texas every Friday night. At promptly 9 P.M. listeners tune in to a familiar theme song and the standard greeting from the show's creator and host, Ray Hill: "Holler down the pipe chase and rattle them bars, 'cause we're gonna do a Prison Show."[50] Broadcast from Houston's Pacifica station KPFT, which Hill claims stands for "Keeping Prison Families Together," the show offers TDCJ prisoners and their families an opportunity to connect.

Since Texas does not allow inmates access to the Internet and permits only one phone call every ninety days, the show is a chance for inmates to hear the voices of their families and friends. During the first hour of the show, Hill, an ex-con who did time in a Huntsville unit in the 1970s, reports on prison issues and interviews guests—including parole board officers, wardens, substance abuse counselors, and criminal defense attorneys. "I teach people how to survive," Hill says. "Prisons are a separate culture that has been evolving for eons."[51] The second hour of Hill's show gives family and friends an opportunity to speak to their loved ones.[52]

Originally a radio talk show about prison politics and ways to help inmates stay straight after they were released, the show had a modest following. One Friday night a woman called from the roadside. She had saved her money for a long time to visit her son in prison, but she had had an accident on the way and could not get there in time for visiting hours. She knew her son listened to Hill's show, so she asked if she could tell him she loved him. Hill said, "Ma'am, he's listening, so why don't you go ahead and tell him yourself?" Immediately, the call-in lines lit up, and the show has created a community on both sides of the walls ever since.[53]

> *"If you get a call, it's like hitting the jackpot. For just a split second you are with them. You are out in the world. And if you don't get lucky, you listen anyway because even when you hear a black mama or wife saying how much they love and miss someone, they aren't black anymore, they are just human. We are all just human."*

A 2002 *Mother Jones* article points out that not all prisoners welcome the show. Inmate Richard "Cowboy" Cain observes, "Most of us don't like pain, which is why we're here. When we go to prison we are separated from all the problems of family and financial responsibility, then you've got this fool on the radio wanting to bring that back to us. It ain't for me."[54]

But this view is not held by many. Jon Buice, serving time for murder, describes the impact of the show on inmates: "If you get a call, it's like hitting the jackpot. For just a split second you are with them. You are out in the world. And if you don't get lucky, you listen anyway because even when you hear a black mama or wife saying how much they love and miss someone, they aren't black anymore, they are just human. We are all just human."[55]

Prison City Close-Up

On the Air: "The Shout-out Show"

A smaller radio station, KDOL 96.1 in Livingston, Texas, also breaks through the prison walls. Airing Sunday afternoons from 2 until 7 P.M., "The Shout-out Show" provides family members, friends, and offenders at the Polunsky unit a radio connection.

KDOL, a community radio station started by Jim and Joy Wolf in 2003, is operated out of the Wolfs' home in downtown Livingston. The concept for the show began when the Wolfs started corresponding with death row offender Greg Summers, a radio listener who requested they play *Irish Blessings*.[56] Other death row inmates began to send in song requests too. In May 2005 KDOL went online via web radio and the Sunday "Shout-out Show" for prisoners at the Polunsky unit quickly grew from a simple request show to a channel of communication for offenders and their loved ones.

Inside, prisoners started telling each other about the show. Offenders cannot call in to give a live shout-out or greeting, so they mail them in each week.[57] The Wolfs receive between thirty-five and sixty letters a week from prisoners containing everything from song requests and thank-you messages to expressions of love and admiration for family and friends.

In addition, the Wolfs also receive nearly 250 requests and shout-outs from inmates' families and friends each week. Sorting through all the letters and emails takes between sixty and seventy hours a week. The Wolfs also have to be careful not to read offender-to-offender correspondence on the air. When an inmate housed in Huntsville wanted a letter read to his son on death row in Livingston, the correspondence was illegal because of laws prohibiting offender-to-offender communication.

KDOL does a special show for those scheduled to die. Starting at 7 on the evening of the execution, the show allows family and friends to call in with words of support for the inmate. Throughout the show, KDOL plays requested songs. This special show started in May 2005 with Richard Cartwright's execution, and it has been continued for every execution since. For most of those shows, family and friends come to the studio.

As a community-based radio station, KDOL relies on donations to stay on the air. Offenders' friends and family members send money to support the station. Inmates at the Polunsky unit also send donations in the only form of currency they are allowed—postage stamps. ✪

Attracting Foreign Aid

In his tenure as governor of Texas and during his first run for the presidency, George W. Bush was well known for his tough-on-crime stance. The United States, along with China, Iran, and Vietnam, leads the world in sanctioned executions.[58] Some international citizens consider the U.S. endorsement of capital punishment to be the ultimate human rights violation. One of the largest organizations to protest the death penalty is the Canadian Coalition against the Death Penalty, which dubbed George W. Bush the "Texecutioner" and Governor Rick Perry "lil Texecutioner" for their roles in carrying out executions in Texas.[59] The organization sponsors protest rallies and supports a website that deplores what it terms inhumane treatment of prison inmates.

Some opponents take a personal role to combat capital punishment. Marcus, of the Texas Defender Service, acknowledges that there are a lot of foreigners performing volunteer work in his office.[60] He thinks that many have a difficult time understanding the U.S. legal system. In many countries if evidence were found that a prisoner was innocent, according to Marcus, one could bring that information to court and get a decision. "They don't create all these procedural barriers to meaningful review."[61]

Even American citizens do not fully understand how our criminal appeal system works, Marcus says. "If you walked into federal court with incontrovertible proof of innocence, chances are you would still lose because innocence is not a claim in habeas. In fact, there was a Supreme Court case where Texas took the position that innocence is irrelevant—and won! As long as someone has a constitutionally fair trial, it is okay to execute him even if he is innocent."[62]

Amnesty International is perhaps the most widely recognized organization opposing the death penalty. Its members range from Hollywood stars to local churchgoers. To Amnesty International, capital punishment is the ultimate denial of human rights, and executions are "premeditated and cold-blooded killings by the state in the name of justice."[63] According to Amnesty International, the death penalty violates the right to life as proclaimed in the Universal Declaration of Human Rights, and is a cruel, inhuman, and degrading punishment.

The Lamp of Hope Project (LHP), founded in 1991, is one of Amnesty International's better-known projects. LHP's mission is to prove the death penalty "a counter productive response to the problems of crime punishment."[64] Prison inmates governed the LHP until 1999, when prisoners were denied access to the Internet. The program's web page supports its goal of "bringing hope to those who believe in life"[65] by addressing victims' rights and the concerns of incarcerated individuals' family members, especially those on death row. It hopes to stop the cycle of violence found in many families with a loved one in prison by breaking the stereotypical image of inmates on death row.[66]

Other global organizations from Europe to Latin America work to increase international understanding and reach out to the U.S. penal system population. Every year thousands of international visitors come to the United States as volunteers. They assist with legal paperwork, visit incarcerated pen pals, and sometimes even marry prisoners.

Many travel to the Polunsky unit to visit condemned convicts, often staying overnight at the nearby Blue Shelter, a guesthouse for friends and family of death row inmates. Owner Christa Haber is a German national with a specialization in youth welfare and psychology. Her main goal is to furnish support to death row inmates and their families.[67]

The organization Lifespark also fights against the death penalty. Begun in 1997 by Swiss banker Evelyne Giordani, Lifespark's 250 members visit and correspond with death row inmates in Texas and across the United States. Visitors who reside more than three hundred miles away are allowed four hours with prisoners, while others are granted a maximum of two hours.[68]

Unlike the limitations on personal visits, prisoners may have as many pen pals as they wish. Douglass Roberts has written thousands of letters since arriving on death row, and he says, "You can sit inside these walls and go insane, or you can get outside through the mail."[69] Some see the prisoners' outreach as entirely self-serving. A guard opines, "The international visitors are gullible Europeans who romanticize the prisoners they write. The prisoners are out for anything they can get—attention, money, or legal help."[70]

Websites for Friends, Fun, and Romance

The world comes to Texas prisoners through the persuasive powers of the Internet even though the incarcerated do not have direct access to the web. To get online, TDCJ inmates need the outside help of an advocacy group or a paid host website, but even with those barriers, prisoners have become very adept at using electronic media.

In his book *About Prison* Michael Santos quotes a prisoner's view of how the web can assist inmates in their return to society: "With the help of my supporters, I have published information on a personal web site. This has provided not just a tool to connect with the world but has proven to be extremely therapeutic. As a long-term prisoner, I find it extremely important to initiate contacts with law-abiding citizens. If I didn't reach outside, my associations would be limited to the felons with whom I'm confined. Such relationships can't be conducive to leading a law-abiding life upon my release."[71]

The number of Internet sites designed to link prisoners with pen pals is multiplying since the service is much in demand.

Websites associated with the penal system can be divided into three categories: blogs, which tell the stories of life in prison to the general public; forums, which offer support and information for family and friends of the convicted; and personal web pages, which connect inmates with pen pals outside the prison. The number of Internet sites designed to link prisoners with pen pals is multiplying since the service is much in demand. The sites commonly feature preincarceration pictures and describe hobbies, interests, goals, and the type of person with whom the inmate wishes to correspond. Crime details are not widely advertised or easily located on inmates' websites. One Texas inmate's page says, "Looking for a female Christian friend to discuss spiritual understanding, fine art and good music," but the TDCJ website for inmates on death row told another story about that prisoner—a man convicted of hacking a pastor and his wife to death with a machete in the church sanctuary.

Responses to inmate web pages must be printed out and mailed to the prisoner, which most companies do for an additional fee. To encourage her students to form friendships in the free population, Mayes has them write to their pen pals. "Most are happy to do it because if they turn it in as an assignment, I grade it, they make the corrections, and the pen pals think they are good writers. The inmates complain about not having anything to read, and the pen pal letters provide that."[72]

There are some benefits for the pen pals as well. Inmates' correspondents generally fall into three groups. The first, mostly European women, help inmates with their legal cases, and in return get a copy of the inmate's birth certificate, thus clearing a path for the women to obtain U.S. visas. The inmates see this as an equal tradeoff.

The second group includes the softhearted and naïve, which makes them easy targets. Mayes tells how a prisoner deceived a student at a small Texas community college. "These men make a killing from softhearted women. They will write multiple women, telling them how wonderful they are and in return the women send them every penny they have. One girl I was teaching had a baby. She was working two jobs—one to support her and the child, and the other to send money to her pen pal inmate who was going to marry her when he got out. She sent more money to him than she kept to live on, and when he got out he didn't even tell her!"[73]

Brush reports that while working in the mailroom she sees many letters to female pen pals. "The pen pal letters are the worst," she says. "You read the same thing over and over again. Several inmates use carbon paper and then do something unique to each person's name. They want money; they need help; they just want to talk; they are falling in love. Those women are crazy because they are being used big time."[74]

Convicts who are thinking ahead want outside contacts to impress the parole board, Brush explains. "One of the things a parole board wants to know is if a support network is waiting on the outside to help the inmates matriculate back into society, and sure they do—the friends they have been writing the past several years."[75]

Women are not the only victims of pen-pal fraud, Brush continues.

> One time, this guy wrote the warden because he had fallen in love with two female prisoners. They told him they were framed by their ex-boyfriends who had instructed them to sit in the car while they went inside to pay for gas. Supposedly, the boyfriends burglarized the store, and the two women were in the wrong place at the wrong time. He wanted to know what he could do to help and was willing to hire the best lawyers to help get these women off. Well, we looked up the women, and they had both been convicted of homicide and armed robbery and neither file listed a male accomplice.[76]

Inmates dub the third category of pen pals "welfares." This group corresponds with inmates who have been disowned by their families and friends, Mayes says. "I had one guy tell me his pen pal was the only family he had, and he wanted someone to care if he died."[77] Sometimes these convicts were once the focus of high-profile cases. For example, famous convicted murderers John Wayne Gacy, Ted Bundy, Erik and Lyle Menendez, and even Kenneth Bianch (the Hillside Strangler) all developed long-term, committed relationships with pen pals.

Prison City Close-Up

Writing Letters:
My Prison Pal

In the fall of 2004, as part of a research assignment, I decided to write to a young man who was sentenced to die. Prior to January 2004, I was pro–capital punishment. But since becoming a pen pal with a death row inmate, I have embarked on a remarkable journey that has taught me a lot about true friendship, forgiveness, and capital punishment in Texas.

As I began my research, I found the TDCJ website listing information about inmates on death row. Surprisingly, I found an inmate with my birthday, with one exception: he was two years younger than me. Since I was only twenty-two, realizing there was someone so young on death row really bothered me. We started out writing a letter a week, but now it is strange if we do not correspond three or four times a week because he is no longer just a pen pal. He is a friend.

In April 2005 I met my pen pal for the first time. The visit was a unique experience. I had never been in a prison before, and I was nervous. Walking through the metal detector, I immediately noticed a sign that did not help my fears. It said, "No hostages exit through this gate." Seeing that, I thought to myself, 'What are you doing?'"

Once he arrived and we began to talk, my nerves calmed. I was not visiting a stranger; I was visiting a friend I had already grown to know through his letters. He was so easy to talk to, and the two hours flew by. When I got up to leave, my pen pal put his hand up to the glass, and I reciprocated the gesture. I really wanted to give him a hug, but contact visits are not allowed on death row, so touching the glass had to suffice.

Since that first visit, I have been to see my pen pal nearly every week, only missing when I had final exams or when others on his list came to visit. Through this process I have realized, from the outside looking in, that it is hard for people to understand that prisoners are not always the cruel, evil, heartless individuals the media portray. Many are young people whose bad choices led to the death of another human being. It is not my place to judge my friend for his past; instead, I choose to accept him for the person he has become.

Texas's state motto is "Friendship," and it can be found almost anywhere in the state, even on death row. ✪

—Tina Baiter, 2005 Sam Houston State University graduate

Marriage behind Bars

For those who form long-term bonds with convicts on death row it is difficult to defend their choice of romantic partners to friends, family, and other critics. Much like getting married in the free population, it takes time, patience, and resources to wed an inmate. "Jennifer" recently became engaged to a man on death row and understands the pain and joy of being in a relationship with an inmate. "We really didn't want to get married while he is in," she says, "but things are not going our way, and they set his execution date in less than a year, so we agreed to go ahead and get married. He believes if we are joined together by marriage, then when I pass on, we will be together for all eternity, and he will be able to find me again."[78]

Jennifer's relationship began like many in the free world: "We began writing each other letters and just fell in love. He was getting a divorce, and I was scared she wouldn't sign the papers, but she did. So now I am waiting for TDCJ to put me on his visitation list. His mother doesn't approve because she is afraid I will take all the visitation times. She has already told me I will get one weekend a month, and the rest are hers. But that is okay as long as we have a chance to be together."[79]

Texas allows contact visits only to trusties, so most prison marriages are by proxy, with a close friend or family member standing in for the incarcerated party.

Texas allows contact visits only to trusties, so most prison marriages are by proxy, with a close friend or family member standing in for the incarcerated party. According to Jim Brazzil, retired TDCJ prison chaplain, TDCJ does not require premarriage counseling for the offender and his future bride, but some guidance is offered. For example, "Nina" has been married to three death row inmates. Each time she was asked why she wanted to marry an inmate. "With my first husband, I was surprised by the question and said something like, ''cause I love him,'" Nina says, "and of course they rolled their eyes thinking there is no way this woman knows what she is getting herself into.

"The second time I was prepared and said 'we both had a desire to make a lifelong commitment to each other and a marriage ceremony would allow us to affirm before each other and God the oaths we have already taken in spirit.' I am sure it took them a while to figure that one out. This last time, my sarcastic nature got the best of me, and I responded, 'the batteries in my vibrator need to be replaced, and I want to be in a blessed marriage before I go to Wal-Mart for another twelve pack.'" The guard closed his book, reminded me I would need a copy of my fiancé's birth certificate and a signed proxy for the marriage to be legal and left the room."[80]

Although she wasn't asked why she wanted to marry an inmate, Jennifer says "they asked him [her future husband] why he was making me marry him, and he said, 'She's not the prisoner—she's the one who is making the choice to marry me.'"[81]

> *"I have no illusions about my looks; I am below average, and he is so good looking. I ask myself, 'what is he doing with someone like me?'"*

"Lonnie," a TDCJ assistant warden who wants to remain anonymous, explains, "We are just trying to make sure there are no misconceptions or unreasonable expectations. Usually people say they want to get married because they love each other, but even when both people are free, love ain't enough to put food on the table and a roof over your head. It may be a long time before they can be together, so we want her to have the financial and emotional resources to provide for herself."[82]

The prison officials' words of caution usually fall on deaf ears. "Most women who decide to marry a man in prison have their minds already made up," Nina points out, "so this so-called 'marriage enrichment' talk isn't going to change much. The women may live to regret it somewhere down the line, but so will millions of other women who marry men who are not incarcerated."[83]

Even the euphoric feeling of being in love cannot erase all the concerns and fears of being engaged to a prison inmate. Jennifer voices her apprehension about meeting her fiancé and especially about greeting his mother, "The scariest thought for me is meeting them face to face. His ex-wife, girlfriends and even his mom are so gorgeous and now there is me. I have no illusions about my looks; I am below average, and he is so good looking. I ask myself, 'what is he doing with someone like me?'"[84] Since the relationship between Jennifer and her future husband developed by correspondence, the two have only exchanged photos.

Jennifer is very anxious about their first meeting:

> I am really worried he will see the plain Jane in person and decide not to marry me. Pictures don't show the real you. I was a nobody in a plain old wrapper. He keeps telling me it isn't what is on the outside that counts. I've never had any man tell me that. He says he doesn't feel handsome because he was always an outsider and now society has said he cannot be rehabilitated and has locked him away, which proves he is useless. I guess it takes a social outcast to understand and love another social outcast.[85]

Nina attempts to lighten Jennifer's mood by instructing her on the proper retort if the first meeting does not work out as well as hoped. "Honey, you tell that man, 'Look at me. Take a *good* look at me. Now do you think I am so nasty and undesirable that I thought I'd have to marry a man in *prison* just to find a husband?'[86] If he doesn't start groveling, then you walk your little butt right out that door."

Despite her levity, Nina understands Jennifer's fear:

> Everyone has her own journey, and each person marries for her own reasons or needs. Hell, for all I know, the need to be in a relationship with a man who is unavailable can be a good thing for a particular woman. Perhaps she is healing from something that would be difficult if not impossible to get over if she were in a physical relationship. I know it was important for me because I had a ton of healing to do, and my prison marriages have given me the security I've needed to face some demons of my own. Some say I am wrong to live my life this way, but this is my life's journey and it is important for me to follow my own path and learn whatever the creator has given me the opportunity to learn.[87]

For brides of death row inmates, "'til death us do part" takes on an ominous tone. The newly engaged Jennifer worries, "I hope we can find counseling to help us make it through the rough times. The other possibility is one I try not to think about, but in the back of my mind I know it can happen. He is on death row; he could be executed.

"Do I really want to be a widow? I believe in my heart of hearts he will come home to me, but as we know, justice isn't only deaf but blind and dumb, too. I feel our love is strong enough to get us through all this, even if the worst possible scenario happens. I made a promise to him and I will not break it."[88]

Nina agrees. "No, you do not want to be a widow. I have been twice—thanks to the great state of Texas, and there is the possibility of a third—but if you truly love the man, it won't hurt any more or less with or without the marriage certificate. Love doesn't care about paperwork."[89]

Everyone deals with the harsh realities in her own way. The widow of a recently executed inmate took her husband's ashes and had diamonds made from his remains. She said, "You are going home with me forever,"[90] and she meant it, literally.

The Feeling That Never Goes Away

I'll talk to you about that, but I don't want to talk to you on the record....Turn that damn thing off! ...Sorry, I would love to talk to you but I need this job.... Please do not use my real name; you don't understand how many people can get hurt.

Many people who rely on TDCJ for their livelihoods are reluctant to speak on the record, despite constitutional protection. Only after a guarantee of anonymity did they agree to share their thoughts and feelings about life in a prison company town. An employee in a TDCJ administrative office says vehemently, "The work is monotonous and repetitive and you know there are better ways to do things, but you do not dare question anything because you will be fired or, worse yet, made a guard. Most people who work here hate it. They just accept it because it is a job, and where else are you going to find a job in this town?"[91]

Another TDCJ employee explains why it is more difficult to get fellow workers to talk than it is prisoners: "You are having a problem getting people to agree to do interviews because they will be fired if they say how they really feel and how it really is up there and everyone knows it. Say something negative, and you are gone on an 'action not becoming of a State employee' charge and we need these jobs."[92]

Equally adamant regarding anonymity, a civic leader who frequently teaches at Sam Houston State University shares his experiences since moving to Huntsville. "I feel sorry for everyone involved: the people who work there, the inmates, and the families," he says.

"It is much worse than it needs to be, and it is getting worse. Other states have prisoners who have done things just as bad, but the prisons are not nearly like it is here. TDCJ seems to view these adults as children who were 'bad' and need to do hard time. There is fear if you give an inch, then people will complain. Politicians don't want that because they might not get reelected."

After a moment to reflect, he continues,

What most people do not understand is what goes on in the prisons does not stay in the prisons; it goes home with every guard, every worker. So now you've got wives and children who are regularly having the hell beat out of them—just look at the domestic abuse rate of Huntsville if you need statistical proof. I think, and I believe other psychologists would agree, the reason the guards are so horrible to everyone is because of what they are exposed to daily. They are told if they show a moment of weakness, then it could all be over. To survive, they just get hard and mean. SHSU feels the effects. The students who are guards bring that personality into the classroom. Most of the teachers do not dare show any emotion because they will be eaten alive. Since I began working here, I have heard words I never dreamed of hearing in a university. I have seen students scream and threaten teachers. It is scary, and it doesn't have to be that way.[93]

When you go inside the prison it is a minefield of mistakes to be made... especially if you are not strong, wise, and experienced.
—Lyndol Wilkinson, associate publisher, TDCJ newspaper the *Echo*

Prison City Close-Up

A Primer:
The ABCs of Prison Marriage

A strong sense of humor—however dark or macabre—is essential for those who are married to death row inmates. The following combines humor from a web blog created by women with loved ones on death row and information from the TDCJ prisoner handbook.

You might be the fiancée of an inmate if...

- *You make new friends and wonder what their guy is in for.*

Each year thousands of Texas couples say "I do" and promise to love and honor for a lifetime. But, if the wedding announcement says the names of all guests must appear on a visitation list, then it is certain one member of the couple is incarcerated in a state prison unit.

- *You come to a door and wait to be "buzzed" in.*

Regardless of its location, the first step to getting married in a TDCJ prison unit is for the incarcerated member of the couple to request a marriage packet from the prison chaplain, which explains the logistics of getting married in a penal facility.

- *You have separated your clothes into two categories, prison wear and not acceptable.*

For security reasons, most prisons do not allow a bride to wear a formal wedding gown. Instead, it is recommended that she choose a practical outfit that follows the prison guidelines for clothing—no open-toed shoes or cleavage-baring garments. The groom, if present, will be dressed in his finest TDCJ-issued jumpsuit. No exceptions.

- *Your new purse is soft plastic, see through, and only large enough to carry a roll of quarters and one key to your car.*

Rings are an important symbol of love and dedication for anyone who has recently become engaged. Prisons only allow plain gold or silver bands with a price limit of one hundred dollars.

- *Your photo album is full of Polaroids and he is wearing the same outfit in each shot.*

Getting married in prison allows the couple to save money on flowers since none are allowed. The couple won't need a big budget for the photographer—most prisons only allow a limited number of Polaroid shots. Some units allow the bride to bring a disposable camera.

• *You think it is normal for his friends to have interesting names like Trigger, Shooter, Spanky, and Diablo.*

Most prisons allow witnesses to stand up for the bride and groom as long as their names appear on the inmate's visitation list. Death row inmates are not allowed more than one visitor at a time, so most marriages are conducted off the premises with a double standing in for the groom. Under no circumstances will another inmate be allowed to participate in the wedding party.

• *Your postal carrier delivers a lot of letters from a man with numbers for a last name.*

Rather than rushing off for a romantic getaway after the ceremony, the couple married in a prison unit is destined to spend the wedding night apart. A website dedicated to providing support to family and friends of the incarcerated recommends that the newlywed on the outside plan a fun evening with close friends. On the site's discussion board, several women have posted recommendations on how to spend the wedding night.

One participant wrote that she went home, mowed the lawn and cooked a steak, while another took her best girlfriend on a cruise that had been planned for her and her new husband. Another woman described how her family and friends threw a large wedding reception, complete with a three-tiered cake decorated with a groom in an orange jumpsuit surrounded by police cars instead of flowers. ✪

—Debbi Hatton

Notes

[1] Ray Hill, conversation with Ruth Massingill, August 28, 2006.
[2] Legislative Reference Library of Texas, SB 60—79th Legislative Regular Session. Available at: http://www.capitol.state.tx.us/tlo/79R/billtext/SB00060F.htm.
[3] *Ruiz v. Estelle*, 503 F.Supp. 1265 (S.D. Tex. 1980), *rev'd in part*, 679 F.2d 1115 (5th Cir. 1992), *modified in part*, 688 F.2d 266 (5th Cir. 1982), cert. denied, 103 S.Ct. 1438 (1983).
[4] Mike Tolson, "A 'Vicious' Generation Brought Fear, Swift Justice," *Houston Chronicle*, March 2, 2005.
[5] Jim Marcus (director, Texas Defender Service), interview by Ruth Massingill, Houston, Texas, August 15, 2005.
[6] Ibid.
[7] Ibid.
[8] 39 U.S.C. § 3623 (d) 1970 provides: "No letter of the first class of domestic origin shall be opened except under authority of a search warrant authorized by law, or by an officer or employee of the Postal Service for the sole purpose of determining an address at which the letter can be delivered, or pursuant to the authorization of the addressee." Title 18 of the United States Code provides criminal penalties for interference with the mail. Section 1701 prohibits the obstruction of the mail and provides criminal penalties for anyone who obstructs or retards the transmission of mailed matter from the time it is deposited in the mail, or placed in a place designated by law, up to the time the mail is delivered to the person to whom it is addressed. Section 1702 makes it a crime for anyone to take "any letter which has been in any post office or authorized depository, or in the custody of any letter or mail carrier, before it has been delivered to the person to whom it was directed, with design to open or destroy the same."
[9] *McCowan v. United States*, 376 F.2d 122 (9th Cir. 197), cert. denied, 389 U.S. 839 (1967).
[10] Rockwall Bullard, "Prisoners' Rights to Unrestricted Use of the Mail," *New England Journal on Prison Law* (1974): 80–102.
[11] *Jackson v. Norris*, 748 F. Supp. 570, 573 (M.D. Tenn 1990), aff'd, 928 F2d 1132 (6th Cir. 1991).
[12] *Gaines v. Lane*, 790 F.2d 1299, 1304 (7th Cir. 1986).
[13] *Nolan v. Fitzpatrick*, 326 F. Supp. 209 (D. Mass. 1971); *Palmigiano v. Travisono*, 317 F. Supp. 776 (D.R.I. 1970).
[14] *Whalen v. Roe*, 429 U.S. 589 (1997).
[15] *Houchin v. KQED, Inc.*, 438 U.S. 1 (1978).
[16] *Bieregu v. Reno*, 59 F.3d 1445 (3d Cir. 1995).
[17] *Palmigiano v. Travisono*, 317 F. Supp. 209 (D.R.I. 1970).
[18] Amy Brush (TDCJ employee), interview by Debbi Hatton, Huntsville, Texas, July 6, 2005.
[19] "TDCJ Approves Changes to Inmates' Correspondence Policies," Media Advisory, April 2, 2004.
[20] Ibid.
[21] Ibid.
[22] Ibid.
[23] Ibid.
[23] Ibid.
[24] Ibid.
[25] Brush interview, 2005.
[26] Jorge Renaud, *Behind the Walls: A Guide for Families and Friends of Texas Prison Inmates* (Denton: University of North Texas Press, 2002).
[27] Brush interview, 2005.
[28] Renaud.
[29] Ibid.

[30] Ibid.
[31] "TDCJ Approves Changes..."
[32] *Bell v. Wolfish*, 441 U.S. 520, 552 (1979).
[33] *Thornburgh v. Abbott*, 490 U.S. 401 (1989).
[34] *Turner v. Safley*, 482 U.S. (1987).
[35] Ibid.
[36] Brush interview, 2005.
[37] *Wagner v. Thomas*, 608 F. Supp. 1095, 1097 (N.D. Tex. 1985).
[38] *Espinoza v. Wilson*, 814 F.2d 1093, 1095 Cir. (1987).
[39] Ronald Kuby and William Kunstler, "Silencing the Oppressed: No Freedom of Speech for Those behind the Walls," *Prison Legal News*, 1995. Available at: http://www.prisonlegalnews.org/Members/issues/pln_1995/9505/02art95b.htm.
[40] Ibid.
[41] Ibid.
[42] Wanda Mayes (teacher, Windham School District), interview by Debbi Hatton, Athens, Texas, July 2, 2005.
[43] *Espinoza v. Wilson*.
[44] Kuby and Kunstler.
[45] Ibid.
[46] Mayes interview, 2005.
[47] Mumia Abu-Jamal, "Live from Death Row," Review by David Gilbert, *Prison Legal News*. (1995). Available at: http://www.prisonlegalnews.org/Members/issues/pln_1995/9509/9509_04c.htm.
[48] Ibid.
[49] Ibid.
[50] Mark Frazier, "Jailhouse Talk," *Mother Jones*, November–December 2002. Available at: http://www.motherjones.com/news/feature/2002/11/ma_146_01.html.
[51] Ray Hill, 2006.
[52] Ibid.
[53] Ibid.
[54] Ibid.
[55] Ibid.
[56] Joy Wolf (local radio station owner), interview by Tina Baiter, Livingston, Texas, August 8, 2005.
[57] Ibid.
[58] Amnesty International—USA, Death Penalty Information Center, Report, 2004. Available at: http://www.amnestyusa.org.
[59] Dave Parkinson, "President George W. Bush: 155 Homicides." Available at: http://www.ccadp.org/serialpresident.htm
[60] Marcus interview, 2005.
[61] Ibid.
[62] Ibid.
[63] Amnesty International.
[64] Karen Sebung, Lamp of Hope Project. Available at: http://www.lampofhope.org.
[65] Ibid.
[66] Ibid.
[67] Christa Haber, Show Life Texas. Available at: http://showlifetex.us/html.
[68] "Special Visits," *Texas Department of Criminal Justice Offender Orientation Handbook*, 78. Available at: http://www.tdcj.state.tx.us/publications/cid/OffendOrientHbkNov04.pdf
[69] Jeannie Kever, "Lifelines to Death Row: Inmates Find Outlets in Letters, Visits from Anti-Death Penalty Activists," *Houston Chronicle*, July 13, 2003, E1.
[70] Ibid.
[71] Michael G. Santos, *About Prison* (Denton: University of North Texas Press, 2004), 120.

72. Mayes interview, 2005.
73. Ibid.
74. Brush interview, 2005.
75. Ibid.
76. Ibid.
77. Mayes interview, 2005.
78. Jennifer [pseudo.], online interview by Debbi Hatton, July 1, 2005.
79. Ibid.
80. Nina [pseudo.], online interview by Debbi Hatton, July 1, 2005.
81. Jennifer interview, 2005.
82. Lonnie [pseudo.], online interview by Debbi Hatton, July 16, 2005.
83. Nina interview, 2005.
84. Jennifer interview, 2005.
85. Ibid.
86. Nina interview, 2005.
87. Ibid.
88. Jennifer interview, 2005.
89. Nina interview, 2005.
90. Wolf interview, 2005.
91. Anonymous interview by Debbi Hatton, July 2005.
92. Ibid.
93. Ibid.

SUMMARY

Taking their best shot: TDCJ guards practice their marksmanship in this 1950s photo.

On Monday, I hope to get to Huntsville....It is said to be healthy there....I have traded for another place within two or three miles of Huntsville. It is a bang-up place!
—Sam Houston correspondence, June 12, 1847

Sam Houston is long buried in the quiet grove of Oakwood Cemetery in Huntsville, but his name and bigger-than-life persona continue to permeate life and culture in the town. Yes, as the preceding chapters clearly show, Huntsville—Prison City—is a bang-up place in every sense. This book set out to explore just what makes Huntsville extraordinary by posing the question *What's going on here?* The answer, understandably, depends on whom you ask.

What's Going on…in the Community?

We're on different sides, but we have a great deal of respect for each other.

Huntsville is a physical as well as a psychological destination. For those acquainted with small towns in America, the town square is familiar, with flowers, rolling hills, and woods—a pleasant backdrop to antique stores, an old-fashioned ice-cream parlor, and restaurants specializing in hearty food and sweetened iced tea. What's not familiar are high fences, red brick walls overseen by guards carrying guns, and inmate squads mowing lawns or moving dirt. This town is *different*. Visitors cannot quickly or easily integrate into the fabric of Huntsville without spending time maneuvering through several layers of society. The journey into Huntsville requires careful observation, open-mindedness, and willingness to park stereotypes at the border.

Leaders have worked hard to build a town model for a community that is at the center of public justice in Texas. They have preserved an eclectic history, erecting a statue to honor war hero Sam Houston as well as commissioning a distinctive mural of musician and former prisoner Leadbelly on the side of a prominent building. The prison system is not hidden nor is it celebrated. While elites realize that many outsiders won't understand their town and what goes on there, they are unwilling to be passive about their past and future. They argue about the death penalty; they understand outsiders' concerns. They are incredibly good-natured about the unsolicited criticism and tired jokes drop-in visitors feel compelled to share with them. Town leaders don't just cope; they recognize their problems, like hypervigilance, drugs, and teen underachievement, and seek strategies for dealing with the challenges they face. Critical analysis and reform is in the speech of some leaders, while pragmatic action and negotiation is in the rhetoric of others. They are neither stupid nor blind, and while there is definitely tension, leaders strive for civil, respectful disagreement.

There is not one but several answers to the question *What's going on here?* The reader is invited to listen to the voices of these leaders and follow the complexities of their responses. Boundaries are blurred, but there is universal agreement that the town has choices about how it can respond to the responsibilities it has been given. Its leaders continue to work on the town's opportunities with a vigor and spirit that is rare for communities with half the challenges Huntsville faces.

What's Going on…in the Command Center?

We all use each other to get the story.

Like a media *ménage à trois*, prisoners, public information officers, and reporters are bound together in a mutually dependent relationship. The prisoners passionately crave media attention, both to feed their egos and to fuel hopes for freedom. Driven by competitive pressures, the media maneuver to feed the public appetite for human interest news and "scoop" their colleagues. The PIOs, caught between the two and with responsibilities to both, must facilitate communication while keeping their PR agenda in mind, shaping proactive messages to enhance the prison's public image.

Day to day, the interaction of the three groups follows an established pattern, but, just beneath the surface, fear is always present. At any moment the routine might be broken by an attack, an escape, a riot, or a natural disaster. The danger is real and ever present, creating a heady undercurrent of trepidation and adrenaline. But, until danger strikes, everyone has a job to do, and sometimes it is easier to concentrate on immediate practicalities rather than dwell on philosophical questions of truth and justice.

Black humor and Southern civility become coping mechanisms in situations too bizarre to be fictional. Political agendas and individual egos often distort or redirect decisions. Prisoners present their own worldviews, appropriately phrased for their purposes. Which perceptions reflect reality? Which are wishful thinking or even deliberate manipulation? It is often left to the PIOs to provide explanations and to cope with long-standing traditions and ingrained stereotypes. And, like anyone caught between conflicting opinions, the PIOs absorb some of the barbs meant for others. Reporters also struggle to set aside their own prejudices and personal beliefs so they can meld facts and impressions to tell the "real" story.

This relationship of dependence and aversion has been in place in Huntsville for so many decades the insiders find it commonplace. They are taken by surprise when outsiders are perturbed or horrified by the prison culture and death rituals carried out in the town.

However, the otherworldliness of life and death in prison will assuredly continue to be a popular media theme; it makes for great stories. Unfortunately, the stories lend themselves to sensationalized treatments, which are easier and more popular than the messy, complex, ambiguous "truths." For all three groups, the greatest danger may lie in becoming both accustomed to and calloused by the realities of life—and death—in Prison City.

What's Going on…behind the Walls?

Prisoners are not always as they're portrayed.

When a person crosses the line from law-abiding citizen to convicted criminal, everything changes. From the physical labels to the psychological boundaries, prison inmates are as alike and as different as those who are free to live as they please. Felons may have begun their careers as petty thieves stealing radios from cars with little thought of advancing to murder—but somehow their lives took that path. Whether small-time criminals or serial offenders, however, they will forever remain someone's little baby, brother, sister, or best friend.

To underestimate the survival capabilities or the communication ingenuity of those who spend their days behind prison walls is imprudent. Prison inmates as well as employees find innovative conduits to converse and to tell their stories. At times the boundaries between the guards and the guarded become indistinct. Inmates obtain tattoos to identify their association with street gangs; guards purchase tattoos symbolizing their allegiance to the brotherhood of police officers. Prisoners develop specialized words to describe their feelings and surroundings, only to have those terms assimilated into society through such avenues as rap music and everyday language spoken in public school hallways.

Nevertheless, prisons are not only for those convicted of crimes. They provide short-term employment for college students and lifelong careers for generations of Huntsville natives. The physical walls represent boundaries that separate the guilty and convicted from the acquitted and innocent. Those walls are easy to identify by their sheer size and strategically placed guard towers. The psychological walls created by the prison system are less visible, but just as real. Family members and loved ones of the incarcerated feel the agony imposed by those invisible barriers as they search for ways to bridge the gulf between themselves and those who have crossed into society's no man's land.

For Further Reflection

Historically, the separation between Huntsville and the prison was blurred. In fact, community members saw the Walls as an appropriate venue for hometown entertainment, sometimes provided by such groups as the Goree Prison Girls Band. Thousands of Texans still wistfully and openly regret the closing of the annual October prison rodeo, in which inmates performed for fans who came to Huntsville from all over the state. Prisoners participated in community parades and worked on large construction projects in the town, and provided general maintenance for parks and roadways.

When prisoners "behaved," they were rewarded with increased community contact and less separation from society. As the preceding chapters have shown, today the border of the prison walls is much more defined, and the prisoners are more separate from society than once was the case. This reflects not only changes in the attitudes of Huntsville residents, but overall societal tensions brought about, at least in part, by increased fear of the incarcerated.

The following invited response from a national authority on media and crime examines national trends and attitudes about crime and imprisonment. It is meant to be a reflective piece for readers who are interested in putting the story of Huntsville into a larger context. While the authors have tried to maintain appropriate neutrality consistent with research methodologies throughout this book, they often encountered individuals who had strong political or ideological opinions about capital punishment. The authors hope readers will enjoy this provocative perspective from outside Texas.

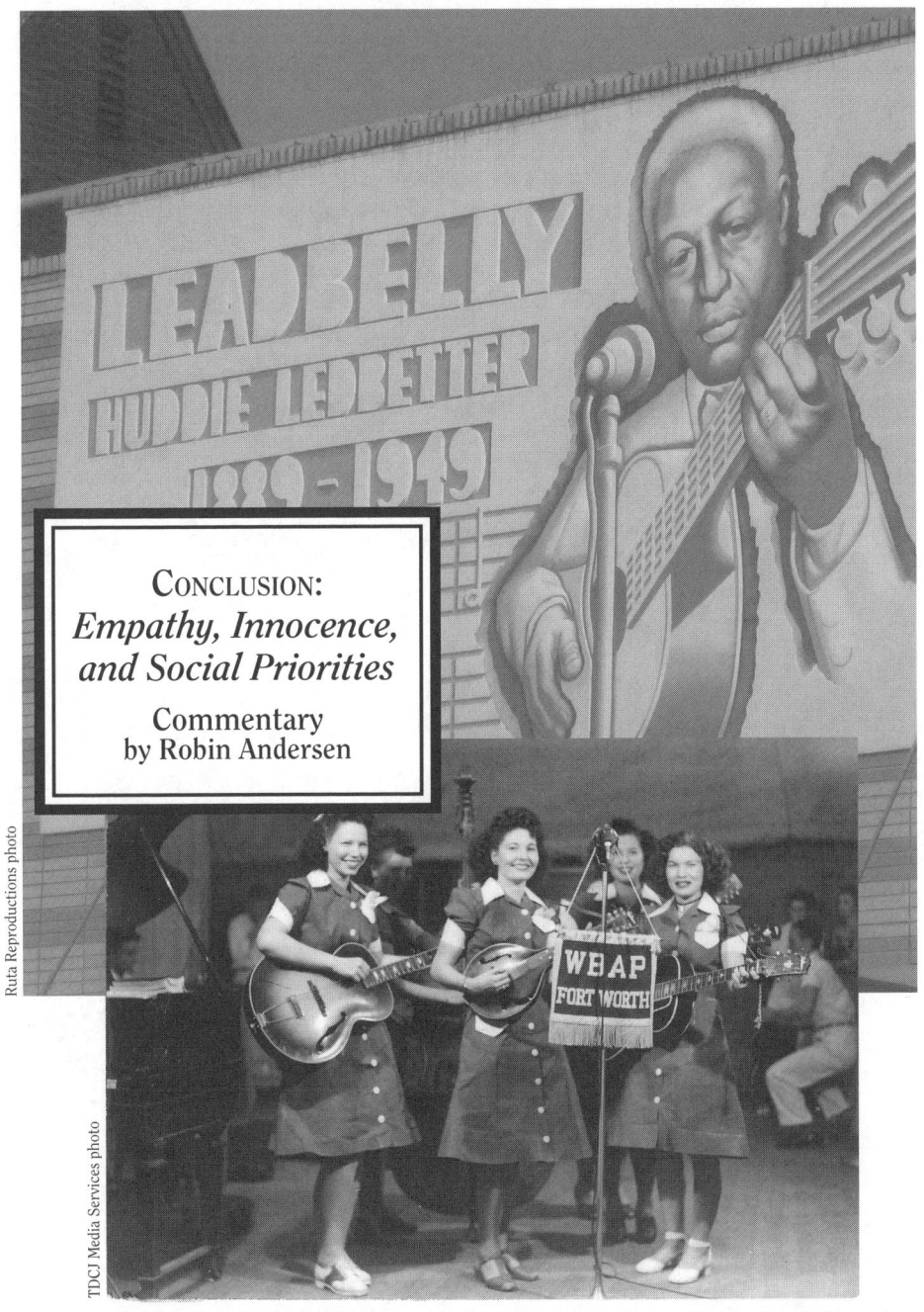

CONCLUSION:
Empathy, Innocence, and Social Priorities
Commentary by Robin Andersen

Blues musician Leadbelly (top) was a reluctant visitor to Huntsville in the 1920s, when he was imprisoned for murder. He pled for clemency with a song and was pardoned by the governor. Now his image resides on a wall in the downtown square.

The Goree Girls Prison Band reached an appreciative local and national audience with "Thirty Minutes behind the Walls" on Wednesday nights, beginning at 10 P.M.

CONCLUSION
EMPATHY, INNOCENCE, AND SOCIAL PRIORITIES

Commentary by Robin Andersen

By taking us behind the Walls in Huntsville, the authors of Prison City *have done an admirable job of presenting the many perspectives of those who come face to face with the death penalty and criminal justice issues in Texas. But trying to answer the ethnographer's question "What's going on here?" may be like the African tale of getting to know the elephant. The many small, fragmented views of the huge beast fail to reveal a complete image of the entire animal. Like the elephant, the larger picture of American criminal justice may be just beyond our grasp, lost in the compelling details of intense experience. Stepping back from that focus by placing Huntsville and Texas within a broader criminal justice landscape, we may take yet another look and try to find "what is going on" in American society with regard to the politics, policies, and depictions of crime, criminals, and the ultimate punishment.*

On February 11, 1968, Johnny Cash walked on stage knowing his performance was being recorded for a live album. Johnny would later tell well-known radio host Terry Gross[1] that he had convinced his producer to do a live album at this venue because the response he always received "was far and above anything I had ever had in my life—the complete explosion of noise and reaction they gave me with every song." He felt that the general public and his fans "ought to share that, feel that excitement too." Those who listened to Johnny sing "Folsom Prison Blues" that winter of 1968 knew those blues well. Johnny was recording the album *Live at Folsom Prison* that day, and the surges of enthusiasm between lyrical pauses were coming from men doing hard time in what was then one of California's highest-security penitentiaries.

Johnny and his band and his wife, June Carter Cash, of the well-known Carter family of folk musicians, performed frequently at prisons across the country in those early years of his career. Cash felt a natural affinity for the offenders behind bars, as he had seen the inside of prison walls on more than one occasion. And the prisoners could identify with Cash, always dressed in black, singing songs like "Dark as a Dungeon" and "Bottom of a Mountain," songs that are, he said, "about the working man and the hard life." Cash understood that "they'd been through the hard life, all of them or they wouldn't be there—the down and outers."[2]

Cash also performed at San Quentin, and he would learn only later that every time he had played there Merle Haggard had been sitting in one of the front two rows. When Haggard was released, he would go on to experience immediate success himself, becoming another legendary country singer.

"Folsom Prison Blues" was a hit for Cash even before he recorded "I Walk the Line," and, as his reputation as a singer who played for prisoners grew, Johnny was invited by a warden in Texas to do a show there. While in Texas, Cash discovered another venue, and he and his band rushed to set up their sound equipment during the intervals between the bucking broncos and the calf-roping events at the annual rodeo held in Huntsville. After writing his autobiography, Cash explained his reasons for playing for the down-and-outers behind bars. He felt a natural empathy for prisoners, and back then, he said, "I thought it would make a difference, that they really were there to be rehabilitated."[3]

Those attitudes toward prisoners are as far removed from present-day public expression as the Huntsville rodeo that was closed years ago. The attitudes held by the man in black with the baritone voice seem to exist in a different world and a different society, one that assumed that a person could be rehabilitated, that rehabilitation was the goal, and that prison could be the site for such transformations. Cash spoke of a world in which it was considered punishment enough to have one's freedom taken away. We have come a long way from the original concept of the role of incarceration, first articulated and lobbied for by Quakers, who saw it as a humane alternative to corporal punishment and disfigurement. Prison, they argued, would allow the offenders, when separated from others, to contemplate and reflect on their behavior, their future, and their ability to live peacefully with others.

But those ideas say as much about the role of prisons as they do about social perceptions of the prisoners themselves. Cash identified with the men behind bars because of his own experiences. He knew well the feeling of hitting bottom. As radio host Terry Gross points out, his life seemed to traverse two very different worlds, wrought with contradictions between the sacred and the profane. He was a Christian, and his first songs were gospel hymns sung as he picked cotton in the fields with his father. And yet as he became famous, he would have his share of troubles. Admitting to his addiction to amphetamines, Cash said, "I was taking the pills and then the pills started taking me."

Leadbelly and David Crosby are also musicians with firsthand experience of failure and ending up in jail. Both are prominently featured in the Huntsville museum. Like Cash, Crosby found himself in jail for drugs, and contemporary attitudes toward addiction are harsh. Yet we hear that Crosby was "one of the all-time nice guys." By virtue of their talent we consider these musicians exceptions, but do they tell us something about the general prison population as well? Cash understood that the qualities of the sacred and the profane are the mixed strands that define us all as human. This philosophy appreciates the complexities of human nature and understands that each person is capable of doing good and bad. So much of what we are capable of depends on the social and cultural circumstances that surround us. Such ideas are frequently articulated in county and folk music, and compellingly expressed in the writing of another musician, folksinger Phil Oaks, in his song "There but for Fortune":

> Show me a prison
> Show me a jail,
> Show me a prisoner whose face has gone pale
> And I'll show you a young man with so many reasons why
> And there but for fortune, may go you or I.

Such lyrics treat of social conditions offering so many reasons why someone might find themselves in jail. Under similar conditions you and I could end up there too. These traditions in folk culture can be referred to as *narratives of inclusion*. They tell stories of people who are down and out, but they could be members of our own communities. Folk songs are often awash in stories of harsh conditions in which human tragedy is mixed with indomitable ingenuity, all played out against a background of confounding and arbitrary inequities. For whatever reasons, bad luck or bad timing, their protagonists sometimes fall from grace. Such notions of shared humanity, together with rehabilitation, assume that redemption, healing, and change are human qualities, and desirable social processes.

Another attitudinal strand in contemporary American culture imagines a very different scenario for those behind bars. *Narratives of exclusion* present offenders as people essentially different from ourselves. They stand as Others, and their lack of shared behaviors and characteristics places them outside our social group and ourselves. We do not empathize with them or feel their pain, because they are essentially different from us, not part of a shared humanity. Sociologists of criminal justice understand that these conceptions are held in tandem with another supposition about the social world, and that is the certainty of fairness. Just-world theory holds that we live our lives on a level playing field and because we are treated equally digression is a personal failure that stems from a lack of character and responsibility. Those who fall short or descend into substance abuse are not like us. Their victimization is self-perpetuating, and excuses such as social conditions, circumstances, or structural injustices do not apply.

In many ways great and small those behind bars have been wrenched from a sense of belonging. They are not like us and are easily Othered, presented through narratives of exclusion. As one guard interviewed for this study of Huntsville said, "They're not in there for skipping Sunday school." The implication that their crimes are much more grievous is underscored by the reference to religious instruction, something prisoners have failed to heed. This process of exclusion leads to dehumanization, and it serves as justification for the treatment that the incarcerated often experience behind bars, even when their crimes are better described as petty, not egregious.

Criminals, Prisoners, and the Media

Depictions of the "criminal" in mainstream media have much to do with social conceptions and attitudes toward the incarcerated. Crime dramas have been a staple of television entertainment since its birth. Week after week this popular programming format features demonized criminals who commit violent crimes including murder, assault, and rape, often depicted in graphic detail. Diligent investigators succeed by the end of the fictional hour in detecting, prosecuting, and putting criminals behind bars for long prison terms. Only then are the streets once again safe. Media research and cultivation theory finds that television's mediated reality is "a credible foundation for belief."[4] Over time, the consequences of a steady diet of crime dramas lead to a variety of strongly held yet often inaccurate assumptions about crime and criminal justice issues.[5] Heavy viewers of crime dramas are more fearful of crime and are more likely to believe they will be victimized.[6] In addition, TV crime dramas emphasize the most serious crime—homicide. People are often surprised to find that violent criminals constitute only a small portion of the prison population. Overall, nearly three quarters of federal prisoners have no history of violence, and more than half (55 percent) are serving time for drug offenses. Only 13 percent are in prison for a violent crime. Of those sentenced for a drug offense in 2002, over half fell into the lowest criminal history category, and in 87 percent of cases no weapon was involved.[7]

News Programming

Trends in American journalism correspond to a misconception of criminal justice issues. Put bluntly, the public has been scared to death by the media. Even a casual news consumer is not unaffected by the flood of stories about scary criminals, unsafe streets, and what some media watch groups term simply "mayhem." Local news usually garners the worst of these criticisms, but the stunning increase in such visceral fare is also now a cornerstone of the flagship network news programs. From 1990 to 1998, for example, the number of crime stories broadcast annually on the NBC, CBS, and ABC evening news programs rose from 542 to 1,392.[8]

The increased popularity of news about violent crime occurred at a time when actual levels of the most violent crimes in society dropped significantly. The disjuncture between the news reality and the social reality of crime is also reflected in the reporting of homicides. In just three years, between 1993 and 1996, the number of murder stories increased by 700 percent. During this same period, the actual murder rate dropped 20 percent.[9]

Media portrayals and public attitudes also correspond to public policy. Public support for longer sentences and more punitive measures have led to rates of incarceration in America that are the highest in the world. Despite falling crime rates since 1991, the rate of incarceration in prison increased by more than 50 percent.

America's Imprisonment Binge

Today the number of persons behind bars exceeds 2 million and costs American taxpayers $57 billion annually. The building and filling of prisons has been conducted at a rate unprecedented in human history, and the American prison system far exceeds any in the industrial democracies. In

1972 federal and state prisons held 196,000 inmates, with another 130,000 in local jails. Since then the national inmate population has risen more than 500 percent.

Mandatory Minimum Sentencing

These numbers are due in large measure to changes in policies that have increased the length of time a person will stay in prison, which has risen by about 30 percent.[10] Measures such as "truth in sentencing" and "three strikes" create mandatory minimum sentencing that remove sentencing judgment from the process. The "three strikes and you're out" law passed in California in 1994 called for twenty-five years to life for any felony conviction following two prior convictions. In 2003 lawyers challenged the constitutionality of the law in two cases that were heard before the U.S. Supreme Court. In one case a man was found guilty of stealing videotapes worth $153 from K-Mart on two separate occasions and was sentenced to fifty years to life. The other man stole three golf clubs from a sporting goods store and was sentenced to twenty-five years to life. The Court found that the law did not represent cruel and unusual punishment and let the sentences stand. Marc Mauer, of the Sentencing Project, notes that as a consequence of the Court's decision, California taxpayers will spend well over $1 million to keep these men in jail for their low-level property crimes.

The War on Drugs

The policies adopted in the mid-1980s that declared a "war on drugs" also led to spiraling incarceration figures. Increased criminalization for drug possession resulted in many low-level dealers and drug addicts serving long prison terms. From 1985 to 2000, nonviolent drug offenses alone accounted for 65 percent of the rise in the federal prison population.[11] Federal crime statistics show that during that same period violent criminals accounted for only 6 percent of the rise in inmate numbers.

The Politics of Race

Even though the vast majority of drug users and a majority of dealers are white and live in suburbs, street-level law enforcement has been carried out primarily in urban minority neighborhoods characterized by severe underemployment.[12] In the book *Breaking Rank*, former police chief Norm Stamper exposes racial profiling and the targeting of young

African Americans.[13] Critics argue that this and other types of selective law enforcement have led to disproportionate arrests and imprisonment of minorities. Nearly half of all prison inmates are now African Americans. Once convicted of a felony, it becomes harder to find a job, and policy critics argue that the war on drugs further undermines already poor, minority communities. They argue that racial and economic equality would be better served by strengthening community policing and dealing with economic and social problems in America.

Lack of Treatment Options

With 70 percent of funding for the war on drugs directed to law enforcement, treatment options for addicts became less available. Doctors and others in public health argue that drug addiction should be considered a medical problem and believe that lack of treatment for addicts exacerbates demand. After years of fighting the war on drugs, millions of Americans continue to consume drugs, and they are readily available. Those in favor of continued criminalization argue that if harsh sanctions are lifted more Americans will become addicts.

But many with criminal justice experience believe that putting users in prison only creates more drug abuse and has devastating social consequences. Jailing persons with substance abuse problems only serves to further destabilize their lives and socialize them into criminal culture. Stamper's most critical words are devoted to the demonization of drug users: "From early on, we teach children that the people who use drugs are monsters and fiends. Well, excuse me, but they're not. Some of them manage to handle it successfully, and many do not. Many abuse the drugs and wind up very ill—psychologically, physiologically, mentally, emotionally. But rather than demonizing them, we ought to be reaching out to help them."[14]

Stamper goes on to articulate what many public policy critics and health advocacy researchers also argue, that we need to "spend much more money on prevention, education, medication and rehabilitation."[15] But these values and social solutions to addiction are rarely given priority in a media environment that continues to emphasize fear and retaliation over more effective and humane policies. Cultural practices and public policies based on such irrational criteria as fear and demonization have led to the contradictions we live with on a daily basis. Celebrities such as Johnny Cash, David Crosby, Merle Haggard, and many others remain objects of public admiration even as so many others languish in prison with long sentences for similar drug use and petty, economic crimes. We would not wish such a fate on those we know and care about, even as we vote for politicians who call for tougher measures on nonviolent and victimless crimes.

Current social conceptions of prisons as places that should be nothing like country clubs relegate those spaces as institutions that mete out perpetual punishment. Our current attitudes toward retaliation, and the lack of compassion in sentencing, leave little room for reflection, drug rehabilitation, or redemption, and ultimately for social and economic equality. As we will see below, this is also the context in which capital punishment has flourished in America.

Guilty until Proven Innocent

On crime dramas, when a cop suspects a perpetrator, the officer is usually correct. Survey analysis has demonstrated that heavy TV viewers typically believe that if someone is arrested they are likely guilty of something.[16] As attitudes toward one of the keystones of due process, the assumption of innocence, have become more skeptical, investigations into innocence claims have resulted in exposing significant cases of wrongful conviction.

Voices of the Innocent

There are significant voices and stories still to be told that will help complete the picture of twenty-first-century American prisons. Those whose convictions have been vacated give us insights into a system of inconsistency and errors. The stories of innocence are haunting, and they cast a long shadow over our sense of fairness and justice. In many cases, it was volunteer attorneys and amateur investigators, not our legal system, who saved prisoners' lives. Almost 400 men have been released from prison mostly in the last fifteen years after DNA and other evidence proved their innocence; 122 of those were on death row.

New York–based attorney Marc Simon felt so strongly about these systematic errors in the criminal justice process that he became a filmmaker to get the information out. His documentary *After Innocence* tracks the lives of seven men who were exonerated after being wrongfully imprisoned for decades.

The film focuses on the struggles to rebuild their lives. It reveals the many roadblocks they encountered once outside the prison walls, telling the stories of a police officer, an army sergeant, and a young father, all sent to prison, some to death row.

After being framed by New York City detective Louis J. Eppolito, it took nineteen years for Barry Gibbs to be exonerated. By the time he was released his mother was dead and most of his friends and family members had moved on with their lives. Unable to return to his job as a letter carrier and not qualified to receive social security, his situation outside seems as bleak as his imprisonment. Exonerees across the United States receive little to no assistance to help them with the transition back into society. There are virtually no government-funded programs or health care, psychological counseling, social services, job training, or housing assistance.

The Death Penalty

On January 31, 2000, Republican governor George Ryan called for a moratorium on the death penalty in Illinois.[17] Northwestern University journalism students had begun to investigate the cases of the men who sat on death row. When the investigations were finished, the students had helped exonerate thirteen people waiting to die. One of them, Anthony Porter, had an IQ of 51, and was two days from execution. Later, someone else admitted to committing the crime of which Porter had been convicted. Results of the student investigation revealed a stunning failure of the justice system in Illinois.

Amid reports of inadequate representation and numerous reversals of capital convictions due to DNA evidence across the country, public support for the moratorium spread. Within a year, 64 percent of the public was in favor of such an action at the national level.

In May 2002 Governor Paris Glendening also called a moratorium in Maryland. Before leaving office in 2003, Governor Ryan pardoned four men and commuted the sentences of 167 death row inmates because he found the death penalty convictions arbitrary, capricious, and immoral.[18]

These broader failures of justice in capital cases on a national scale are beyond the scope of individual public information officers, who must focus on presenting the press with details and facts about the condemned at their respective institutions. Media professionals often tell the stories of those on death row without including the context and background needed to see the big picture and all its complexities. Increasing opposition to capital punishment in high-profile cases has served to bring these broader, controversial issues to the media's attention.

Gary Graham

We learn in these pages that the execution of Gary Graham presented problems for the public information officer and staff at Huntsville. The PIO details the unusual degree of media interest and notes that the sensationalism surrounding Graham's case disrupted the systematic process that usually allows executions to take place with a degree of relative calm. Attention to Graham's case was the result of the problems brought to light by appeal lawyers and anti–death penalty advocates. Amnesty International argued that Graham's case was egregious and demonstrated significant legal problems with his conviction.

Though Graham was arrested when he was twenty, he was seventeen years old at the time of the murder for which he was convicted. Graham's lawyer, Ron Mock, has become well known in Texas over the years for having more clients sent to death row than any other attorney. Accused of sleeping during trial and smelling of drugs and alcohol, Mock represented a dozen defendants who were sentenced to death. He was subsequently barred from practicing law until 2007, and permanently barred from ever trying death penalty cases again.

There was no physical evidence to tie Graham to the crime, and he was convicted on a single eyewitness account. Not only was the veracity of the eyewitness questioned, but during his trial Graham's lawyer failed to call two other witnesses who said the shooter was not Graham. While Graham had prior arrests, those juvenile crimes certainly did not warrant the death penalty. Graham's case exemplifies the ongoing problems with capital convictions, due process, and the disproportionate application of the death penalty to poor black men.

Women and Texas

As noted in these pages, women are the fastest-growing sector of the prison population. Texas has also executed women for the first time in over a century.

The Case of Frances Newton

On September 14, 2005, the State of Texas executed Frances Newton for the April 1987 murders of her husband, Adrian Newton, and her two children. Her death was a significant milestone. Newton was the first African-American woman put to death in Texas since the Civil War. It is not disputed that Newton's trial counsel was egregiously incompetent. She was assigned the same court-appointed lawyer as Gary Graham. During Newton's trial Mock called no witnesses, nor did he conduct any independent investigation into the murders. The first charges brought by the prosecution were never challenged in court, even though the case against her was thin and appeal lawyers found significant evidence challenging her conviction.

One of the most popular programs on prime-time television is *CSI, Crime Scene Investigation*, now with three different series on CBS. Week after week, the public is reassured that capable and honest investigators confirm irrefutable evidence that leads to real perpetrators of egregious crimes. The young appealing stars single-mindedly follow rigorous scientific procedures that always lead to the truth and expose the killer(s). With increasing frequency, however, this formula bears little resemblance to criminal justice realities. As was mentioned in these pages, sometimes the local press reports on forensic errors, but they stand little chance of changing dominant perceptions of the technical proficiency of prosecutorial evidence.

In criminal justice circles, the Houston Police Department's crime lab is widely regarded as extraordinarily unreliable. It was closed down in 2002 for improper procedures and contamination. In Newton's case, the lab's ballistics report was key. Without it, it is doubtful Newton would ever have stood trial.[19] The only other physical evidence offered by the prosecution was the presence of nitrates found on the lower part of Newton's dress. While the state argued that the presence of nitrates was gunpowder residue, Newton's attorney never introduced other explanations for nitrates, such as the fertilizer her toddler was exposed to earlier that day. On the evening of the murders Newton's hands were tested for gunpowder, but no residue was found.[20] In addition, during the appeal process the assistant D.A. admitted that a second gun had been found at the crime scene all those years ago, but it was never entered into evidence.

The case against Newton was largely circumstantial. She had taken out a life insurance policy on her husband and her daughter less than a month before, yet there was no plausible motivation offered for the killing of her seven-year-old son.[21] The police also knew that Adrian Newton was a drug dealer who was in debt to a supplier. Despite this information, the possibility that the deaths were drug-related was not investigated.

The group of students and law professors at the Innocence Project who took up Newton's case felt that she had a strong innocence claim, and that her case had never been thoroughly or independently investigated.

The lawyers who handled her appeal argued that there was a complex and overwhelming array of facts and circumstances that challenged the accuracy of her conviction. But, as in the case of Graham, evidence supporting her innocence was never heard in court. After Texas governor Perry allowed a 120-day reprieve, the U.S. Supreme Court rejected the appeal because the court deadlines had expired.

Newton's case embodies core problems with the death penalty in the United States in general and in Texas in particular. As one of her lawyers noted bitterly, "I think she was innocent, but you don't get much of a chance when you're poor, Black and convicted in Texas."[22]

Indeed, even some prison officials in Texas question the fairness of death penalty convictions, as Denis Johnson noted in *Five Executions and a Barbeque*. In 2000 death row inmates were transferred to a new, modern structure that sits fifty miles outside of Huntsville in the town of Livingston. The building was named the Terrell unit after Charles T. Terrell, a former director of prisons in Texas.[23] In a letter to the *Dallas Morning News*, Terrell expressed regrets that the building bore his name and doubted the "fairness of capital punishment as it's currently administered in Texas." His request that his name be removed was granted, and the death row structure is now called the Polunsky unit.

George W. Bush

During his five years as the governor of Texas, Bush was nicknamed by opponents "Governor Death" and "the Texacutioner." He oversaw the execution of 152 people, far more than any other state. When questions about the death penalty were directed toward Governor Bush during his bid for the White House in 2000, he often repeated the same phrases that went largely unchallenged by journalists. He said, "Everybody who has been put to death in Texas has been granted full access to the law" and "everyone who has been put to death has been guilty of the crime charged."[24]

Yet Texas has no public defender system. The former governor vetoed a bill allowing counties to establish public defender offices, leaving judges to appoint defense attorneys. The problems of disproportionate racial application of capital prosecutions and convictions, unequal representation, and lack of a clemency process have plagued the Texas death penalty system, as they have nationally.

Public Opinion and the Death Penalty

It is often referred to as an immutable fact that the death penalty is popular nationwide, particularly in Texas. But fluctuations in opinion polls demonstrate that American opinion about capital punishment is qualified and certainly subject to change. The height of favorable attitudes toward capital punishment was 1994, when certain polls showed an 80 percent approval rating.[25] Toward the end of the 1990s the number stabilized at about 75 percent.

In recent years, news of inequities and error rates have caused its popularity to slide to 64 percent, the lowest level in twenty-seven years. When poll respondents are asked if it could be assured that convicted persons would receive a sentence of life in prison without the possibility of parole, support for the death penalty falls below 50 percent. In most states with the death penalty, however, life without parole is not an option. In Texas, for example, "prosecutors have successfully lobbied against legislation that would give juries the option of life without parole instead of the death penalty."[26]

Most telling is the case of Karla Faye Tucker, the pickax murderer frequently referred to in Texas. News of her execution gained national as well as international press attention. She was a petite, polite, articulate young woman, and the first female to be executed in Texas since 1863. She had undergone a religious conversion, expressed remorse for her crime, and said she was not afraid to die. The brother of one of her victims saw no point in her execution. There was enormous pressure on then-governor Bush to grant her clemency. Although opinion favored the death penalty in the abstract, when it came to Tucker only 45 percent of the public thought it should be applied to her.

Tucker presented an appealing subjectivity, and through media interviews and stories of her conversion she was no longer a faceless integer or a crazed demon. Instead she became one of the few death row convicts to be depicted in the popular media as a person. Her process of redemption was perceived as authentic, and her story evoked compassion, even in those in Texas who said they favored capital punishment. Her case illustrates that media treatment and exposure can result in changing perceptions and opinions.

Press coverage, however, far more frequently plays an important role in shoring up support for the death penalty. Analysis of news reports discussed in these pages demonstrates how stories about executions tend to present a positive attitude toward the death penalty. Fear of crime and demonized criminals, especially black criminals, are prominent features of mainstream media. The excellent body of work by Robert Entman and others over the years has demonstrated how imagery affects public perceptions about race and criminality, and Frank Gilliam and others have noted that crime stories on local news overrepresent black perpetrators and underrepresent blacks as victims of crime.[27]

These depictions correspond to the disproportionate application of capital punishment based on race, a fact that has caused many criminal justice professionals and officials to become critics of the death penalty. One district attorney in Milwaukee, E. Michael McCann, argues that the death penalty is applied unfairly to minorities, pointing out how rarely wealthy white men are put to death.

"Those who 'have labored long in the criminal justice system know, supported by a variety of studies and extensive personal experience, that blacks get the harsher hand in criminal justice and particularly in capital punishment cases,' Mr. McCann wrote in "Opposing Capital Punishment: A Prosecutor's Perspective, published in the *Marquette Law Review* in 1996."[28] According to the NAACP Legal Defense and Educational Fund, 43 percent of the people on death row are African Americans. In addition, the death penalty has been employed much more often when the victim is white. One study of death penalty convictions, published in 2000, found that 82 percent of the victims in capital cases were white, while only 50 percent of homicide victims were white.[29]

The "Wolf Pack"

We have learned that high-profile criminal cases of violent crime often result in renewed calls for the death penalty. It is worth recalling the Central Park jogger case in New York, in which a white female investment banker was viciously attacked, raped, and left for dead. Though no physical evidence was found to implicate them, police focused on four young black teenagers, who under questioning all confessed to what came to be called a "wilding." The popular phrase used in the media to describe these young men became *wolf pack*.

In the midst of the media sensationalism that surrounded the case, Donald Trump spent $85,000 on television ads calling for the reinstatement of the death penalty in New York. Years later, a single individual would admit to the crime, and the young men would be exonerated. Reviewing their videotaped confessions during the trial to vacate their convictions, it became obvious in hindsight that the boys were repeating the scenario presented to them by investigators. Had they been white and middle class, they most certainly would have had a lawyer whose legal protections might have prevented the coerced confessions.

Dead Man Walking: Forgiveness and Reconciliation

The movie *Dead Man Walking* is based on the life and work of Sister Helen Prejean. Played by Susan Sarandon, the nun attempts to retrieve the lost souls of those who have committed the most egregious crimes. Her struggle is to bring the murderer Matthew Poncelet (played by Sean Penn) out of denial, back to his humanity, and save his soul. The nun urges the murderer to admit his crime and take responsibility. His only hope for redemption is through forgiveness. In a highly emotive ending, he admits to the killings and seems to find peace. Sister Helen stays with him spiritually and emotionally during his execution.

But Sister Helen's efforts with the victim's family members are not as successful. Their grief is painful to watch. They seem utterly destroyed and unable to reconcile their loss. The movie ends with Sister Helen kneeling in a church pew, praying with the father of one of the slain teenagers. The execution of Poncelet has not released him or healed his wounds. The world makes as little sense after the execution as it did before. The loss of his child remains an open wound. The impulse for revenge has been unsatisfying.

The most forceful argument frequently brought to bear to justify capital punishment is the justice needs of the family. When humanitarian concerns are raised about state executions, compassion is usually redirected toward the feelings of the victim's family members. We are told to feel sorry for them. They will find well-being only if the perpetrator is put to death. In *Dead Man Walking*, that promise is revealed to be false.

Many of those who have lost family members to violent crime have found that the promise of healing through execution is another painful misconception. One group, Murder Victims' Families for Reconciliation (MVFR),[30] makes this assertion explicitly in its mission statement, saying, "[We] challenge the assumption that all survivors of murder victims want and need the death penalty in order to heal." Revenge has not always been viewed as the most reliable path to justice, or to breaking the cycle of violence.

As a strategy for ending crime and violence, the death penalty seems to be failing. This is borne out in another measure of the death penalty. Capital punishment is often said to be a deterrent to crime, yet in recent years state execution rates can be correlated to increased violence. In 2003 Texas had a murder rate above the national average. Consider a *New York Times* survey that found that states without the death penalty have lower homicide rates than states with the death penalty.[31]

The gap between the cumulative murder rates of death penalty and non–death penalty states actually widened in 2003, from 36 percent in 2002 to 44 percent in 2003. Overall, the murder rate of the death penalty states increased from 2002, while the rate in non–death penalty states decreased.[32]

The Cycle of Violence

These numbers seem to support a position that views capital punishment not as a deterrent but as part of a cycle of violence. This debate was reinvigorated when Stanley "Tookie" Williams was put to death by lethal injection in California on December 13, 2005. Many argued that by granting Williams clemency, Governor Arnold Schwarzenegger, frequently criticized for popularizing graphic violence and killing fantasies in his movies, had an opportunity to help break the cycle of gang violence so prevalent in the state. Williams was the former leader of the notorious gang the Crips. While in prison he repudiated his former life and became a powerful voice for young people, writing children's books and counseling teenagers against gang violence.

The clemency debate was driven as well by the execution of Vietnam combat veteran Kenneth Boyd in North Carolina on December 2, the thousandth state killing since the Supreme Court reinstated capital punishment in 1976. In denying clemency, Schwarzenegger insisted that the many years Williams worked as an antigang mediator meant little in the absence of an admission of guilt, and Tookie Williams always insisted he was innocent of the four killings he was convicted of.

It is doubtful that the governor would have changed his mind if Williams had uttered a last-minute confession, but the history of death row cases reveals that guilt, even with confession, is profoundly error-prone, and thus a poor guide to mercy. As the history of nonviolent action and philosophy teach, only when the cry for revenge is transformed into a call for mercy will the cycle of violence abate.

Growing Ambivalence

During the execution of Tookie Williams, California executioners had trouble finding a suitable vein in which to inject a lethal combination of drugs. Medical professionals explained that the problems most likely resulted in excessive and unnecessary pain for an additional twelve minutes. Williams's death contributed to a growing sense of unease among doctors and anesthesiologists who are increasingly unwilling to participate in execution by lethal injection on the grounds they have signed the Hippocratic oath promising to do no harm. There is mounting evidence that lethal injection often results in unseen pain. Investigative journalist Vince Beiser reported that "some condemned people might not get enough anesthetic to actually put them to sleep—leaving them conscious but, paralyzed by the second drug, incapable of screaming or convulsing as their hearts are squeezed to a stop."[33] Autopsy evidence has shown that some inmates had concentrations of anesthetic that could have left them conscious as their lives were taken.

A study published in the British medical journal the *Lancet* found that twenty-one out of forty-nine toxicology reports of executed prisoners showed concentrations of anesthetics "consistent with awareness."[34] A Columbia University anesthesiology professor testified at a Connecticut hearing that if a person were still conscious when the potassium chloride hit his or her body the pain would feel like "boiling oil or branding with a red hot iron."[35] Since a physician must determine or declare death in twenty-eight death-penalty states, and must oversee the process in others, as more medical professionals refuse to participate in capital punishment, some prisoners' death sentences are being repealed. These revelations, together with doubts raised by failures of justice in capital cases, have led to fewer executions in recent years. The number of executions fell from ninety-eight in 1999 to sixty in 2005, nineteen of which were in Texas. By the fall of 2006, Texas had executed twenty people.

Social Priorities

The answer to crime, public safety, and a less-violent society will not be constructing more and more prisons, but building a society in which every person has the opportunity to participate in economic and social life with dignity and responsibility. These are words taken from a statement of the Catholic bishops of the United States, titled "Responsibility, Rehabilitation, and Restoration: A Catholic Perspective on Crime and Criminal Justice": "In many states, education, health and human services, and public transportation budgets remain stagnant or decline while more and more prisons are built." Indeed, by the mid-1990s, the National Criminal Justice Commission evaluated criminal justice policies, issuing a report highly critical of U.S. prison spending, arguing that alternative policies and funding would better serve public safety, as well as social justice needs. The commission offered specific crime prevention initiatives that could replace more expensive prison construction: "Many means of reducing violence occur outside the formal justice system. Classes in conflict resolution, educational and recreational opportunities, drug treatment, counseling, job training, improved street lighting, and many other techniques can reduce violence in a community. The development of such programs is limited only by a jurisdiction's creativity and financial commitment."[36]

The resources needed to construct a society in which every person has the opportunity to participate in life are being used to incarcerate increasing numbers of people. Many prison reform advocates including academics, economists and policy advisors have demonstrated the correlation between increased prison spending and decreased funding for social services, education and public welfare. As the Commission argued "In order to fund jails and prisons, state and local governments have been forced to divert money from education and welfare spending."[37] The state of California illustrates these trends. In 1979, 18 percent of California's state budget went to education, and only 3 percent was spent on prisons. By 1994, education and prisons cost where each 8 percent of the budget. By 2003, California experienced a fiscal crisis with a ballooning deficit amounting to $38.2 billion. Governor Gray Davis slashed many state programs including education, health care, and workforce development, but the 25-year prison budget boom remained intact, with a budget drop of only 1 percent. When Davis was recalled in 2003, California spent $5.1 billion on prisons, more than only other state.[38]

As Jonathan Kozol has argued eloquently over the years, as a society we are willing to spend tens of thousands of dollars a year to incarcerate young people, after we have failed them by spending only a few thousand to poorly educate them. This misdirected social priority is compounded when we deny educational programs to prisoners. In 1995 the federal government stopped funding the Pell grants that made education possible in many facilities, even though, as we have learned, education radically reduces recidivism rates. But as the authors of *Prison City* found, those stories do not garner much interest in the press.

Prison Reform

Those in favor of reforming the current prison system include a wide range of professionals in the criminal justice system, from police officers to judges and from legal aid workers to prison wardens. They argue that there are less expensive, more humane, and more effective ways to reduce crime at the community and policing levels. Those concerned with social and racial injustice, together with the expanding numbers of family and community members affected by what critics call the U.S. incarceration binge, are also vocal supporters of prison reform.

A great deal more compassion is needed when these criminal justice policies are debated, instead of the usual media spotlight on fearsome individuals whose cases never tell the whole story of crime and punishment in America. The media would serve the public far better by presenting criminal justice issues through a reasoned discourse instead of sensationalizing scary villains and trivializing executions with generic accounts of their last meals.

Sam Houston found his eternal rest at Oakwood Cemetery in Huntsville, but his willingness to tackle controversial issues and speak his mind even when his views were unpopular still lives in this East Texas town.

Notes

[1] *Fresh Air with Terry Gross*, Interview first aired in April 1997 on National Public Radio. Rebroadcast on Thanksgiving Day, 2005, to correspond to the release of the film about Cash's life *Walk the Line*.

[2] Ibid.

[3] Ibid.

[4] Robert M. Entman and Andrew Rojecki, *The Black Image in the White Mind: Media and Race in America* (Chicago: University of Chicago Press, 2000).

[5] Craig Haney and John Manzolati, "Television Criminology: Network Illusions of Criminal Justice Realities," in *Readings about the Social Animal*, edited by Elliot Aronson (San Francisco, California: W. H. Freeman, 1981), 125–36.

[6] George Gerbner and Larry Gross, "Living with Television: The Violence Profile," *Journal of Communication* 26, no. 2 (1976): 73–99.

[7] "New Incarceration Figures," Sentencing Project. Available at: http://www.sentencingproject.org/pdfs/1044.pdf.

[8] W. Lance Bennett, *News: The Politics of Illusion* (New York: Longman, 2001), 14.

[9] Richard Morin, "An Airwave of Crime: While TV News Coverage of Murder Has Soared – Feeding Public Fears – Crime is Actually Down, *The Washington Post National Weekly Edition*, August 18, 1997, p. 34.

[10] Marc Mauer, *Race to Incarcerate* (New York: New Press, 2006).

[11] Ibid.

[12] For a more complete discussion of racial disparity in the conduct of the war on drugs, see Robin Andersen, *Consumer Culture and TV Programming* (Boulder, Colorado: Westview, 1995), chapter 8.

[13] Norm Stamper, *Breaking Rank: A Top Cop's Exposé of the Dark Side of American Policing* (New York: Nation, 2005).

[14] Laura Barcella, "Seattle Confidential," AlterNet, June 15, 2005. Available at: http://www.alternet.org/module/prentversion/22196.

[15] Ibid.

[16] Haney and Manzolati.

[17] In 1999 the American Bar Association, a group of 400,000 lawyers, had renewed a call for a moratorium on executions because of concerns about racial disparity and the failure to provide adequate counsel and resources to defendants.

[18] Republican governor Gary Johnson declared New Mexico's death penalty to be bad public policy in 2002. The men waiting on New Mexico's death row could not afford to hire their own lawyers.

[19] With regard to the lab's accuracy, the Houston chief of police is quoted as saying, "Let's just stop the execution until we go through all the substances in the crime lab."

[20] Gunpowder residue cannot be washed away or quickly removed from skin after a gun has been fired.

[21] As the National Coalition to Abolish the Death Penalty points out, "The state was not able to provide a viable motive for his death. She also allegedly killed her 20-month old daughter for an additional $50,000 in insurance benefits. While a problematic marital situation may serve as motive for Newton's husband's murder, the killing of her two children is still speculative and largely unexplained by the state." See "Do Not Execute Frances Newton!" September 14, 2005. Available at: http://www.demaction.org/dia/organizations/ncadp/campaign.jsp?campaign_KEY=1132.

[22] "Remembering Frances Newton: We Vow to Continue the Fight," *New Abolitionist* (Chicago, Illinois: Campaign to End the Death Penalty), November 2005, 16.

[23] Cited in Denis Johnson, "Five Executions and a Barbeque," *Rolling Stone*, August 17, 2000.

[24] Lily Hughes, "We'll keep fighting! Texecutioner in the White House," *New Abolitionist*, January 2001, Issue 18. Available at; http://www.nodeathpenalty.org/newab018/index.html.

[25] Bradley Brooks, "Countdown to 1,000th Execution," *Journal News*, November 25, 2005, 3B.

[26] Raymond Bonner and Ford Fassenden, "Absence of Executions: A Special Report: States with No Death Penalty Share Lower Homicide Rates," *New York Times*, September 22, 2000. Available at: http://nytimes.com/search/restricted/article?res=FB091FFE355F0C718EDDA00894D8404482.

[27] Frank D. Gilliam, Jr., et al., "Crime in Black and White: The Scary World of Local News," *Harvard International Journal of Press/Politics* 1, no. 3 (1996): 6–23.

[28] Ibid.

[29] Ibid.

[30] "Death Penalty Facts." Available at: http://www.mvfr.org/DeathPenaltyFacts.htm.

[31] Bonner and Fassenden.

[32] "Deterrence: States without the Death Penalty Fared Better over Past Decade." Available at: http://www.deathpenaltyinfo.org/article.php?&did=1705#STATES%20WITH%20THE%20DEATH%20PENALTY%20V.%20STATES%20WITHOUT.

[33] Vince Beiser, "A Guilty Man," *Mother Jones,* September–October 2005, 38–39.

[34] Ibid.

[35] Ibid.

[36] Steven Donziger, editor. *The Real War on Crime: The Report of the National Criminal Justice Commission* (New York: HarperPerennial, 1996) pp. 224-5.

[37] Ibid. p. 48

[38] Van Jones and Nativo Vigil Lopex, "Easy Choice on Deficit: Trim Prison Spending;" The *San Francisco Chronicle*, November 19, 2003. Van Jones, executive director of the Ella Baker Center for Human Rights, also pointed out that California voters, by a ratio of 3 to 1, wanted to cut prison spending.

REFERENCES
Primary Sources

Interviews

Blumenthal, Ralph (Southwest bureau chief for the *New York Times*), interview by Ruth Massingill, Houston, Texas, May 23, 2005.

Brazzil, Jim (TDCJ prison chaplain and current program administrator for Victim and Community Support and Education), interview by Tina Baiter, Huntsville, Texas, July 18, 2005.

Brown, Charles (former TDCJ public information officer), interview by Melody A. Davison, Huntsville, Texas, June 23, 2005.

Brush, Amy (TDCJ employee), interview by Debbi Hatton, Huntsville, Texas, July 6, 2005.

Collins, Mary Evelyn (Sam Houston State University professor and local activist), interview by Ardyth Sohn, Huntsville, Texas, March 23, 2005.

Cox, Brian (TDCJ psychologist, Windham School District), interview by Tina Baiter, Huntsville, Texas, March 2005.

Crawford, Gary (former Huntsville city council member), interview by Melody Davison, Huntsville, Texas, June 21, 2005.

Davis, Andrew (TDCJ webmaster), interview by Ruth Massingill, Austin, Texas, March 18, 2005.

Dial, Janet (former death row reporter), interview by Ruth Massingill, March 17, 2004.

Dobbs, Frank (Huntsville native and independent filmmaker), interview by Ruth Massingill, Huntsville, Texas, March 12, 2005.

Ellis, Judy (Elkins Lake neighborhood leader), interview by Ardyth Sohn, Huntsville, Texas, March 23, 2005.

Evans, Bob (director, Division of Continuing Education, Windham School District), interview by Ruth Massingill, Huntsville, Texas, March 9, 2005.

Evans, Kevin (city manager), interview by Ardyth Sohn, Huntsville, Texas, March 21, 2005.

Fitzgerald, Larry (former TDCJ public information manager), interview by Ruth Massingill, Huntsville, Texas, April 7, 2003, and Austin, Texas, March 17, 2005.

Graczyk, Mike (Associated Press reporter), interview by Tina Baiter, Huntsville, Texas, June 7, 2005.

Griffith, James (Polunsky unit principal, Windham School District), interview by Tina Baiter, Livingston, Texas, March 8, 2005.

Haynes, Marjie (director, Division of Instruction, Windham School District), interview by Ardyth Sohn, Huntsville, Texas, March 23, 2005.

Hilla, Derek Ian (TDCJ inmate and editor of the *Echo*) interview by Ruth Massingill, Huntsville, Texas, October 4, 2006.

Kiser, Bambi (communications coordinator, Windham School District), interview by Ardyth Sohn, Huntsville, Texas, March 23, 2005.

Linney, Jake (Texas Department of Criminal Justice employee), interview by Melody Davison, Huntsville, Texas, July 8, 2005.

Lyons, Michelle (TDCJ public information officer), interview by Ruth Massingill, Huntsville, Texas, February 12, 2003, April 23, 2004, and March 29, 2005.

Longmire, Dennis (criminal justice professor and anti–capital punishment activist), interview by Melody Davison, Huntsville, Texas, June 21, 2005.

Marcus, Jim (director, Texas Defender Service), interview by Ruth Massingill, Houston, Texas, August 15, 2005.

Mayes, Wanda (Windham School District teacher), interview by Debbi Hatton, Athens, Texas, July 2, 2005.

Monday, Jane (city leader and former mayor), interview by Ruth Massingill, Huntsville, Texas, December 2, 2003.
Prew, Kelly (*Huntsville Item* reporter), interview by Tina Baiter, Huntsville, Texas, March 10, 2005.
Russell, George (Huntsville business owner and local activist), interview by Ardyth Sohn, Huntsville, Texas, March 21, 2005.
Thompson, Eric (reporter for Pacifica affiliate KPFT), interview by Ruth Massingill, Conroe, Texas, June 20, 2005.
Viesca, Mike (former TDCJ director of public information), interview by Ruth Massingill, Austin, Texas, December 15, 2003, and March 18, 2005.
Walt, Kathy (spokesperson for Texas governor Rick Perry and former *Houston Chronicle* reporter), interview by Ruth Massingill, Huntsville, Texas, December 14, 2003, and Austin, Texas, March 17, 2005.
Walters, Charles Freddy (overseer of Hospitality House), interview by Tina Baiter, Huntsville, Texas, March 21, 2005.
Weeks, David (Walker County district attorney), interview by Ardyth Sohn, Huntsville, Texas, March 21, 2005.
Wilkinson, Lyndol (associate publisher of the *Echo*), interview by Melody Davison, Huntsville, Texas, June 26, 2005, and by Ruth Massingill, Huntsville, Texas, September 22, 2006.
Willett, Jim (former warden), interview by Ruth Massingill and Ardyth Sohn, Huntsville, Texas, March 22, 2005.
Winn, Jamie (local body artist), interview by Debbi Hatton, Huntsville, Texas, July 6, 2005.
Wolf, Joy (local radio station owner), interview by Tina Baiter, Livingston, Texas, August 8, 2005.

Published Sources

Books

Andersen, Robin. *Consumer Culture and TV Programming*. Boulder, Colorado: Westview, 1995.
Bennett, W. Lance. *News: The Politics of Illusion*. New York: Longman, 2001.
Cohen, Bernard C. *The Press and Foreign Policy*. Princeton, New Jersey: Princeton University Press, 1967.
Donziger, Steven, ed., *The Real War on Crime: The Report of the National Criminal Justice Commission*. New York: HarperPerennial, 1996.
Entman, Robert M. and Andrew Rojecki. *The Black Image in the White Mind: Media and Race in America*. Chicago: University of Chicago Press, 2000.
Gay, L.R., Geoffrey Mills, and Peter Airasian. *Educational Research*. Columbus, Ohio: Pearson Prentice Hall, 2006.
Green, Terisa. *The Tattoo Encyclopedia: A Guide to Choosing Your Tattoo*. New York: Fireside, 2003.
Haney, Craig and John Manzolati. "Television Criminology: Network Illusions of Criminal Justice Realities," in *Readings about the Social Animal*, edited by Elliot Aronson. San Francisco, California: W. H. Freeman, 1981.
Horn, Laurence R. *Descriptions in Context*. New York: Garland, 1997.
Jacobs, James B. *Stateville: The Penitentiary in Mass Society*. Chicago: University of Chicago Press, 1977.
Kraus, Sidney et al., "Critical Events Analysis," in *Political Communications: Issues and Strategies for Research*, edited by Steven H. Chaffee. Beverly Hills, California: Sage, 1975.
Lynd, Robert S. and Helen M. Lynd. *Middletown*. New York: Harcourt, Brace, 1929.

Marquart, James W., Sheldon Ekland-Olson, and Jonathan R. Sorensen. *The Rope, the Chair, and the Needle: Capital Punishment in Texas, 1923–1990.* Austin: University of Texas Press, 1994.
Mauer, Marc. *Race to Incarcerate.* New York: New Press, 2006.
Owens, Virginia Stem and David Clinton. *Living Next Door to the Death House.* Grand Rapids, Michigan: William B. Eerdmans, 2003.
Protess, David and Maxwell McCombs, Eds. *Agenda Setting: Readings on Media, Public Opinion, and Policy Making.* Hillsdale, New Jersey: Lawrence Earlbaum, 1991.
Reid, Don. *Have a Seat, Please.* Huntsville: Texas Review Press, 2001.
Renaud, Jorge. *Behind the Walls: A Guide for Families and Friends of Texas Prison Inmates.* Denton: University of North Texas Press, 2002.
Rhodes, Lorna A. *Total Confinement: Madness and Reason in the Maximum Security Prison.* Berkeley: University of California Press, 2004.
Santos, Michael G. *About Prison.* Denton: University of North Texas Press, 2004.
Stamper, Norm. *Breaking Rank: A Top Cop's Exposé of the Dark Side of American Policing.* New York: Nation, 2005.
Sykes, Gresham. *The Society of Captives.* Princeton, New Jersey: Princeton University Press, 1958; repr., New York: Atteneur, 1966.
Valentine, Bill. *Gang Intelligence Manual: Identifying and Understanding Modern-Day Violent Gangs in the United States.* Boulder, Colorado: Paladin, 1995.

Articles

Abu-Jamal, Mumia. "Live from Death Row." Review by David Gilbert. *Prison Legal News*, 1995.
Beiser, Vince. "A Guilty Man." *Mother Jones*, September–October 2005.
Bernstein, Jake. "They Shot More than a Messenger." *Texas Observer*, February 18, 2005.
Britt, B., E. Panepento, and I. Wilson. "The Incidence of Tattooing in a Male Criminal Population." *Behavioral Neuropsychiatry* 4, 1972.
Bullard Rockwall. "Prisoners' Rights to Unrestricted Use of the Mail." *New England Journal on Prison Law*, 1974.
Cartwright, Gary. "Dan Rather Retorting." *Texas Monthly*, March 2005.
Casriel, Erika. "Bush and the Texas Death Machine." *Rolling Stone*, August 3, 2000.
Cohen, Fred. "The Laws of Prisoners' Rights: An Overview." *Criminal Law Bulletin*, 1997.
"From Death Row: Texas Set to Execute First African-American Woman since Civil War." *Democracy Now*, August 25, 2005.
Frazier, Mark. "Jailhouse Talk." *Mother Jones*, November–December 2002.
Gerbner, George and Larry Gross. "Living with Television: The Violence Profile." *Journal of Communication* 26, no. 2 (1976).
Gilliam, Frank D. Jr., et al., "Crime in Black and White: The Scary World of Local News," *Harvard International Journal of Press/Politics* 1, no. 3 (1996).
Halmari, Helen and Jan-Ola Ostman. "The Soft-Spoken, Angelic Pickax Killer: The Notion of Discourse Pattern in Controversial News Reporting." *Journal of Pragmatics*, 2001.
Harrison, Paige and Jennifer Karberg. "Prison and Jail Inmates at Midyear 2003." *Bureau of Justice Statistics Bulletin*, May 2004.
Hughes, Lily. "We'll keep fighting! Texecutioner in the White House," *New Abolitionist*, January 2001, Issue 18.
Johnson, Denis. "Five Executions and a Barbecue." *Rolling Stone*, August 17, 2000.
Kuby, Ronald and William Kunstler. "Silencing the Oppressed: No Freedom of Speech for Those behind the Walls." *Prison Legal News*, 1995.
O'Neill, Kevin Francis. "Muzzling Death Row Inmates: Applying the First Amendment to Regulations That Restrict a Condemned Prisoner's Last Words." *Arizona State Law Journal* 2 (winter 2001).

Miscellaneous

ACLU. "Executions and Exonerations by State since 1976." February 6, 2004. Available at: http://www.aclu.org/capital/general/10425pub20040206.html.

Fabelo, Tony. "Elderly Offenders in Texas Prisons," Criminal Justice Policy Council Report, 1999.

Halmari, Helena. "Discourse of Death: The Function of the Local Newspaper Coverage of Huntsville, Texas, Executions in Language and Ideology: Selected Papers from the 6th International Pragmatics Conference," vol. 1, edited by Jef Verschueren, International Pragmatics Association, Antwerp, Belgium, 1999.

Mauer, Marc. "Comparative International Rates of Incarceration: An Examination of Causes and Trends." June 20, 2003. Presented to the U.S. Commission on Civil Rights.

"Women in Prison," Bureau of Justice Statistics Special Report. Available at: http://www.ojp.usdoj.gov/bjs/abstract/wopris.htm.

"Year by Year Death Row Statistics," Texas Execution Information Center Statistics. Available at: http://www.txexecutions.org/stats/asp.

In addition, numerous agency and organizational publications, press releases, and websites as well as news reports and relevant court cases are referenced in the chapter notes.

Contributors

ROBIN ANDERSEN, PH.D., teaches Communication and Media Studies at Fordham University and is the Director of the Peace and Justice Studies Program. She has written numerous journal articles and book chapters about the ways in which media influence public opinion and social policy. She also writes about the impact of advertising and consumer culture on American society. She is the author of *A Century of Media: A Century of War* (Peter Lang Publishing, 2006), *Consumer Culture and TV Programming* (Westview Press, 1995) and coeditor of *Critical Studies in Media Commercialism* (Oxford University Press, 2000). She is frequently interviewed as an expert source on media issues for radio, television, and newspaper reporting. She is also featured in numerous educational documentaries.

MELODY DAVISON is a writer, editor, and graphic designer. She is an experienced professional whose award-winning firm, Gryphon, has provided innovative solutions to communications needs for a variety of clients. She has a Bachelor of Journalism with Honors from the University of Texas at Austin.

DEBBI HATTON is an instructor of Speech Communication at Sam Houston State University. She has graduate degrees in Speech Communication, Theatre, and History from the University of Texas—Tyler.

TINA BAITER is a graduate of Blinn College and of Sam Houston State University. She also studied as a Rotary Ambassadorial Scholar at the University of Edinburgh in Scotland, and she completed a summer of language study at the Universidad Iberoamericana in Puebla, Mexico. After graduation, Baiter served as editor of the *Madisonville* (Texas) *Meteor* before taking a position as the marketing coordinator for Smith-Blair, Inc., in Texarkana, Arkansas.

INDEX

About Prison (Santos), 209
Adickes, David, 1
After Innocence (Simon), 238
agenda-setting, 50–51, 95
AIDS, 89, 184
Amnesty International, 126, 129–30, 240
Archie, Mae and Horace, 27
argot, 173-75
Aryan Brotherhood, 179
Associated Press, 67, 83, 109–10
Austin College, 19
Austin Hall, 143. *See also* Sam Houston State University
Austin, 16-17, 24, 68, 105
Avery, Ann, 189

Bedias Indians, 30
Beiser, Vince, 247
Bell v. Wolfish, 202
Beto, George, 108
Bianch, Kenneth, 211
Bieregu v. Reno, 200
Big Sam, 1, 31
Black Guerrilla Family, 180
Blumenthal, Ralph, 83–86, 95
body art, 176, 178. *See also* tattoos
Bonnie and Clyde, 30
Boyd, Kenneth, 246
Brazzil, Jim, 47–48, 171, 173, 213
Breaking Rank (Stamper), 236
Bridge, Warren, 114
Brown, Charles, 74, 78, 84, 94
Brush, Amy, 179, 200–02, 211
Bryant, Salatheia, 132
Bundy, Ted, 211
Bureau of Justice Statistics, 122
Burke v. Levi, 183
Bush, Gov. George W., 4, 58, 70–71, 126, 130–31, 201, 208, 242–43
Buxxkemper, Felix, 32
Byrd unit, 31

Cain, Richard, 206
Canadian Coalition Against the Death Penalty, 208
capital punishment:
   cruel and unusual, 105; career maker for district attorneys, 90; crime deterrent, 108, 246; fairness of, 242, 244; Huntsville news coverage, 19, 48–49; medical professional's role in, 247; protests, 16, 44, 59, 123, 132–33, 208–09. *See also* death penalty, death row, executions
Carter, Robert Anthony, 81
Cartwright, Richard, 207
Cash, Johnny, 231, 237
Cash, June Carter, 232
Chappell, William, 113
Cobb, Raymond, 36–37
Coffin v. Reichard, 173
Collard, Lemuel, 26
Collins, Mary Evelyn, 24
country club myth, 87, 116
Cox, Brian, 122
Crawford, Gary, 52–54, 87
Criminal Justice Policy Council, 89
Crosby, David, 30, 182, 233
Crossroads Baptist Church, 45
Cunningham, Hugh, 18

Dan Rather Scholarship Fund, 17
Davis, Andrew, 84–85
Davis, Gov. Gray, 248
Dead Man Walking, 245
death penalty:
   history of, 105–7; media stance regarding, 50, 80, 110, 124, 126; moratorium, 94, 239; public support for, 58, 66, 70, 86, 90–91, 94 –96, 104, 124, 128, 198, 243. *See also* capital punishment, death row, executions
death row:
   correspondence, 212; costs of, 90; demographics, 124, 244; education, 92; escape from, 97–98; exonerations, 95, 238–39; juvenile crimes, 36; legal counsel, 94; living conditions, 88, 164–66; marriage, 213–219; media coverage, 70, 73, 83, 85–86, 106, 239, 243; profits from, 73–74; women on, 105, 122–23, 240–42. *See also* capital punishment, death penalty, executions
Dallas Morning News, 242
Death Penalty Information Center, 90

Demographics Daily, 43
Dial, Janet Parker, 120–21, 124–25, 128
Dirty White Boys, 179
DNA testing, 70, 94–95, 113, 238–39
Dobbs, Frank, 69, 78–79
Dobbs, Velda, 79

Echo, the, 76, 157; 172, 181–82, 184–85, 190–92, 217.
Educational Filmstrip Network, 19
Educational Video Network, 20
Elkins Lake, 25, 31
Ellis unit, 31, 97, 105, 145, 167
Ellis, Edward, 114
Ellis, Rodney, 70, 198
Entman, Robert, 244
Eppolito, Louis, 239
Espinoza v. Wilson, 203–04
Espy, M. Watt, 107
Estelle unit, 31-32, 146
Evans, Bob, 92
Evans, Kevin, 20–22, 24, 26, 65
executions:
    decrease in, 247; history of in Texas, 108, 124, 208; last meals, 111–12; last words, 113–15; media coverage, 48–49, 70, 80–81, 84–85, 103, 109, 110, 117, 121, 124–6, 129–134, 240, 243; media escorts, 69; public relations, 116–119; states by time frame, 106; support for, 94, 124; urban legends, 115–16. *See also* capital punishment, death penalty, death row

Facts You Should Know, 183
Family Faith Church, 173
First Amendment rights, 113, 171–72, 179, 183–86, 188, 199–200. *See also* U.S. Supreme Court
Fitzgerald, Larry, 44, 50, 72, 74, 78, 87, 89–90, 97–98, 111–18, 123–26, 128, 130–34
framing, 7, 50, 86

Gacy, John Wayne, 211
Gaines v. Lane, 200
gangs in prison, 179–80
Gallagher, Rob, 107
Gatesville, 103, 105

Gibbs Brothers, 27
Gibbs v. King, 188
Gibbs, Barry, 239
Gilliam, Frank, 244
Giordani, Evelyne, 209
Gite, Lloyd, 132
Glendening, Gov. Paris, 239
Goree Prison Girls, 148, 226, 229
Goree unit, 29, 79
Graczyk, Mike, 67–68, 72, 80–82, 110, 132
graduations in prison, 154–59
Graham, Gary, 118, 123, 129–34, 240–42
Graves, Rachel, 111
Gray, Pleasant, 30
Griffin, Richard, 54
Griffith, James, 93
Grimes County, 66
Gross, Terry, 231
Groundhog Day syndrome, 164–66
Groundhog Day, 165
Gurule, Martin, 97–98

Haber, Christa, 209
Hadden v. Howard, 188
Haggard, Merle, 232, 237
Halmari, Helena, 48–49
Harris County, 94–95, 147
Have a Seat, Please (Reid), 109
Haynes, Marjie, 34
Hays, Byron, 55
Hemphill, Albert Lee, 110
Hill, Ray, 205–06
Hilla, Derek Ian, 190-92
Hoge, Harry, 158
Homestead restaurant, 26
Horn, Laurence, 174
Hornets, 141
Hospitality House, 45-47. *See also* Huntsville
Houchin v. KQED, Inc., 200
Houston Chronicle, 73, 82, 94, 108, 111, 132, 189
Houston, Joshua, 22
Houston, Sam, 2, 6, 8, 15-16, 19, 21, 23– 24, 26-27, 29, 223, 249. *See also* Big Sam
Houstonian, 17
Huntsville Item, 48–50, 63, 69, 73, 80–81, 84, 96, 108-09, 120, 132

Index

Huntsville: community outreach, 47–48; company town, 41, 145; description, 15; downtown churches, 172–73; educational concerns, 25; employment figures, 22; inter- national image, 19, 103-04; jokes about, 71; leadership, 52; support for death penalty, 66; tourist attractions, 26–30. *See also* capital punishment, *Huntsville Item*, Sam Houston, hypervigilance, Texas Department of Criminal Justice
hypervigilance, 25, 32, 35

Innocence Protection Act, 94
Ivins, Molly, 18

Jackson v. Norris, 200
Jackson, Jesse, 133
Jagger, Bianca, 134
jailhouse lawyers, 172, 181, 188
Janowitz, Morris, 42
Joe Byrd Cemetery, 29, 134. *See also* Peckerwood Hill
Johnson v. Avery, 188
Johnson, Denis, 125–26, 242
Johnson, Ken, 55
Johnson, Kia, 113
Johnson, Lyndon, 71
Jones v. North Carolina Prisoners' Union, Inc., 180, 183–85
Justice, William Wayne, 181

Kayse, Judy, 53
KDOL, 206
King, John, 72
King's Candies, 27
Kiser, Bambi, 69, 76–77, 93, 154–59,191
Kiwanis, 142
Kozol, Jonathan, 248
Krystyniak, Frank, 71
Ku Klux Klan (KKK), 53, 133
Kuby, Ronald, 203
Kunstler, William, 203

La Citta di Morte, 19
Lake Livingston, 17, 119
Lamp of Hope Project, 208
Leadbelly, 28, 30, 229, 233

Ledbetter, Huddie William, 28. *See also* Leadbelly
Lee College, 155, 157–58
Liberty Bound, 20
Lichtenstein, Andrew, 177
life without parole, 175, 198–99, 243. *See also* capital punishment
Lifespark, 209
Linney, Jake, 55-56
Live at Folsom Prison, 231
Livingston, 37, 45, 105, 119, 207
Livingston, Charlie, 114
London Daily Mail, 81
Longmire, Dennis, 44, 57, 58–59, 71, 82, 123, 132
Lupar v. Stoneman, 183
Lynd, Robert and Helen, 50
Lynn, Loretta, 29
Lyons, Michelle, 69–78, 80, 82, 84–85, 88–89, 97–98, 103, 108, 112–15, 117, 119–21, 123, 126, 132, 163

mandatory minimum sentencing, 236
Marble, Guy, 181–82
Marcus, Jim, 83, 88–89, 91, 94–95, 187–89, 198–99, 208
Marquart, James, 130
marriage in prison, 213–19
Masters, Linda, 32–34
Mauer, Marc, 236
Mayes, Wanda, 32–33, 176–77, 179–80, 203–04, 210–11
McCann, Michael, 244
McCombs, Maxwell, 51
McConnell unit, 164
McCowan v. United States, 199
McFarland, George, 189
Menendez, Erik and Lyle, 211
Metro Source, 117
Mexican Mafia, 178–79
Middletown, 50–51
Miranda Act, 47
Mix, Tom, 29
Mock, Ron, 123, 240
Monday, Jane, 22, 24, 28, 33, 35
Money magazine, 43
Mountain View unit, 105
Mumia Abu-Jamal, 205

Murder Victims' Families for Reconciliation, 245
Murray, Bill, 165

NAACP, 53, 244
narratives of exclusion, 234
narratives of inclusion, 233
Nelson, Willie, 29
New Zion Missionary Baptist Church, 27, 140
Newton, Frances, 123, 240–42
New York Times, 83, 86, 95, 98, 246
Nowlin, Bill, 157–60

O'Neill, Kevin, 114
Oaks, Phil, 233
Oakwood Cemetery, 223, 249
Old Sparky, 105, 115, 141, 162
Ostman, Jan-Ola, 49
Owens, Virgina and David, 19, 79
Owings, Margaret, 37-38

Pacifica Radio, 81, 127–28, 205
Palmigiano v. Travisono, 200
Peckerwood Hill, 29, 134, 140. *See also* Joe Byrd Cemetery
pen pal inmates, 210–12
Perry, Gov. Rick, 56, 82, 198, 201, 208
Pittman v. Hutto, 183
Pollis, David, 55
Polunsky unit, 37, 72, 93, 105, 119–20, 127, 205, 209, 242
Poncelet, Matthew, 245
Porter, Anthony, 239
Prejean, Sister Helen, 245
Prew, Kelly, 73, 75, 94-96, 80, 90, 109, 120–21, 123
Price, Brian, 111
prison museum. *See* Texas Prison Museum
prison rodeo. *See* Texas Prison Rodeo
prisoner-to-prisoner correspondence, 185–87
Procunier v. Martinez, 185
Pruett, Robert, 164–67
public information. *See* public relations, Texas Department of Criminal Justice
public relations, 16, 22, 28, 30, 49, 67, 74–75, 95, 132

Randleman, Mike, 111
Rather, Dan, 17–18
Rating Guide to Life in America's Small Cities, 43
Ray Hill Prison Show, 197, 205-06
recidivism, 32, 76, 90, 92–93, 122, 190, 248
Reeves, Reginald, 113
Reid, Don, 63, 109–10, 113, 115
Renaud, Jorge, 10, 183, 191
research methods, 5–7, 234
Resendiz, Angel Maturino, 73
Reuters, 117
revolving door, 89
Reynolds, Charles, 105
Rhodes, Lorna, 42
Roberts, Douglas Alan, 127
Roberts, Douglass, 209
Rockwell Chapel Band, 156, 159
Rolling Stone, 82, 125–26
Ronald, James, 114
Rose, Christine, 20
Ruiz v. Estelle, 181, 198
Ruiz, David, 10
Russell, George, 15–17, 19–20, 162
Russellville, 20
Ryan, Gov. George, 239

Salt Creek Massacre, 29
Sam Houston. *See* Houston, Sam
Sam Houston Avenue, 27, 28, 150, 152
Sam Houston Museum, 26, 150
Sam Houston State University, 15, 17–19, 22, 24, 26, 42, 44, 48, 55–56, 66, 71, 121, 130, 132, 154–59, 190, 216. *See also* Austin Hall.
Santos, Michael, 209
Sarandon, Susan, 245
Satanta, 29
Saturday Night Live, 205
Schwarzenegger, Gov. Arnold, 246
Sentencing Project, 236
Sharpton, Rev. Al, 130, 134
Shenanigans, 87
Shout-Out Show, 207
Simon, Marc, 238
Sorge, Wayne, 132
Stamper, Norm, 236, 237
State Counsel for Offenders, 189

Steamboat House, 24
Stuart, Julia, 81
Summers, Greg, 207
Sykes, Gresham, 43

tattoos, 49, 141, 150–52, 176–77, 178, 179–80, 190, 226. *See also* body art
Terrell unit, 242
Terrell, Charles, 242
Texan Café, 27, 150
Texas Correctional Industries, 23
Texas Defender Service, 83, 88, 187, 198, 208
Texas Department of Corrections, 147
Texas Department of Criminal Justice: employment in Huntsville, 22, 145–47; media guidelines, 118, 120–21, 124; media relations, 50–51, 68, 75, 77–88, 81, 83, 111–12, 116–17, 119, 126, 128, 131–34; mission, 68; public information staff qualifications, 68–69; recruiting employees, 13, 54–55. *See also* the *Echo*, death row, public relations, the Walls, Windham School
Texas Monthly, 27
Texas Prison Museum, 24, 30, 126, 141
Texas Prison Rodeo, 20, 28–29, 79, 148, 227, 232
Texas State Network, 117
Texas Syndicate, 169, 179
Thompson, Eric, 81, 83, 88, 90, 93–94, 96, 127, 128
Thornburgh v. Abbott, 203
Todd, Larry, 67
Tribute to Courage, 1. *See also* Big Sam
Tucker, Karla Faye, 49–50, 111, 123, 131, 243
Turner v. Safley, 185–86, 203

United Press International, 109
U.S. Supreme Court, 36, 58, 105, 133, 171, 180, 184, 202, 208, 236, 242. *See also* First Amendment rights
Universal Declaration of Human Rights, 208
Universal Ethician Church, 17
University Heights Baptist Church, 36
University of Texas at Austin, 18, 51
Urban Cowboy, 20
urban legends, 104, 115

Victim and Community Support and Education, 47
victim notification services, 48
victim offender mediation dialogue, 48
victims' rights, 47–48, 50, 68, 111, 209
Viesca, Mike, 67–68, 70–71, 75, 85–86, 89–92, 95, 108, 116, 128
Voodoo Tattoo, 150–52, 178, 180

Wagner v. Thomas, 203
Walker County Courthouse, 31
Walls, the, 6, 15, 25, 27–29, 35, 42, 44, 53, 71–72, 80–81, 86, 97, 104–05, 108, 116–18, 127, 131–32, 142–44, 147, 149, 172–73, 191
Wal-Mart, 22, 53, 145
Walt, Kathy, 70, 73, 75, 82, 108–09, 114–16, 120–21, 124–25
Walters, Freddy, 45–46
Ward, Annie Mae, 27
websites as used by inmates, 37, 209–211
Weeks, David, 36-37, 41, 43–44, 54
Whalen v. Roe, 200
Wild West, 79, 86, 96, 198–99
Wilkinson, Lyndol, 181–82, 184–85, 191, 217
Willett, Jim, 30, 134
Williams, Stanley "Tookie," 246-47
Windham School, 31–32, 69, 76–77, 92–93, 154, 160, 176, 191, 203
wolf pack, 244
Wolf, Jim and Joy, 207
Woodall, Patsy, 63
Woodland Home, 26
writ writers, 188
Wynne unit, 31, 77, 155, 157, 161, 191

Zuniga, Rey, 156